CORNISH STUDIES

Second Series

FIVE

INSTITUTE OF CORNISH STUDIES

Sardinia Pilchardus
(The Pilchard)

EDITOR'S NOTE

Cornish Studies (second series) exists to reflect current research conducted internationally in the inter-disciplinary field of Cornish Studies. It is edited by Dr Philip Payton, Reader in Cornish Studies and Director of the Institute of Cornish Studies at the University of Exeter, and is published by the University of Exeter Press. The opinions expressed in *Cornish Studies* are those of individual authors and are not necessarily those of the editor or publisher. The support of Cornwall County Council if gratefully acknowledged.

CORNISH STUDIES

Second Series

FIVE

Edited by

Philip Payton

UNIVERSITY
of
EXETER
PRESS

First published in 1997 by
University of Exeter Press
Reed Hall, Streatham Drive
Exeter, Devon EX4 4QR
UK

British Library Cataloguing in Publication Data
A catalogue record of this book is
available from the British Library

ISBN 0 85989 551 3
ISSN 1352-271X

Typeset by Kestrel Data, Exeter, Devon

Printed and bound in Great Britain by
T.J. International, Padstow, Cornwall

Contents

RESEARCH NOTE

INTRODUCTION

In his recent polemic *The Battle For Scotland* (London, 2nd ed., 1995, p. 8), Andrew Marr notes the important role of 'eminent professional historians who have been opening up Scottish history and popularizing it'. In our more modest Cornish way, a similar grouping of historians and other social scientists has been opening up and popularizing the history and identity of Cornwall. Ella Westland (amongst others) has recognized this, writing in her major collection *Cornwall: The Cultural Construction of Place* (Penzance, 1997, p. 2) of 'The recent shift evident in Cornish Studies . . . and its readiness to engage with new theoretical discourses', a shift manifested in the activities of 'a group of academics growing around the nucleus of the Institute of Cornish Studies— represented in publications like the new series of . . . *Cornish Studies*'.

This edition of *Cornish Studies*, the fifth in the series, draws together important elements of this new work, focusing in varying degrees and in various ways upon the increasingly academically significant issue of identity. Andy Seward, in his article, stresses Williams' and Hill's observation (*Sport and Identity in the North of England*, Keele, 1996, p. 1), that 'In the 1990s the problem of identity is becoming a central, even fashionable, one among historians and other social scientists'. In so doing, Seward offers an important benchmark by which we may measure and judge Cornish Studies as an area of academic inquiry, for the inference is that its practitioners should be aware of and participate in this growing imperative, the 'problem of identity'.

This is a theme echoed in Philip Payton's article, 'Cornwall in Context: The New Cornish Historiography' (developed from a paper delivered recently at the University of Wales Cardiff) which discusses the relevance and success of Cornish Studies in terms of its ability to construct interdisciplinary, comparative perspectives and to penetrate wider academic discourses. Here the emphasis is on wider historio-graphical trends—the 'British problem', the nature of industrial regions, the politics of territorial identity, the 'crisis' in Celtic Studies—and the manner in which Cornish Studies has been able to learn from and contribute to these identity-related issues. It seems an obvious point, but it is worth re-emphasizing that, in this increasingly identity-led world where political visibility (and economic development) in regional, national and international contexts is so often a function of the successful deployment of identity, the elucidation of such identity is potentially a major resource for administrators and planners.

Be that as it may, Dick Cole in his provocative article offers a major challenge to those who would deny (or assert) Cornwall's 'Celtic identity' on the basis of genetic traits supposedly inherited from the murky Dark Ages. As well as reminding us that ethnic identities are social (not biological) constructs, he argues that those anthropologists who have attempted to answer the question 'How Celtic are the Cornish?' by examining genetic evidence have been seriously misled by their embrace of now outdated assumptions about the early history of this island—namely, that a homogenous Celtic race was displaced in what is now England by an equally homogenous Anglo-Saxon people, the Celts surviving in numbers only in their western and northern fastnesses of Cornwall, Wales and Scotland. Cole shows that the terms 'Celtic' and 'Anglo-Saxon' are themselves ambiguous and value-laden, to be approached cautiously and with qualification by academics, but he also draws attention to the fact that archaeologists now consider that the 'Anglo-Saxon invasion' probably numbered no more than 100,000 souls—an elite which was able to impose its cultural attributes upon the indigenous populations.

Clearly, it is foolish to try to analyse (let alone judge the 'validity' of) modern ethnic identities by recourse to genetic data (although, paradoxically, myths of origin may be of extreme significance to those ethnic identities themselves). Cole's intervention has alerted us to another key area of historiographical debate where there is an important role for Cornwall to play, not least with his assertion that we should be sceptical of historical 'narratives which concentrate on migration and population replacement as the principal impetus behind change'. Although an archaeologist concerned with prehistory and early history, Cole has raised an issue of at least equal importance for the modern or contemporary historian. That is to say, our examination of the characteristics of 'globalization' requires the comparative consideration of the relative impacts of, on the one hand, the diffusion of communications and new technologies by 'hegemonic' cultures and economies, and, on the other, large-scale migrations and ethnic conflicts —everything from the European colonization of North America,

Australasia and Southern Africa to the 'Holocaust', the mass movement of peoples in Europe after the First and Second World Wars, and (most recently) the examples of Yugoslavia and Rwanda.

Cole's inference that, in our efforts to elaborate the Cornish identity, we should look again at the history of early Cornwall is reflected in David Harvey's illuminating discussion of the tithings framework in Cornwall in the medieval period. The *Oxford Companion to Local and Family History* (David Hey ed., Oxford, 1996, p. 441) tells us simply that the tithing was the medieval system whereby groups of households (usually tenfold) were responsible to the manorial court leet (which dealt with petty law and order and the administration of communal agriculture) for the good conduct of each member. Harvey, however, indicates that the tithing in Cornwall (and especially West Cornwall) represented not only this form of judicial and production control, but also an important territorial device which formed the basic Cornish administrative unit of the medieval period and was the primary subdivision of the Cornish Hundred. He argues that the tithing system (otherwise common in England) acquired this 'territorialization' only in south-western Britain, and then only on a systematic basis in Cornwall, hinting—as Harvey puts it—'at an earlier relationship with strategies of economic exploitation and political influence in the landscape'.

The distinctive characteristics of medieval Cornwall are also observed in Lynette Olson's discussion of the late medieval, early modern Cornish language miracle play, *Beunans Meriasek* (the Life of St Meriasek). She argues that the common theme which ties together the otherwise highly disparate three sections of the play is that of 'tyranny', a theme which may have had a particular political resonance in post-1497 Cornwall (when the play was almost certainly performed in the aftermath of the Cornish rebellions of that year) but which also had literary meaning in its own right. She notes that *Beunans Meriasek* is a 'very Cornish' play (it is written in the Cornish language, is set partly in Cornwall and in Brittany, and celebrates a relatively obscure Cornu-Breton saint rather than a universal figure) but concludes that its treatment of 'tyranny' does in fact have universal applicability—it is primarily a religious treatment, 'sincerely meant and sincerely taken, with a good deal of fun and entertainment in the process'.

Moving to the later modern period, Bernard Deacon looks again —in a discussion of 'proto-industrialization and potatoes'—at the history of nineteenth-century Cornwall, offering a revised narrative which suggests that the key decade of change was not (as conventional wisdom has insisted) the 1860s but rather the 1840s, 'the decade when Cornwall decisively moved from a proto-industrial to an industrial society'. However, as Deacon notes in his conclusion, this mid-century modernization was arrested by the crises of the 1860s and the 1870s and the inability of the Cornish economy to diversify. Thus interpreted, the Cornish experience is curiously unique, a somehow 'intermediate' position between that of Ireland (in which a hitherto expanding economy was unable to recover from the catastrophic impact of the 1840s) and the North of England (where the economic recession of the 1840s was superseded by the long summer of mid-Victorian prosperity).

The contrast between Ireland and the North of England has been sketched ably by Christine Kinealy in her *This Great Calamity: The Irish Famine 1845–52* (London, 1994, Chapter 9). The 1830s and 1840s had been a time of unprecedented economic dislocation and social unrest in Britain, and acute depression hit the economically and (after 1832) politically important North of England in 1847, also the height of the Irish potato crisis. Like Cornwall, the North had recovered by the late 1840s, the Great Exhibition of 1851 marking the new era of industrial resurgence. In Ireland, however, 1851 was the seventh consecutive year of famine and shortage, a major landmark in the growing economic (and thus political) disparity between Britain and Ireland. And in Cornwall, despite the experience of the late 1840s and 1850s, industrial modernization had faltered by the 1860s, prompting a new era of mass emigration and heralding the onset of de-industrialization. Deacon's contribution, then, is to further emphasize the distinctive characteristics of the Cornish industrial experience but also to place that experience within the comparative context of events elsewhere in these islands at a time of crucial socio-economic change.

One effect, it has been argued, of the industrial crisis experienced in Cornwall in the second half of the nineteenth century was the Celtic-Cornish Revival, the movement which (it has been contended) determined to look back over the 'failure' of the industrial period to a time when Cornwall was unequivocally 'Celtic'. The emphasis in recent Cornish historiography on this important cultural (and, by implication, economic) shift has been accompanied by a concern on the wider academic stage to reconsider the whole notion of 'Celticity'. Amy Hale engages with both these trends in twin articles designed, first of all, to investigate how notions of Celticity have been deployed (and contested) in Cornwall, and, secondly, to examine the organizational origins of the Celto-Cornish movement itself. She concludes that, despite the contested nature of 'Celticity' and its sometimes controversial application in Cornwall, 'Celtic expressions in Cornwall are meaningful, multi-vocalic, and constantly undergoing change and negotiation'.

Hale further demonstrates, in her analysis of the origins of the

Cowethas Kelto-Kernuak (the first of Cornwall's Revivalist organizations, formed in the early twentieth century), that the aims of the early Revivalists were unswervingly 'pre-industrial', focusing firmly as they did on antiquities, wrestling and hurling, and the Cornish language and its literature. She notes how the early Cornish Revivalists were much influenced by wider Pan-Celtic debates, and she observes that it is in Cowethas Kelto-Kernuak that we see the first division into sub-categories of cultural symbolic systems in Cornwall, a division based on class in which the Revivalists failed to draw upon the existing values and traditions of a largely industrial Cornish society. She notes 'the potential conflict between Cornwall's industrial heritage and popular perceptions of Celts as non-industrial peoples' but she also warns that 'to assume that Celtic revivalist traditions in Cornwall arose only in response to the economic crisis brought about by the collapse of the mining industry, reduces the emotional and aesthetic components of their genesis'.

This objection is echoed in part in Ronald Perry's discussion of the relationship between the Celto-Cornish Revival and economic development in Edwardian Cornwall. He questions the extent to which the Revivalists were in fact ideological 'revolutionaries' who were deliberately rejecting the experience of recent industrial history in preference for a more distant Celtic golden age, and suggests instead that they were for the most part 'establishment antiquarians' who saw no conflict (or even connection) between their Revivalist and economic activities. Perry argues that, in the years up to the First World War, Cornwall seemed to be recovering from its economic cataclysm, with the extractive and associated engineering activities apparently re-emerging, with horticulture prospering, and tourism on the increase. In such a climate, relatively comfortable middle-class Revivalists did not need to ask themselves difficult questions about the relationship between rural, pre-industrial images of Celticity and the reality of industrial Cornwall, nor were they confronted with difficult choices about their personal or collective identities. However, Perry does raise the possibility of at least the potential for self-doubt and inner-conflict amongst these Revivalists, asking, for example, whether it was their commitment to 'old-fashioned, Cornish Free-Trade Liberalism' that made them 'shy away' from the 'protectionist solutions proffered by other Celtic groups' in Scotland, Wales and Ireland.

This suggestion of a 'political' contrast between the early Cornish Revivalists and their counterparts elsewhere in the Celtic world is pursued vigorously by Garry Tregidga in his treatment of the relationship between the Revival and Cornish politics in the period 1886–1939. Tregidga suggests that the impact of the 'Irish Question' is central to our understanding of the subject, arguing that the religious and strategic 'threat' of Irish Home Rule (as it was perceived in late Victorian, early Edwardian Cornwall) led to a Liberal Unionist dominance in Cornwall which left the Revivalist movement (with its own Unionist leanings) in no position to develop a political agenda of its own. Paradoxically, however, the issue of Irish Home Rule also stimulated interest in the idea of Home Rule All Round in which Cornwall, like Scotland and Wales, might also achieve a measure of self-government. Similarly, the Liberals in the inter-war period, no longer the party of government, began to adopt Celtic imagery as part of a wider strategy to develop an anti-metropolitan stance in Cornwall, a practice they were to promote with greater effect in the years after 1945. This, in turn, argues Tregidga, coincided with the emergence in the pre-war years of a new generation of Revivalists which was more proactively political in its perspectives, setting the stage for the politicization of the Revival in the period after the Second World War.

The issue of identity creation and contestation in modern Cornwall is addressed at a more theoretical level by Rob Burton, who argues that in the Gramscian notion of 'cultural hegemony' we have an important tool for understanding the otherwise contradictory, para-doxical, complex, even confused elements of Cornish cultural identity. Antonio Gramsci (1891–1937), a Sardinian Marxist, spent ten years of his life in Fascist prisons and 'clinics' in Italy, and during this period of incarceration he wrote his *Prison Notebooks*, first published in 1948–1951. His main aim was to reconstruct Marxian theory, attempting to refute the standard Marxist conception of the economy as the base upon which society's political and social structures are built, and arguing instead that it was 'cultural hegemony' which allowed a ruling class to impose its authority upon other classes. Thus all ideological struggles are struggles for hegemony, a cultural battle to win hearts and minds. In this analysis, Gramsci identified the Italian proletariat as a subordinate group which was simultaneously able to hold two distinct conceptions of the world—one which was the 'official' view-point of the 'cultural hegemonic group', and the other which was its own 'popular' view. The latter was vigorous and spontaneous, a 'passion to exist' which occasionally burst through in defiant 'flashes' but which was as incoherent as it was turbulent, a lack of systematic articulation making it vulnerable to the dominance of the 'cultural hegemonic' group.

Burton holds that the Cornish are a similar subordinate group, exposed to the 'cultural hegemony' of the English state but also with its own 'popular' view of the world. He argues that myriad fragments of different (and often conflicting) ideologies and traditions have been brought together to mould the contemporary Cornish identity, an apparently *ad hoc*, eclectic, even contradictory culture which none-theless has its own spontaneous life and a 'mosaic of meaning' which somehow makes sense. Burton turns to history and folklore to find evidence of this, and further adds that the 'text' which we must read to fathom this complex identity includes not only those historical and folkloric attributes but also the deliberations of those who have sought to comment upon them. Thus the perspectives of writers as diverse as F.E. Halliday on the one hand, and Bernard Deacon and Philip Payton on the other, are seen to offer insights which might be interpreted as Gramscian but—more importantly—are also vital parts of the wider cultural 'text'.

For Burton, examples of Gramscian 'flashes' are to be found in the behaviour of 'Trelawny's Army', the throng of Cornish rugby supporters who in the 1980s and 1990s have lent passionate support to the Cornish side in the county championships. Andy Seward in his article agrees that rugby football has had, and indeed continues to enjoy, a particular role in both the construction and expression of popular identity in modern Cornwall. He draws upon a wide literature survey to indicate the increasing interest expressed by historians, sociologists and others in the relationship between sport and identity, and to suggest the comparative importance for Cornwall of specific studies of sport (including rugby) and identity already conducted in Wales, Scotland, Ireland and English regions.

He begins by considering the Cornish 'folk' sports of hurling and wrestling (the former with a code of 'laws' which made it almost a form of proto-rugby, the latter a strenuous contact sport which may have anticipated the 'scrum'), and sets the arrival of rugby in Cornwall and the foundation of the Cornwall Rugby Football Union against the backdrop of wider socio-economic change in late nineteenth-, early twentieth-century Cornwall. Seward argues that rugby football developed as an important popular outlet (perhaps the only one) for a persisting Cornish identity in the 'making-do' culture of the 'paralysis' years before the Second World War, stressing the importance for Cornwall of its 'international' status in meeting and playing other constituent teams from the British Empire family—Australia, New Zealand, South Africa. He adds that rugby has continued to play a significant role in asserting the strength of Cornish identity in the face of rapid socio-economic change since 1945, remarking that it is the meaning given to a particular sporting event (rather than the event itself) which is of social and cultural significance.

Finally, in a Research Note designed as a prelude to a broader investigation of Cornish Studies and the National Curriculum, F. Roff

Rayner and F.L. Harris—two practitioners of Cornish education with a formidable fund of experience in the field—come together with the Director of the Institute of Cornish Studies to dwell upon the educational implications of what Sir Geoffrey Holland has called 'the curious paradox' of the increasing significance of local identities at a time of burgeoning globalization. Recognizing the difficulties experienced by both teachers and Local Education Authorities in responding to this paradox, the authors nonetheless take their inspiration from the decidedly Cornish flavour of the *Cornwall Education Week Handbook* produced as long ago as 1927, suggesting that it is an example of what might be achieved in the very different climate of the 1990s where there is a clear need to accommodate Cornish Studies within the prescriptive constraints of the National Curriculum. Although the discussion is aimed principally at teachers in Cornish schools, it has in a sense a wider applicability for all those concerned with the recognition, respect for, and articulation of the myriad identities that at the end of this millennium comprise our 'global village'.

Philip Payton,
Reader in Cornish Studies and
Director,
Institute of Cornish Studies,
University of Exeter,
Truro, Cornwall.

CORNWALL IN CONTEXT: THE NEW CORNISH HISTORIOGRAPHY

Philip Payton

INTRODUCTION

The General Election of 1997 will be remembered as one of the great landmarks in modern British political history—comparable to 1832, 1906 and 1945—and, irrespective of what the long-term fortunes of the new government might be, the election result will be seen inevitably as the turning point when the British electorate 'came home' to Labour. However, there is another way of reading the outcome of this election, and that is to see it as the triumph (or at least assertion) of the 'Other Britain' over the dominance of Tory England.

As commentators have been quick to point out, the Conservative Party has been reduced electorally to the party of rural, lowland shire England, something not unlike its pre-1832 and indeed pre-1707 identity as England's 'Country Party'. Meanwhile, the 'Other Britain'— from urban and northern England to Scotland, Wales, Cornwall and Northern Ireland—represents not only the huge reservoir of Labour's electoral support but also the territorial heartlands of parties which are in their several ways the voices of the periphery: from the Liberal Democrats to Sinn Fein and the Ulster Unionists. In Cornwall, Andrew George, the newly elected Liberal Democrat MP for St Ives, observed in his victory address 'that the Celtic nations of Scotland, Wales and Cornwall were a Tory-free zone'.[1] The *Guardian* newspaper took a similar view, in particular emphasizing the strong Scottish influence in the new Cabinet. Tongue in cheek, it commented that 'It looks like a successful Scottish invasion, achieving by stealth what their forefathers failed to do in 1745'. But it struck a more serious note when it observed 'pundits and and columnists [such as Polly Toynbee] complaining loudly about a Celtic Mafia'.[2] The *Guardian* warned against the emergence of a 'Little Englander' mentality in the reaction to new assertions of Scottishness (or Celticity), and it was significant that when William Hague announced his candidacy for the Conservative Party leadership, he stressed as his credentials his intimate knowledge of both the North of England and of Wales. Born and bred in the North but also—as former Welsh Secretary—with extensive experience of Welsh issues, his point was that he was uniquely placed to understand (and thus lead a Tory fight-back in) the 'Other Britain'.

THE BRITISH PROBLEM

One effect, then, of the 1997 General Election result was to re-emphasize the significant territorial dimension of British (or, more correctly, United Kingdom) politics, reminding observers abroad and at home (not least the Conservative Party) of the inherent diversity of these islands. The experience of 1997 was a far cry from the conventional wisdom of 1960s' political scientists (epitomised in Jean Blondel's famous dictum that 'Britain is probably the most homogeneous of all industrial countries'[3]), while the re-assertion of the 'Other Britain' in this election was a sharp reminder that even at the end of the twentieth century notions of 'Britishness'—the 'British problem' as academics have termed it recently—remain contested and unresolved. Robin Cohen has referred to the 'fuzzy frontiers' of British identity, describing the ambiguous boundary between 'Englishness' and 'Britishness' and noting that 'The Celtic fringe . . . is a familiar but inexplicit internal boundary. For the English, the boundary is marked by irresolution, uncertainty, incongruity, derogation or humour.'[4] Ian McBride, meanwhile, refers not to 'fuzzy frontiers' but to 'ethnic allegiances co-existing in concentric circles, with different patterns emerging in different contexts' (politics, economics, religion, sport, and so on), pointing to 'the persistence of such concentric loyalties within the United Kingdom . . . [and thus] . . . the unresolved nature of Britishness itself'.[5]

As well as considering the persistence of the 'British problem' into the 1990s, scholars have of late developed a historical perspective of the origins and changing nature of Britishness. McBride (writing in 1996) notes that 'in the past five years or so, Britishness has been pushed to the centre of historical debate'.[6] Hugh Kearney's insistence upon a 'Britannic' approach to the history of these islands, replacing an anglocentric perspective with a new emphasis upon the separate but intertwined experiences of four (at least) nations, was followed by Linda Colley's widely acclaimed and enormously influential *Britons*, published in 1992.[7] In this seminal work, Colley indicated that

Britishness was a post-1707 construct conditional upon the link between commerce, industry and empire, forged in war and underpinned by Protestantism, an identity which was superimposed upon an array of internal differences but did not imply the integration or homogenization of disparate cultures within these islands. To this was added the approach of John Morrill and other historians of the early modern period, who tackled the issue of state formation in the period c1534–1707 in what they termed the 'Atlantic Archipelago', seeking to transcend the limitations of compartmentalized English, Welsh, Irish and Scottish histories by taking a 'holistic' view of historical development in these islands.[8]

Paradoxically, this breaking-down of 'national' histories also facilitated a more vigorous approach to regional history, enabling historians to set regional distinctiveness within the experience of the 'Archipelago' as a whole. Helen M. Jewell's *The North–South Divide* was one such study, an investigation of the origins of Northern consciousness in England which argued that the North constituted a distinct culture zone long before the Industrial Revolution re- invented its separate identity.[9] But this was not to underestimate the impact of industrialization in perpetuating, reinforcing and re-inventing regional distinctiveness, as economic historians and historical geographers such as Jack Langton and Pat Hudson have emphasized.[10] Thus earlier assumptions that industrialization had promoted social, cultural and political uniformity in Britain have been replaced by a new orthodoxy which insists that industrialization gave new meanings to regional identities, the often highly specialized and distinctive forms of industrial activity that characterized specific localities becoming defining cultural icons. One might add that the process of de-industrialization has been similarly important in perpetuating regional distinctiveness, especially in the realms of 'heritage tourism' where— quite apart from the huge socio-economic structural problems caused by industrial decline—the co-option of hitherto derelict industrial artefacts by a redefining tourist industry has led to new constructions of what John Urry has termed the 'tourist gaze': the unusual or distinctive that draws tourists to particular destinations.[11]

CORNWALL AND BRITISHNESS

The historiographical trends sketched above have had a considerable impact upon our approach to studying Cornwall's past (and present), precipitating what in is effect a major review of how that history might be written and read. The present author's *Cornwall*, published at the end of 1996, is an attempt to bring those trends to bear upon our consideration of Cornish history, a synthesis which itself sketches the new Cornish historiography. However, it is not the purpose of this article to present a précis or discussion of the book *Cornwall*, but rather to highlight key areas where the study of Cornish history has engaged with, learnt from, and (one hopes) contributed to the new discourses. Implicit in this is the suggestion that such engagement should be our over-arching research strategy for the future. Not only should Cornish Studies as an area of academic enquiry seek to keep abreast of relevant developments in the wider academic world, but, if the study of Cornwall is itself to have relevance beyond the Tamar, then it should be set firmly in a comparative context.

An exciting aspect of all this is the manner in which the study of early modern Cornwall has been able to participate in the elucidation of state formation in the Atlantic Archipelago. In an intriguing paradox, it has been argued that although the Cornish were early converts to the Tudors' 'British project', they were at the same time resistant to the intrusions of the Tudor state and the threat that these posed to the political and cultural accommodation of Cornwall.[12] This resistance explained both the Cornish rebellions of 1497 and 1549 and the events of their aftermaths, which ranged from the accommodating Charter of Pardon of 1508 to the savage repression of Cornwall in the mid-sixteenth century. Mark Stoyle has taken up these themes, wedding them to his own consideration of the Civil War in Cornwall and setting this synthesis, in turn, within the wider 'Britannic' consideration of the 'War of the Three Kingdoms'.[13] As Stoyle has observed, within a period of no more than 150 years the Cornish rose on no fewer than five occasions. He remarks:

> Why should have this been so? Few historians have thought to ask. Rather than viewing these periodic eruptions as part of an ongoing tradition of popular protest, most scholars have preferred to see them as isolated, almost unrelated events. Yet . . . the frequency with which Cornwall was convulsed by rebellion during the Tudor and Stuart periods can only be explained in terms of that county's unique position within the early modern British state.[14]

Indeed, in his consideration of the 1648 rising against the Parliamentarians, we have more than an echo of the 'Curse of Cromwell' and Roundhead behaviour in Ireland:

> Having dragged their sullen captives to Penryn, the Parliamentarians paraded them through the town in a humiliating show, preceded by three Roundhead soldiers who carried, upon the points of their

swords, 'three silver balls used in hurling'. Hurling (a form of handball) was regarded as 'a sport peculiar to Cornwall' at this time, so the significance of the soldiers' action is obvious. By parading violated hurling balls through Penryn, of all places, they were making the clearest possible statement about the final defeat of the ancient Cornish culture which had endured in this region for so long.[15]

And yet, the triumph of Parliament in Cornwall did not mean the end of a distinctive place for Cornwall within the Archipelago, for in the ensuing period—with its re-invention of Britishness in the manner described by Linda Colley—the Cornish were to play their own particular role within a new 'British project' based on commerce, industry and empire. In this, like the Lowland Scots, they were to deploy separate ethnic identity to their own particular advantage. The maritime dimension of this process offers intriguing possibilities for further research, and a major gap in our treatment of Cornish history is the absence of a thoroughgoing maritime history of Cornwall. Nevertheless, there are fascinating pointers. Recent work by June Palmer has emphasized the significance of eighteenth-century Cornish trading contact with a wider Atlantic world, while the emphasis on a distinctive Cornish place in the expansion of the Royal Navy prompts consideration of the paradox that, for the British state, Cornwall was—geographically and strategically—both a far- flung periphery and the focus of close governmental attention.[16]

CORNWALL AS AN INDUSTRIAL REGION
Until recently, the image of industrial Cornwall has sat unhappily alongside wider constructions of Cornish identity, not least in the estimation of Cornish Revivalists with their own ideological view of 'Cornishness' as essentially rural, Celtic, even Catholic, in which the modernity of industrialization was often left unaddressed. When the industrial era was tackled, it was generally as a discrete period in its own right, largely unconnected to what had gone before (or, indeed, had come afterwards), to be explained simply as a function of the 'Industrial Revolution'. To this was added a particular kind of industrial archaeological antiquarianism, more interested in things than people (intent on investigating artefacts rather than understanding socio-economic history), and suspicious of—even hostile to—attempts to place the Cornish industrial experience in any kind of explanatory framework. Of late, however, just as recent scholarship has offered a more sophisticated critique of the notion of industrial revolution (leading, amongst other things, to the new emphasis on diversity mentioned above), so Cornish academics have looked anew at the

process of industrialization in Cornwall. This has been at two levels, attempting first of all to contextualize the Cornish industrial experience within a wider explanation of Cornwall's history, and then setting that experience within broader models of regional economic specialization and cultural differentiation.[17] Bernard Deacon has been at the forefront of this process. He explains:

> The converging work of some economic historians and economic geographers helps to contextualise Cornwall, one of Europe's early industrial regions. Langton (1984) and Hudson (1989, 1992) argue that industrialisation produced distinct place identities as economic specialisation increased the differences between places at the same time as they were being inserted into an emerging global economy. Industrial regions thus gave rise to cultural regions. However, this approach emphasises material structures over discourses and images of regions, the economic over the cultural. To balance this I therefore combine this model of industrial regions with the work of Passi (1986, 1991) who brings together material factors and discursive represen- tations in a model of regional identity formation which stresses the role of insiders and outsiders in the construction of identities and that of social institutions in the reproduction of those identities over time.[18]

Deacon has put this approach successfully to the test in his chapter in Ella Westland's important collection, *Cornwall: The Cultural Con- struction of Place*, published in 1997, where he concludes that in the nineteenth century working-class reaction to rapid economic change combined with a proactive middle-class pride in Cornwall's industrial prowess to produce a vigorous and assertive Cornish identity. This, in turn, was reproduced in 'county' institutions, in newspapers, in novels, and in chapels, the workplace and the home. Deacon considers that at times this pride verged on arrogance, a fact noted (as Deacon records) by one observer who in 1857 wrote that:

> The thorough Cornishman's respect for his own shrewdness and that of his clan is unbounded, or equalled by his profound contempt for 'foreigners' from the east . . . this feeling increases ludicrously in intensity as we advance further west.[19]

Amongst other things, this more holistic approach to Cornwall's industrial experience allows us to revisit the nineteenth-century 'Great Emigration' with new perspectives in mind. Although much has already been written on this subject, especially in the period from the late 1960s to the mid 1980s, the emphasis has been almost exclusively on the

Cornish experience overseas (especially in North America and Australia), with correspondingly little attention given to the emigration process itself and its connection with the characteristics of industrial Cornwall. Time is ripe, therefore, for a review of the historiography of the 'Great Emigration', an opportunity to assess how historians have approached the subject thus far and to suggest new avenues of approach. There are indications that this is beginning to happen already, alongside a parallel desire to consider Cornwall's experience together with those of other peripheral (but not necessarily industrial) emigration regions in these islands.[20]

THE POLITICS OF TERRITORIAL IDENTITY

Long before the study of territorial and ethnic politics had risen to the academic prominence that it enjoys today, Adrian Lee and Colin Rallings were two political scientists prepared to point to the distinctive qualities of Cornish political behaviour, identifying not only a small but persistent nationalist movement but also other indices of 'difference'—not least that which they termed the politics of 'anti-metropolitanism'.[21] Thus, when the wider academic community had woken up to what Michael Keating described as 'the wave of "peripheral nationalist" movements which, confounding most orthodox wisdom, swept through advanced western countries in the 1960s and 1970s', upsetting 'many of the textbook theories of politics in western nations'[22] and pointing to diversity rather than homogeneity as the defining characteristic of those states (at least in their territorial dimensions), Cornwall found itself on the scholarly agenda.

Again, both theoretical work and case studies undertaken elsewhere helped in the construction of models to explain the Cornish experience. Early attempts included the co-option of both Anthony D. Smith's *Theories of Nationalism* and Michael Hechter's *Internal Colonialism*,[23] but a more thoroughgoing and comprehensive model was achieved through the application of the centre–periphery approach as elaborated by Stein Rokkan and Derek Urwin. Wary of the then prevalent mono-causal explanations of peripheral protest or regional distinctiveness, they argued for 'a broader approach which stresses the dichotomy between centre and periphery, seeking to place ethnic variations in a general framework of geopolitical location, economic strength and access to the loci of decision-making'.[24] Thus:

> the whole problem of territory and identity, of the centre–periphery dimension, goes far beyond a consideration only of ethnicity or the sudden rise of a nationalist party . . . a more rigorous, systematic,

historical and comparative perspective is necessary if we are to disentangle what is a complex mosaic.[25]

This suggestion was the cue that prompted the present author's contribution, *The Making of Modern Cornwall*, a volume which reviewed Cornwall's history from a centre–periphery perspective, borrowing the Rokkan and Urwin approach but also developing Sydney Tarrow's model of 'phases of peripherality' with an insistence 'that the effects of industrial change were of crucial significance in determining the distinctive social, economic and political characteristics of modern Cornwall'.[26] Here, in addition to an 'Older Peripheralism' of territorial and cultural isolation and a 'Second Peripheralism' of economic and social marginality associated with industrialization (and de-industrialization), there was a 'Third Peripheralism' of rapid post-war change that had apparently threatened assimilation into the expanding core of southern England and yet had resulted in both growing socio- economic and political distinctiveness *and* a sharpening of Cornish ethnic identity.

At much the same time that this view was being constructed, Ronald Perry was publishing the fruits of his extensive investigation of 'counterurbanization', an analysis of the massive post-war in-migration into Cornwall that had occurred against the background of both central government regional development policies and the creation in Cornwall of a 'branch factory' economy.[27] Perry, an economist, was thus in the forefront of the construction of what we might call the 'new Cornish social science' (with its heavy emphasis on the empirical and the applied), and in practice this social science was wedded swiftly to the new Cornish historiography as the work of historians, political scientists and economists converged with that of sociologists, geographers, anthropologists, environmentalists, psychologists and cultural studies practitioners. Central to the new coalescence were names such as Malcolm Williams, Mary McArthur, Paul Thornton, Alys Thomas, Peter Wills, Alan Kent, Lyn Bryant, John Hurst, Adrian Spalding, Caroline Vink, Amy Hale, Allen Ivey and Peter Mitchell, a number of these (and others) brought together in 1993 in the volume *Cornwall Since The War: The Contemporary History of a European Region.*[28]

CORNWALL AND THE CELTIC WORLD

The success of this coalescence and the international attention that the new Cornish historiography has been able to attract, have led to a new self-confidence in Cornish Studies as an area of academic endeavour, resulting in the New Cornish Studies Forum (a loose association of academics throughout the United Kingdom) but also in a determination to exercise academic leadership in areas where Cornwall is now clearly well placed to do so. This is nowhere more apparent than in the field of Celtic Studies, where Malcolm Chapman's by now famous (or infamous) deconstruction of the notion of 'Celticity' has posed a fundamental challenge to the *raison d'être* of Celtic Studies as a subject area and to the wider belief that within these islands there are 'Celtic nations' and 'Celtic cultures'.[29] Although Chapman's assertions have been treated with a certain scepticism—or at least reservation—by many observers, his impact upon the world of Celtic Studies is everywhere apparent. For example, in a recent (1997) British Museum publication *Britain and the Celtic Iron Age*, by Simon James and Valery Rigby, doubt is expressed as to the relevance of 'Celtic' as a concept to describe either pre-Roman or post-Roman Britain. Thus:

> One of the key questions underlying the study of this period is: can Iron Age Britain be called 'Celtic' in any meaningful sense? The idea of a Celtic past in Britain before, and indeed after, the Roman period is an established part of British popular history . . . Yet currently many scholars are challenging this idea as misleading, if not actively wrong.[30]

And yet, James and Rigby recognize that the issue of ethnicity and identity resists simplistic or dogmatic deliberation, and, while expressing doubt as to the existence of some primordial Pan-European Celtic cultural commonwealth, conclude instead that:

> The Iron Age, then, is surely best considered in terms of a hierarchy of identities. Local ones were, we can reasonably infer, the most important to peoples of the time. Britain was home to a group of developing societies related to their neighbours in Ireland and on the Continent, but also distinctive; 'Briton' is more a geographical than a cultural or political label. It may also still sometimes be useful to think of them as part of a wider world we choose to call 'Ancient Celtic'.[31]

CONCLUSION
However, James and Rigby also conclude that:

> The Ancient Britons appear never to have called themselves Celts. Only we have decided to describe them so. Even 'British' as a common label may seem anachronistic . . . common British national identity—as opposed to Scottish, Welsh or English—is a remarkably modern phenomenon, belonging especially to the years following

the Act of Union between Scotland and England/Wales in 1707. Throughout recorded history, there have always been multiple ethnic or political identities within the island, not uniform Britons, never mind generic Celts.[32]

At a time when, even in the local government elections of 1997, Cornwall proved 'a pundits nightmare'[33] and exhibited a particularist pattern of electoral contestation and electoral behaviour, we are entitled to consider that Cornwall remains a distinctive element of the multiplicity identified by James and Rigby. It is this distinctiveness which demands the further development of the new Cornish historiography but which also allows Cornish Studies to play its role in the comparative elucidation of identity-related issues within the Atlantic Archipelago, and indeed Europe and the wider world. One might further conclude that, in helping us to better understand the nature of Cornwall in its British, European and global contexts, Cornish Studies thus pursued is 'not merely an academic exercise, for such a process cannot fail to inform, influence and guide planners and policymakers at every level—should they care to listen'.[34]

NOTES AND REFERENCES

1. *West Briton*, 8 May 1997.
2. *Guardian*, 8 May 1997.
3. Jean Blondel, *Voters, Parties, and Leaders: The Social Fabric of British Politics*, London, 1963, 6th ed., 1974, p. 20.
4. Robin Cohen, *Frontiers of Identity: The British and the Others*, London, 1994, p. 12.
5. Ian McBride, 'Ulster and the British Problem', in Richard English and Graham Walker (eds.), *Unionism in Modern Ireland: New Perspectives on Politics and Culture*, London, 1996, p. 1.
6. McBride, 1996, p. 2.
7. Hugh Kearney, *The British Isles: A History of Four Nations*, Cambridge, 1989; Linda Colley, *Britons: Forging The Nation, 1707–1837*, Yale, 1992.
8. For example, see Brendan Bradshaw and John Morrill (eds.), *The British Problem c.1534–1707: State Formation in the Atlantic Archipelago*, London, 1996.
9. Helen M. Jewell, *The North-South Divide: The Origins of Northern Consciousness in England*, Manchester, 1994.
10. John Langton, 'The Industrial Revolution and the Regional Geography of England', *Transactions of the Institute of British Geographers*, NS 9, 1984; Pat Hudson, 'The Regional Perspective', in Pat Hudson (ed.), *Regions and Industries: A Regional Perspective on the Industrial Revolution in Britain*, Cambridge, 1989; Pat Hudson, *The Industrial Revolution*, London, 1992.

11. John Urry, *The Tourist Gaze: Leisure and Travel in Contemporary Societies*, London, 1990.

12. Philip Payton, *Cornwall*, Fowey, 1996, Chapter 6.

13. Mark Stoyle, *Loyalty and Locality: Popular Allegiance in Devon during the English Civil War*, Exeter, 1994; Mark Stoyle, '"Paragons or Pagans?"': Images of the Cornish during the English Civil War', *English Historical Review*, Vol.CXI No.441, April 1996; Mark Stoyle, ' "Sir Richard Grenville's Creatures": The New Cornish Tertia, 1644–46', in Philip Payton (ed.), *Cornish Studies: Four*, Exeter, 1996.

14. Mark Stoyle, 'Cornish Rebellions, 1497–1648', *History Today*, Vol. 47(5), May 1997.

15. Stoyle, 1997.

16. June Palmer, *Cornwall, The Canaries and The Atlantic*, Truro, forthcoming; Nicholas Rodger, '"A Little Navy of Your Own Making": Admiral Boscawen and the Cornish Connection in the Royal Navy', in Michael Duffy (ed.), *Parameters of British Naval Power, 1650–1850*, Exeter, 1992; Payton, 1996, Chapter 8.

17. Payton, 1996, Chapters 9 & 10.

18. Bernard Deacon, ' "The Hollow Jarring of the Distant Steam Engine": Images of Cornwall between West Barbary and Delectable Duchy', in Ella Westland (ed.), *Cornwall: The Cultural Construction of Place*, Penzance, 1997; Langton, 1984; Hudson, 1989; Hudson, 1992; Anssi Paasai, 'The Industrialization of Regions: A Theoretical Framework for Understanding the Emergence of Regions and the Constitution of Regional Identity', *Fennia*, 164, 1986.

19. Deacon, 1997, p. 21, citing Herman Merivale, 'Cornwall', *The Quarterly Review*, 102, 1857.

20. For example, see Tanya Louise Cresswell, 'Emigration from the Western Isles of Scotland and Cornwall in the Mid-Nineteenth Century', unpub. MA (Hons). dissertation, University of Aberdeen, 1995.

21. Colin Rallings and Adrian Lee, 'Cornwall: The "Celtic Fringe" in English Politics', unpub. paper, ECPR Workshop, Brussels, 1979; Colin Rallings and Adrian Lee, 'Politics of the Periphery: The Case of Cornwall', unpub. paper, Conference of the Political Studies Association workgroup on UK Politics, Aberystwyth, 1977.

22. Michael Keating, *State and Regional Nationalism: Territorial Politics and the European State*, London, 1988, p. 1.

23. Anthony D.Smith, *Theories of Nationalism*, London, 1971; Michael Hechter, *Internal Colonialism: The Celtic Fringe in British National Development*, London, 1975. Early applications of these approaches were, respectively, Philip Payton, 'The Ideology of Celtic Nationalism', unpub. BSc(Hons) dissertation, University of Bristol, 1975, and Bernard Deacon, 'Is Cornwall an Internal Colony?', in Cathal O'Luain (ed.), *For A Celtic Future*, Dublin, 1983.

24. Stein Rokkan and Derek W.Urwin, *The Politics of Territorial Identity: Studies in European Regionalism*, London, 1982, p. 2; see also Stein

Rokkan and Derek W. Urwin, *Economy, Territory, Identity: Politics of West European Peripheries,* London, 1983.

25. Derek W. Urwin, 'The Price of a Kingdom: Territory, Identity and the Centre–Periphery Dimension in Western Europe', in Yves Mény and Vincent Wright (eds.), *Centre-Periphery Relations in Western Europe,* London, 1985, p. 167.

26. Philip Payton, *The Making of Modern Cornwall: Historical Experience and the Persistence of 'Difference',* Redruth, 1992, p. 3; see also Sydney Tarrow, *Between Centre and Periphery: Grassroots Politicians in Italy and France,* New Haven, 1977, p. 16. For a preliminary attempt to place the politics of territorial identity in Cornwall in a wider 'UK estate' comparative context, see Philip Payton, 'Inconvenient Peripheries: Ethnic Identity and the "United Kingdom Estate"—The Cases of "Protestant Ulster" and Cornwall', in Iain Hampsher-Monk and Jeffrey Stanyer (eds.), *Contemporary Political Studies 1996,* Vol. 1, Belfast, 1996.

27. Ronald Perry, with Ken Dean, Bryan Brown and David Shaw, *Counter-urbanisation: International Case Studies of Socio-economic Change in Rural Areas,* Norwich, 1986.

28. Philip Payton (ed.), *Cornwall Since The War: The Contemporary History of a European Region,* Redruth, 1993

29. Malcolm Chapman, *The Celts: The Construction of a Myth,* London, 1992.

30. Simon James and Valery Rigby, *Britain and The Celtic Iron Age,* London, 1997, p. 1.

31. James & Valery, 1997, p. 85.

32. James & Valery, 1997, pp. 84–85.

33. *West Briton,* 8 May 1997.

34. Payton (ed.), 1996, p. 1; for a recent example of contemporary Cornish Studies impacting upon socio-economic debate see the *In Pursuit of Excellence 'Green Book',* Truro, 1997.

THE CORNISH: IDENTITY AND GENETICS—AN ALTERNATIVE VIEW

Dick Cole

'The whole countrie of Britaine is divided into iiii partes, whereof
the one is inhabited of Englishmen, the other of Scottes, the third
of Wallshemen, the fowerthe of Cornish people.'

Polydore Virgil in the Sixteenth Century[1]

Who were the Cornish anyway?
Celts and Druids—mere superstition
the Tamar—just another river
Carn Kenidjack, Lanyon Quoit, Portherras—
just funny names.

People say they used to fish
and mine for tin and china clay
and that they didn't like strangers.

Grannie T.
turns in the family grave
spitting.[2]

Penny Windsor

INTRODUCTION

This short article sets out to review the recent debate concerning studies
of the biological and genetic make-up of the Cornish people, much of
which was conducted through popular and non-academic channels such
as the regional (sic) press during 1991, 1992 and 1995.

Much has traditionally been written about the physical characteristics of Cornish people, and most of what has appeared has been

based on assumptions that have had little evidence to support them. For example, James Whetter, writing in 1971, considered that during the Romano-British period, 'though little research has been done on the subject one imagines the population of Kernow at this stage . . . consisted of the tall, brown, or fairhaired Celts, mainly farmers, in the centre and east; darker, stockier Veneti colonists around the coast and in the west; on the open moorland solidly built, round-head types, the Bronze Age survivors'.[3] Similarly, there is no evidence for the age-old myth that the dark complexion of many Cornish people can be traced to Spanish incursions at the time of the Armada (1588) or perhaps also the later Mounts Bay raid in 1595.[4]

For the purposes of this review, however, there are a number of pieces of recent genetic/physical research which are relevant, although the most widely reported (and the research on which I shall concentrate) was the work of R.G. Harvey, M.T. Smith, S. Sherren, L. Bailey and S.J. Hyndman, who collectively published an article entitled 'How Celtic are the Cornish?: A Study of Biological Affinities' in the *Journal of the Anthropological Institute* in 1986 (Vol. 21, No. 2). Other recent surveys include the work of Professor Robert Sokal of the State University of New York, which was reported in 1992. Studying blood samples, he noted there was a correlation between the genetic indicators of Cornish people and those living in Devon, which 'picks off Devon and Cornwall from the rest'.[5] Meanwhile, Phyllis Jackson has undertaken a study of regional feet shapes. The author, a retired chiropodist, has argued that a slim foot predominates in Scotland and Ireland. She notes, 'this shape of foot prevails also in Wales and the Cornish peninsula, including some people from Devonshire; it is unfortunate that I have never seen a Breton foot, but I would be very surprised if the same shape has not prevailed'.[6]

By looking primarily at the research of Harvey et al., I intend to demonstrate that, by failing to incorporate recent archaeological investigations regarding the *Adventus Saxonum* (the settlement of the Anglo-Saxons in Britain)—for example, population change, cultural shifts—into their work, they have made conclusions which are inappropriate and not sustainable.

It is not the purpose of this article to criticize the actual methodology of the genetic/scientific testing, especially as Harvey, Smith and their colleagues have cautiously qualified their results by stating that the 'evidence is hard to quantify . . . gene frequencies themselves are unreliable as indicators of historical origin or process'.[7] Nevertheless, it is necessary to question the proffered conclusions, which Smith claims were furnished 'with observed data from archaeology and history'[8] but which were, in fact, structured uncritically around a particular historical metanarrative that is becoming increasingly open to question and reinterpretation.

'HOW CELTIC ARE THE CORNISH?'

In May 1984, over 250 Cornish people took part in an anthropological project to study the physical and genetic attributes of the Cornish, and to compare these results to similar studies from other parts of Britain and Europe. The published report also maintained that it set out to investigate whether Cornwall's 'rich and multifarious Celtic heritage extend[ed] to the biological realm'.[9] Its final conclusions maintained that:

> such characteristics as general body size, head size, hair and eye colour point to greater affinities with the Celtic language-speaking peoples of Wales, Ireland and Scotland than with the neighbours of the Cornish to the east. On the other hand, the blood group evidence shows that the Cornish sample occupies a somewhat intermediate position between 'Celtic' and 'Anglo-Saxon' populations, but with a definite tendency to be aligned with the latter.[10]

A number of other potentially distinctive Cornish traits were also noted but Harvey et al. stated quite categorically that 'the sample is small and we have endeavoured to interpret the results in an appropriately cautious manner', adding 'How Celtic are the Cornish? Our title is provocative: we would not presume to measure on the yardstick of heredity that which might be more satisfactorily be assessed through genealogy, geography, dialect and culture'.[11] Nonetheless, they felt it necessary to further add that:

> to approach the question from another side is no less than fair—the Cornish are Celtic; they might therefore be expected to share the genetic characteristics of the other Celtic populations of Western Europe. That they do so to so slight an extent is testimony to the power of successive Celtic revivals, including the present Cornish language revival, and to the selective retention of cultural traits and manipulation of kinship links in promoting the Celtic identity of a population whose interest in and validation of its roots tends, not unnaturally, to be genealogical rather than genetic.[12]

SOME RESPONSES

The contents of the research first came to the attention of the non-academic world when one of the contributors, Malcolm Smith, delivered a paper at an annual meeting of the British Association for the Advancement of Science, held at Polytechnic South-West (now the University of Plymouth) in 1991.[13] The press promptly seized on the data, which it began to vigorously misinterpret. Press coverage was selective and targeted; Smith's paper was seen as perfect ammunition for an assault on Cornish institutions and aspects of Cornishness or Cornish identity. Amongst all the headlines and soundbites, perhaps the most telling was the BBC *Spotlight* quip which mocked that 'the Cornish are no more Celtic than your average Brummie'.[14]

Interpretations from what might be called the 'Cornish perspective' were also to a degree selective. Some academics, such as Philip Payton, reminded observers of the reported physical similarities between the Cornish and the other Celtic peoples—a fact not reported by the media who themselves had concentrated solely on the blood group evidence. The prominent nature of the press coverage, particularly in 1991, also led to a plethora of responses to newspaper letter pages, local radio phone-ins, and so on. As Payton has noted, angry Cornish people insisted that 'ethnic identity had little to do with biology and everything to do with culture, self-perception and historical experience—including contemporary socio-economic conditions'.[15] Later, in 1995, Ann Sandercock effectively reopened the debate when she delivered a presentation to a gathering of Cornish language speakers at a Cornish language weekend at Maen Porth, Falmouth. She argued that the number of distinctive genetic features in Harvey's study were evidence of the Cornish being sufficiently 'distant from other groups to be unique'.[16]

AN ALTERNATIVE VIEW
Harvey and his colleagues argued that the basis for their particular study was to compare the Cornish people with the populations of the other Celtic countries. They noted that 'it is likely that the Cornish population had an appreciable Celtic ancestral component linking it by descent with the Welsh and Irish' , and set out to investigate if this would be 'detectable in the modern population'.[17] By association, difference between these populations and non- Celtic peoples was also investigated.

In discussing whether the Cornish population might still exhibit clear 'genetic evidence' of 'Celticness', the study dismissed genetic drift and natural selection and argued that migration was the 'most probable and tractable cause of gene frequency change'. At the same time, however, Harvey and his colleagues warned against assumptions of genetic homogeneity, stating that 'the disparate tribal subdivision of Celtic mainland Britain at the coming of the Romans' was unlikely to have led to such homogeneity within areas of Celtic culture.[18] This, of course, echoed recent scholarship which stressed that the term 'Celtic' was (like all other ethnic identities) a social construct, a term used both anciently and in modern times (often by 'non-Celts') to describe a heterogeneous group of peoples who nonetheless exhibited perceived linguistic and other cultural similarities. There could be no such thing as a 'Celtic gene', nor could assumptions about the biological affinities of 'Celtic peoples' be understood as anything more than part of a wider social construct.

The difficulty that Harvey et al. encountered (and this is a serious flaw in their published paper) is that, while they appeared to recognise the illegitimacy of attempting to define 'Celtic' in genetic terms, they nevertheless persisted in asking the question 'How Celtic are the Cornish?' with a view to answering it in a largely biological manner. In other words, they were trapped by exactly those assumptions that they had themselves identified and warned against. Despite their apparent awareness of scholarly objections, they proceeded to structure their study around traditional (but by now contested) assumptions of homogeneity, making little attempt to distance themselves from un-critical approaches to 'Celticness'.

To this uncritical embrace of 'Celticness' was added a similar inability to deal adequately with that other value-laden term, 'Anglo-Saxon'. Indeed, their failure to incorporate a new and radically different view of the *Adventus Saxonum* into their research would serve to fundamentally undermine their conclusions. For inherent within their work is the assumption that the modern-day English population should represent genetic difference from the Cornish, Welsh, Irish; with the Cornish representing the indigenous population and the English representing a new, genetic population which migrated to Britain between the fifth and sixth centuries. In other words, the geneticists were again falling into an old trap. They were accepting, again rather uncritically, the traditional (even 'right-wing') historical view that Britain was the 'political and cultural product of conquest and colony'.[19] England, the traditional historians had argued, was formed by the large-scale migration of hordes of Germanic settlers and the replace-ment of the indigenous Celtic population, leaving genetically distinct populations in opposed Anglo-Saxon and Celtic areas.[20]

Many archaeologists now refuse to accept this interpretation and are arguing that the *Adventus Saxonum* actually involved a limited number of Anglo-Saxon settlers, and moreover was an 'elite takeover of a disintegrating society rather than a mass replacement of popula-tion'.[21] Chris Taylor has rather sarcastically summarised the discredited story thus:

towards the end of the Roman period, as the Roman Empire weakened and fell apart, Saxon raiders attacked the country in large numbers. In the early 5th century the Roman army and administration were withdrawn and Saxon bands swept over the country burning, pillaging and destroying all in their path. A few remaining Romano-British people were massacred or driven west into Wales leaving an empty but potentially rich countryside for the Saxons. These early Saxons quickly found the best sites to live on. They picked out suitable places on dry gravel, at spring heads, or in sheltered valleys, and laid out the first English villages.[22]

The reality was somewhat different and archaeologists no longer give credence to this somewhat mythical version. As Taylor again notes, the Germanic settlers were not moving into a new country but a very old one; full of settlements, field systems and, most importantly, people. He agrees with Charles Thomas that 'during the fifth century no more than 100,000 Saxon settlers came to this country. While this may seem to be a considerable number, when this figure is compared with the estimate of a late Roman population of perhaps five million it pales into insignificance'.[23] In failing to consider such archaeological discussions, the geneticists have tied themselves to some very outdated ideas. It is a serious problem; developments in the past have so often been explained in narrow ethnocentric terms. This has led to numerous narratives which concentrate on migration and population replacement as the principal impetus behind change.

In attempting to explain Cornwall's genetic profile, and its tendency to demonstrate a closeness to some of the 'English' evidence, Malcolm Smith's interpretation hinged on two aspects of Cornwall's history; 'one is evidence for Celtic colonisation from Ireland and Wales . . . the second kind of relevant information relates to movement of people from England to Cornwall during historical times'.[24] It is clear from the published literature that Malcolm Smith and the others never seriously considered the implication that a similarity between the genetic indicators of areas that are not deemed similar in modern ethno-cultural terms, might actually point to evidence surviving from an underlying and somewhat stationary population that largely predates the development of modern entities such as Cornwall and England. Similarly, when the work of Professor Robert Sokal was reported in 1992 and suggested there was some evidence of genetic similarities between Cornish people and the population of Devon, *The Times* interviewed Malcolm Smith and printed a statement that said the Celtic tradition of Cornwall was not 'based on a large number of Celtic settlers'.[25]

The reinterpretation 'Anglo-Saxon England' is perhaps the best-known case of recent archaeological reassessment, in which change (political, social, landscape, cultural) was formerly explained in narratives concentrating on the movement of particular populations but which is now being re-examined. However, it is not the only case. Others include the late Neolithic/early Bronze Age period, when changes in material culture (the introduction of beakers) and shifts in burial tradition were explained until recently as the creations of a whole new ethnic people known as the 'Beakers'; these developments are now more usually interpreted as due to a 'shift in social emphasis'.[26] Also, landscape change in South Pembrokeshire ('Little England beyond Wales') has been explained by Anglo-Norman/Flemish settlement in the eleventh century—but now even the extent of such landscape change is itself in doubt.[27] Similarly, 'the impact of the Danes in the Danelaw in the 9th and 10th centuries . . . is essentially one of lordship appropriation and control rather than one of extensive settlement of Scandinavian farmers'.[28]

In the case of the research of Harvey and his team in Cornwall, they persisted in attempting to use the perceived migration of peoples to explain genetic differences between modern ethno-cultural groups. But as archaeologists, we are now in the position of being able to argue that some of these population movements never actually took place (e.g. the Beaker Folk) while others, like the Anglo-Saxon conquest, were not dependent on the same scale of movement of a (genetically) different, ethnic population as hitherto believed.

Unlike Harvey's team, some scientists are using genetic evidence to actually challenge the histories used uncritically in the research in Cornwall. In studying Anglo-Saxon England, Martin Evison, a research consultant in the Department of Forensic Pathology at Sheffield University, has written that if there were

> a convincing argument for the displacement or destruction of the native population . . . we might expect to find that gene frequencies in England resemble those of the 'Anglo-Saxon' homelands in northern-central Europe. Current research by population geneticists, however, suggests the opposite. For example, a particularly distinctive genetic variant common in Frisia and Schleswig turns out to be rare in all parts of Britain, including the South-East, one part of the country where the historical, archaeological and linguistic evidence for displacement is at its greatest . . . in other words, the genetic evidence does not support the hypothesis of the widespread destruction or displacement of the native population by invaders from what is now northern Germany.[29]

CONCLUSION—WHOSE GENETIC MATERIAL?

So where do such archaeological studies leave the geneticists? If the likes of Chris Taylor and Charles Thomas are correct, when they say only 100,000 'English settlers' moved into Britain in the fifth century, how much will studies of the genetic differences between modern ethno-cultural groups really tell us about their origins? How much value is there in comparing the modern Cornish population to that of England, or any other country, when so much of the underlying population—and by association its genetic material— predates the foundation of the modern political or cultural groups under study? How much of the genetic material of the average English person today, for example, will originate in the early Dark Age/pre-English period? Alternatively, how much of the genetic material of a modern Cornish person or English person will have originated in the even darker, 'pre-Celtic' past?

The conclusion must be that our modern cultural and political identities were not formed through the mass migration of people but as a result of more complex and complicated factors such as assimilation, acculturation and accommodation. Any genetic study must, therefore, accept this reality—otherwise it is likely to be undermined by poorly informed historical and archaeological speculation.

NOTES AND REFERENCES

1. Cited in J. Whetter, *The Celtic Background of Cornwall*, St Austell, 1971, p.17.
2. Extract from the poem 'Relatives' in *Radical Wales*, No. 20, Winter 1988, p. 11; permission to reproduce this poem is gratefully acknowledged.
3. Whetter, 1971, p. 5.
4. G. Pawley White, *A Handbook of Cornish Surnames*, Truro, p. 11.
5. *The Times*, 17 July 1992.
6. J. Jackson, 'Footloose in Archaeology', *Current Archaeology*, 144, Aug.–Sept. 1995, pp. 466–67.
7. M.T. Smith, 'Cornish Genes and Celtic Culture', *Cornish Worldwide*, 5, 1992, pp. 6–7.
8. Smith, 1992, p. 6.
9. R.G. Harvey, M.T. Smith, S. Sherren, L. Bailey and S.J. Hyndman, 'How Celtic are the Cornish?: A Sudy of Biological Affinities', *Journal of the Anthropological Institute*, Vol. 21, No. 2, June 1986, p. 178.
10. Harvey et al., 1986, p. 198.
11. Harvey et al., 1986, p. 198.
12. Harvey et al., 1986, pp. 198–199.
13. A version of this paper was later published as Smith, 1992.
14. P. Payton, 'Post-war Cornwall: A Suitable Case for Treatment?', in P. Payton (ed.), *Cornwall Since the War: The Contemporary History of a European Region*, Redruth, 1993, p. 13.

15. Payton, 1993, p. 13.
16. D. Williams, 'Who are the Cornish?', *Western Morning News*, 20 May 1995; letter from A. Sandercock, *Cornish Guardian*, 29 June 1995.
17. Harvey et al., 1986, p. 179.
18. Harvey et al., 1986, p. 179.
19. D. Austin 'The Proper Study of Medieval Archaeology', in D. Austin and L. Alcock (eds.), *From the Baltic to the Black Sea*, London, 1990, p. 15.
20. Not all historians accepted this view. As early as the late nineteenth century 'liberal' historians such as Seerbohm argued for a large-scale continuity of landscape and people into the Anglo-Saxon period, but until recently these views had been sidelined by the dominant 'Tory' historical view, which included nationalist concepts at 'the very core of Englishness'. For a discussion of this debate and the problems of historiography in this period, see Austin and Alcock (eds.), 1990, pp. 9–42.
21. C. Taylor, *Village and Farmstead*, London, 1983, p. 111.
22. Taylor, 1983, p. 109.
23. Taylor, 1983, p. 111.
24. Smith, 1992, pp. 5–6.
25. *The Times*, 18 July 1992.
26. B. Molyneaux, *Prehistory*, Newport, 1993, p. 41.
27. R. Cole, 'Carew Newton and Houghton Farm—A Study in South Pembrokeshire Settlement Patterns', in *Carew Castle Archaeological Project: 1993 Season Report*, 1993, pp. 27–31.
28. D. Austin (ed.), *Carew Castle Archaeological Project: 1994 Season Report*, 1994, p. 46.
29. M. Evison, 'Lo The Conquering Hero Comes (Or Not)', *British Archaeology*, 23, April 1997, pp. 8–9.

THE TITHING FRAMEWORK OF WEST CORNWALL: A PROPOSED PATTERN AND AN INTERPRETATION OF TERRITORIAL ORIGINS

David Harvey

INTRODUCTION

The judicial tithing system constituted the backbone of Norman law-giving and can be seen as the mechanism through which central government held dominion over the population. In many ways it was a system of compulsory collective responsibility, through which a sort of joint bail was fixed for individuals, not after their arrest for a crime, but rather as a safeguard in anticipation of it.[1] Importantly, however, the tithing in Cornwall not only represented an income generating mechanism and form of judicial control, but became territorialized. The Cornish tithing framework, therefore, appears to be a uniquely systematic and universal territorial device which formed the most basic administrative unit in the medieval period, and was the primary subdivision of the Cornish hundred until the sixteenth century.[2]

In 1284 there were 308 tithings in Cornwall, as opposed to about 200 parishes, and Pool argues that no link between the two forms of territory existed.[3] Tithings often appear to have a strong relationship with manorial patterns but Pool points out that tithings and manors were not necessarily coterminous and prefers to relate the form of the territorial tithing to that of the *vill* rather than to any land holding association.[4] It is important to note, therefore, that although the civil administrative and judicial system of the tithing may have been closely related to the system of early land holding, just as with the *vill* and manor, the two institutions should not be confused.

Pool's exhaustive and informative paper outlined the function of this system in the later medieval period and charted its decline through to the early modern period.[5] This paper included a survey of many sources relating to the tithing system and an extensive appendix of the basic tithing assessments from a wide range of material. The paper was built upon the foundations laid by an earlier paper which concentrated on the transcript and interpretation of a sixteenth-century manuscript relating to the operation of the tithing system in Penwith.[6] These works constitute the only serious attempt to investigate the territorial tithing system and have drawn some important conclusions as to the later operation, context and demise of this system. His cautious map of Penwith tithings constitutes an important and unique aid to our understanding of the territorial aspects of later medieval administrative and judicial control in Cornwall and suggests the value of further interpretative work.[7] Pool, however, does not really attempt to examine the origins of this territorial system nor explore some of the implications of the relationships and assessments to which he refers.

Although not concentrating his analysis upon the origins of the tithing, Pool does state that 'how and when these groups became, in Cornwall at any rate, territorial sub-divisions of the hundreds, is a matter of some mystery, though it is not hard to suggest the probable sequence of events'.[8] However, Pool does not actually give us much help in the 'sequence of events'. His perception of the tithings as subdivisions of the hundreds assumes that the tithings were territorially later and completely dependent on the hundreds. Pool for instance focuses on police duties and noted that for 'practical reasons' people had to live close to each other. He concludes by arguing that it was this that eventually led to territorial tithings. However, he provides no explanation as to why such a tithing system that existed right across England only became territorialized in the South West, and why it only became systematically so in Cornwall. The simple conception of people living close to one another does not provide adequate explanation for the fragmented forms, variable sizes or basic pattern of the territorial tithing.[9] The evolution and development of boundaries and land units cannot be understood in such simple terms.

This article, then, aims to extend the analysis of the actual territorial pattern of tithings in West Cornwall. Working from Pool's initial Penwith map, and using additional information, the tithing patterns of both Penwith and Kirrier can be uncovered to some extent. The map of tithing units produced from this exercise forms the basis for further explorations into the meaning of the tithing assessments and the origins of the framework. The notion of the tithing as a semi-independent expression of 'community' is elaborated and the problematical 'Cornish acre' unit of assessment is analysed with a view to achieving a more meaningful interpretation. The origins of both the assessments and the territorial framework are investigated with the view that the tithing framework may have represented the vestiges of an earlier system of landscape organization. This proposed earlier scheme provides a context within which to perceive later territorial developments as well as providing a useful framework within which to place the early sites, settlements and practices that are of interest to archaeologists, historians and geographers.

TITHING PATTERNS: SOURCES AND INTERPRETATION

In 1699, Joel Gascoyne produced a map of Cornwall that was the first county map in Britain to include parish boundaries.[10] By this time the parochial framework had become the basic unit of civil administration. The tithings, on the other hand, had fallen out of public use and were unrecognized in such cartographic surveys. The reconstruction of the tithing pattern, therefore, is a very difficult task. A fairly accurate representation of the framework is, however, made possible by using a multitude of various sources, many of which offer information that is indirectly related to tithing delineation.[11] Though a clearly recognized territorial framework is implicit, very accurate boundaries are obviously difficult to ascertain. The possibility must be noted that the territorial tithings may have been assessed and recognized in more complex ways than the simple area of land within accurately surveyed boundaries. Therefore the 'territorial reconstruction' of tithings is necessarily vague. This recognizes the interpretational problems inherent in using such multiple sources, and the potential problems surrounding the comprehension of how these territorial units were perceived. The basic map of proposed tithings is displayed in Figure 1, followed by some comment on the processes of how this map was produced and the nature of the source material that was used.

Although systematic survey-style extents survive for only three tithings, other lines of evidence can indirectly provide some useful information as to the position, size and pattern of the tithings.[12] The hundred court proceedings of 1333, for instance, note the location of the crime in five cases which place five tenements within their respective territorial tithing units.[13] The Eyre Court proceedings of 1201 for instance, suggest that Kerthen Wood in St. Erth parish should be placed within Roseworthy tithing.[14] Similar pieces of evidence can be found in the Assize Rolls of 1284 and 1302.[15] Many of the cases describe crimes and other occurrences being committed within certain tithings and such pieces of information help to form a picture of the pattern of tithings. In all the material covered, there appears to be only one

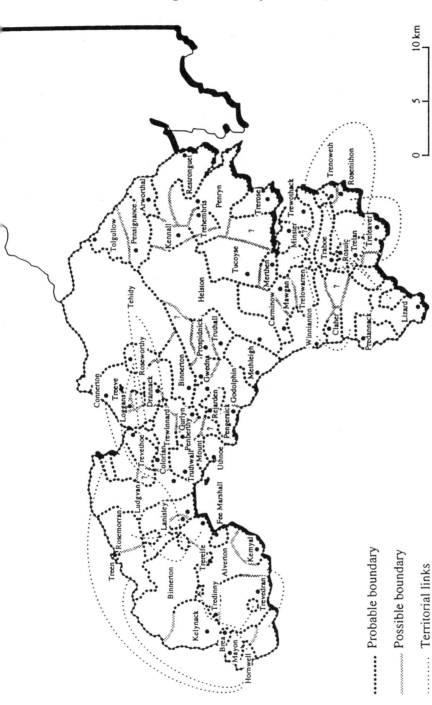

Figure 1: Basic tithing pattern
(Penwith based largely on Pool 1959)

•••••••• Probable boundary

⸝⸝⸝⸝⸝⸝⸝ Possible boundary

·········· Territorial links

instance where a portion of land was specifically designated as being in two entirely different tithings at different times.[16] The rarity of this phenomenon and apparent uniqueness of Rosemorder tend to support the notion of antiquity and persistence in territorial form.

As Thomas points out, the evidence certainly points toward a close and fundamental link between the manor and the tithing in Cornwall.[17] However, when Pool related the tithing names with manorial names that were entered into Domesday Book, no satisfactory relationship could be found other than within the example of Penwith hundred.[18] He goes on to suggest that the many minor differences that seem to occur between the two territorial frameworks are due to the conservative nature of public law and the judiciary to which tithing bounds were subject. As a community institution, defined within the realms of public law, tithings, as with *vills*, are 'not to be disturbed' by later private actions, and so their boundaries became fixed and relatively inflexible at an early date, and (like parishes) were not usually affected by later manorial changes. This raises the possibility that the tithing structures may represent a pattern of archaic land holding or communal territory, fossilized by public law, and also necessitates some further analysis of the relationship between the manor and the tithing.

TABLE 1
A summary table of the tithing/manor associations in Penwith and Kirrier

Tithing name	Associated manor/ sub-manor	Location of tithing centre
In Penwith		
Alverton	Alverton	Madron
Binnerton	Binnerton	Crowan
Brea	Brea	St Just
Collorian	Collorian?	Ludgvan
Connerton	Connerton	Gwithian
Drannack	Drannack (Connerton?)	Gwinear
Fee-Marshall	Fee-Marshall? (Alverton)	Paul
Gurlyn	Gurlyn?	St Erth
Hornwell	Hornwell (Corva)	Morvah?
Kelynack	Kelynack	St Just
Kemyal	Kemyal (Alverton)	Paul
Lanisley	Lanisley	Gulval
Loggans	Trevethoe and Lelant?	Phillack
Ludgvan	Ludgvan-Lease	Ludgvan

Mayon	Mayon?	Sennen
Mount	St Michael's Mount	St Hilary (Marazion)
Penberthy	Penberthy?	St Hilary
Perranuthnoe	Uthnoe	Perranuthnoe
Rosemorran	Rosemorran (Lanisley)	Gulval
Roseworthy	Roseworthy (Tregony)	Gwinear
Tehidy	Tehidy	Illogan
Tredinney	Tredinney (Alverton?)	St Buryan
Treen	?? (Hornwell?)	Zennor
Treeve	?? (Connerton)	Phillack
Tregony	Tregony (Roseworthy)	Madron?
Trereife	Trereife? (Alverton)	Madron
Trevedran	St Buryan	St Buryan
Trevethoe	Trevethoe and Lelant	Lelant
Trewinnard	Trewinnard?	St Erth
Truthwall	Truthwall (ex Mount?	)Ludgvan

In Kirrier

Arworthal	Arworthal	Perranarworthal
Carminoe	Carminoe (Winnianton?)	Mawgan
Claher	Claher (Winnianton?)	Mullion
Godolphin	Godolphin	Breage
Gwedna	Pengwedna?	Breage
Helston	Helston in Kirrier	Wendron
Kennall	Kennall?	Stithians
Lizard	Trethevas (Rosuic)	Landewednack
Lucies	=Rosuic	
Mawgan	Mawgan (Winnianton?)	Mawgan
Merthen	Merthen (Winnianton)	Constantine
Methleigh	Methleigh	Breage
Minster	Minster (Penryn)	Manaccan
Pengersick	Pengersick?	Breage
Penryn	Penryn	Gluvias
Pensignance	Pensignance	Gwennap
Predannack	Predannack (Rosuic)	Mullion
Prospidnick	Prospidnick?	Sithney
Rejarden	Binnerton?	Germoe
Restronguet	Restronguet (Cosawes)	Mylor
Rosenithon	St Keverne/Achevran?	St Keverne
Rosuic	Rosuic	St Keverne
Tolgullow	Tolgullow	Gwennap
Traboe	Traboe	St Keverne
Trehembris	Carnsew (Penryn)	Mabe

Trelan	Trelan?	St Keverne
Treleaver	Reskymer Meneage	St Keverne
Trelowarren	Trelowarren (Winnianton?)	Mawgan
Trenoweth	Trenoweth?	St Keverne
Trerose	Trerose (Penryn)	Mawnan
Trewothack	Trewothack? (Winnianton?)	St Anthony
Truthall	Truthall?	Sithney
Tucoyse	Tucoyse	Constantine
Winnianton	Winnianton	Gunwalloe

Table 1 displays the territorial links between the tithings and the land holding record. Almost every tenement which we can place within a certain tithing seems to have independent evidence placing it within a certain manor or sub-manor that is associated with that tithing. Private manorial power sometimes seems to have compromised the judicial independence of the tithing institution in the later medieval period, as in the case noted in the Cartulary of Launceston Priory where the Prior won a decision in 1357 that meant that his tenants did not have to supply a tithingman nor contributions for tithingmen.[19] The existence of a formal application and judicial decision being made about this case does, however, illustrate the important differences between a private landed estate and a public, hundredal and communal institution.

The strong territorial relationship with land holding, together with the specific reference to tithing locations, tithingman's tenements and the few tithing extents have formed a picture of the territorial framework of the tithing institution in West Cornwall. Small inaccuracies are certain, but the degree of error has been recognised, and so the basic maps should only be seen as approximate.[20] With the use of the Penheleg manuscript, Pool managed to produce a map of tithings in Penwith.[21] With some corrections noted in the following year, this map appears to be the only previous attempt to cartographically portray these important territories. My investigations have highlighted some limitations and problems in Pool's analysis and have led to an improved map of the Penwith tithings as shown on Figure 1. This work paved the way for a similar project on the previously untouched hundred of Kirrier (also illustrated on Figure 1). It is important to note that possibly not all of the tithings portrayed in the maps would have been recognized at the same time. For instance, a fair number of tithings do not seem to be consistently portrayed throughout the records. Kemyal, for example, is described in the Penheleg manuscript as a separate territorial entity, yet does not appear in the *Extenta Acrarum* documents of the thirteenth and fourteenth centuries. Pool, however, notes that it does appear in the Assize Rolls of 1284 and 1302, suggesting its recognition in some form, though not in a form that warranted an assessment in Cornish acres, and thereby inclusion in the *Extenta Acrarum*.[22] The land holding unit associated with the Kemyal area was a sub-manor of the large Alverton estate and so possibly the tithing of Kemyal would have been included under the large assessment for Alverton tithing in the *Extenta Acrarum*.

The lines on the tithing maps therefore should not be seen as exact, fixed and detailed boundaries but simply as representations of territorial limits. Some degree of intra-tithing flexibility seems to be implied by the court proceedings of all dates, with tithing subgroups apparently recognized in some cases. Subgroups seem to be implied relatively often in connection with some of the larger tithings such as Binnerton, Alverton or Tehidy. In 1302 for instance, the borough of Helston (within the tithing of Helston, associated with the manor of Helston-in-Kirrier) claimed view of frankpledge within the borough at the session of Eyre.[23] This implies some sort of sub-recognition within the basic tithing framework.

EXPLOITATION AND THE INSTITUTIONAL FUNCTION OF THE TITHING SYSTEM

The framework of tithings illustrated in the map on Figure 1 represent the basic network of units that held general recognition by public authority. These tithing units represent expressions of public administration and are territorially closely associated with the land-holding pattern. The tithings, however, expressed more aspects of societal organization than mere civil administration. The Cornish territorial tithings were vehicles of communal identity and, in a similar way to the functions of the English *vill*, comprised aspects of economic organisation.[24] Tithings of such a diverse nature as Tehidy and Treen, for instance, cannot have been seen in the same way in terms of communal identity and economic exploitation, even though they may well have held the same status and function in terms of hundredal and judicial organisation. This map therefore should simply be seen as a basic guide to the general pattern of tithings and their location with respect to each other in the context of local civil administration. The tithing framework may be perceived both as a system through which people were exploited through various taxes and dues by people at a higher level in the hierarchy, and as a framework, akin to the system of English *vills*, through which the landscape was economically exploited. The tithing system can also be seen as a territorial mechanism through which aspects of community and society were expressed.

At a local level, the tithing appears to hold some degree of independence. The allocation of its taxation requirements do not seem to be stipulated from above, and its selection of officers such as that of tithingman, though observing certain customs and traditions, does not appear to be dictated by another authority.[25] In addition, the early court proceedings show evidence that tithings held certain investigative powers in the sense that the decision to raise a hue was initially taken at this level.[26] All this suggests a certain level of community self-organization and freedom of movement for the officers. This is especially illustrated in the numerous cases where a hue would be raised, a suspect chased, captured and held; all done within the authority of local tithing operation.

Extending from this argument is the notion that such semi-independent communal units held certain privileges in fund raising and maintained often unusual quasi-judicial rights. Pool noted the apparently common practice of generating a surplus smoke silver for the tithingman.[27] The number of disputes that arise from the attempts by various tenements to get out of supplying a tithingman suggests that the office was not popular, indicating that the surplus smoke silver actually offset 'expenses' incurred by the individual tithing 'authorities'. Many other dues, payments and rights appear in the records, many of which were probably either forgotten or were subsumed within tenant's rents as the archaic forms of public tribute and personal connection gave way to notions of property and rental value in a capitalist society. The payment of *berbagium*, for instance, which in Cornwall is associated with a manorial due on Duchy tenants, has been related to a common theme of early services within an administrative district akin to that of the hundred.[28] Pool recognized the tithing system as the framework in which such rights and dues as those connected with wrecks, porpoises and sharks, and 'straying beasts' were organized.[29] Perhaps more importantly it also provided the framework in which the collection of tin fines were undertaken.[30] Such hundredal rights, which seem even to have extended to the payments of marrowbones and loaves of bread for hunting hounds, appear almost as a relic of archaic tribute practices.[31]

The expressions of exploitation embodied within the tithing system have been recognized but their meaning in terms of the origin and form of the territorial framework of organization needs to be considered further by investigating the systematic assessments that were made of the tithing system. The *Extenta Acrarum* documents for instance provide us with a complete set of assessments in 'Cornish acres'. The term 'Cornish acre' has not been satisfactorily interpreted. A short discussion by Hull reviews the problem, simply suggesting that a Cornish acre represented somewhere between 40 and 200 English statute acres, and most probably either 64 or 120.[32] This, however, is unsatisfactory in that it appears to assume a simple unidimensional and linear relationship relative to statute English acres which may not actually exist in reality.[33] The two versions of the *Extenta Acrarum* provide slightly differing assessment figures.[34] Table 2 clearly displays the apparent discrepancy in the simple association between Cornish acres and area, suggesting a much more complex relationship than is normally recognized.

TABLE 2
The theoretical size of Cornish acres in West Cornwall

| Hundred | Statute Acres (1911 census) | Extenta Acracum versions | | 'Acres per Cornish acre' (1345) |
| | | (1284) | (1345) | |
		in Cornish acres		
Penwith	99,293	535.5	573.5	184.7
Kirrier	104,629	372.5	363.5	287.8

(From a comparison of the *Extenta Acrarum* and actual statute acreage).

One possibility is that Cornish acres only measured a certain portion of the total land area, though the similar soil, climate and proportion of moorland in each hundred suggests that such a form of measurement would not provide such a large difference in the two sets of figures as seems to be displayed. There is the possibility that Cornish acres took into account aspects of each hundred that were not related to areas of land, such as fishing or tin production for instance. It certainly appears however that the Cornish acreage figures represent some form of estimation that was based upon more than mere land area, though this does seem to have been an important component.[35] In order to uncover the basis of such a difference between the two sets of assessments we should investigate the marked differences between the two hundreds. A very realistic explanation therefore may be seen in the private nature of the Penwith hundred. This was the only hundred in Cornwall that became detached from royal or Duchy interests. The private hundredal jurisdiction was granted by William II outside of royal authority in about 1090 and was comprehensively confirmed by a charter to the Arundell family of 1227.[36] Therefore, it seems realistic to assume that the Penwith assessments were artificially changed under this private jurisdiction. An analysis of the other seven hundreds of Cornwall reveals a Cornish acreage relationship very much in line with that of Kirrier, leaving Penwith as the anomaly.[37]

The production of a detailed record of the hundredal rights and jurisdictions of Penwith in the form of the Penheleg Manuscript (1580) reveals the specific nature of the private interests of this hundred, with traditional dues and rights appearing to survive the longest and be recorded latest in Penwith, as the hundredal lords struggled to maintain and make the most of their privileges.[38] The apparent difference in the Cornish acreage assessments may therefore be related to this practice. The actual purpose of the *Extenta Acrarum* lists of 1284 and 1345 is not known but the basis for inclusion seems to be somehow linked to status that reveals the operation of some sort of hierarchy within the tithing system.[39]

INTERPRETING THE ASSESSMENT MATERIAL

Both the smoke silver and the Cornish acreage figures allude to an expression of exploitation, and suggest a large degree of artificiality. The smoke silver assessments represent the exploitation of the population via a household or tenement tax and in Kirrier display an almost complete repetition in certain figures.[40] The Cornish acreage figures suggest some sort of assessment of economic status that is at least partly a function of land area. Interestingly however, the more dependable figures for Kirrier reveal a repetition of 3-, 6-, 9- and 12-acre tithings. This repetition is consistently mirrored in the seven more eastern hundreds (as illustrated in Figure 3 on page 44), but not in Penwith and requires further investigation.

The tithings with the largest Cornish acreage also tend to cover the largest areas and those paying the most smoke silver appear to contain relatively larger numbers of tenements. Inconsistencies do appear however. In Kirrier, some tithings seem to have a very large smoke silver assessment for the number of Cornish acres that they were assessed for, while others seem to pay much smaller smoke silver contributions than would be expected from their Cornish acreage. In the St Keverne area, for instance, there appears a complex pattern of tithing units.[41] Figure 2 seems to show a complex relationship between Cornish acreage and smoke silver with Traboe and Rosuic appearing to be anomalous. It appears that the actual area of Rosuic was mostly outside the parish, and largely composed of moorland, which may well have had few smoke silver paying-tenements. Traboe appears to occupy similar land of a similar size to Treleaver, while Rosenithon, Trenoweth and Trelan all seem to occupy relatively smaller pieces of land. The

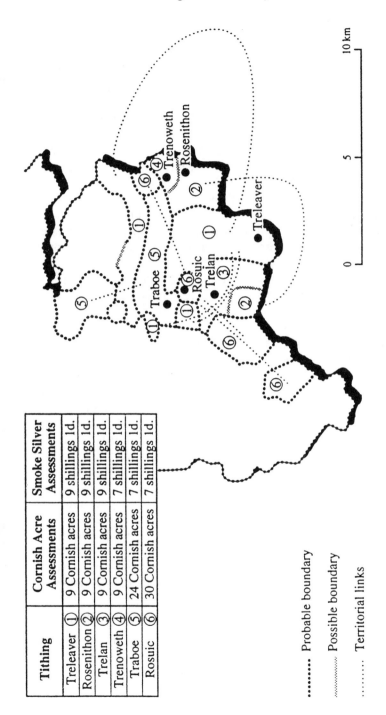

Tithing		Cornish Acre Assessments	Smoke Silver Assessments
Treleaver	①	9 Cornish acres	9 shillings 1d.
Rosenithon	②	9 Cornish acres	9 shillings 1d.
Trelan	③	9 Cornish acres	9 shillings 1d.
Trenoweth	④	9 Cornish acres	7 shillings 1d.
Traboe	⑤	24 Cornish acres	7 shillings 1d.
Rosuic	⑥	30 Cornish acres	7 shillings 1d.

•••••••• Probable boundary

⋯⋯⋯⋯ Possible boundary

⋯⋯⋯⋯ Territorial links

*Figure 2: The Tithing framework in the St Keverne area
(Penwith based largely on Pool 1959)*

assessments certainly appear to be dependent upon some status or function beyond that of simple land area and number of tenements. The fact that these tithings, which are positioned so close to each other, are all assessed in the same way seems to indicate that they are related in some way, perhaps as component parts of a larger entity.

In attempting to account for the apparent 'excessively' large Cornish acreage assessments for certain tithings, the tithings of Minster in Kirrier and Fee-Marshall in Penwith serve as useful examples. From the reconstruction it appears that the tithing of Minster (12 Cornish acres, 5s. 1d. smoke silver) was territorially located mostly in the small parish of Manaccan.[43] The manor of Minster held rights over the Helford river from Calmanasack to the sea with the ferry at the Passage. It seems likely, therefore that the acreage assessment took this valuable right into account.[44] The Penwith tithing of Fee-Marshall was assessed at 23 Cornish acres in 1284, and 25 Cornish acres in 1345.[45] Although this tithing is relatively small, it does seem to contain Newlyn and Gwavas, and so perhaps held some rights to fishing.[46] In 1276, it was called 'Marescalli de Alverton', suggesting a close relationship with the tithing of Alverton.[47] The large Cornish acreage assessment for Alverton of 64 acres, may reflect its high status, and/or its valuable fishing fleet based at Mousehole.[48] The rights to porpoises and to wrecks show a long lasting maritime interest by the hundredal authorities, which is perhaps reflected in the Cornish acreage assessments of the late thirteenth and early fourteenth centuries. The imposition of elevated acreage assessment that appears to have occurred in the private hundred of Penwith may also account for the change in the Cornish acreage assessment for the tithing of Fee-Marshall between 1284 and 1345. It is suggested that the increase from 23 to 25 assessed Cornish acres may reflect an increase in the value of the fishing industry over this period.

The assessment figures tend to emphasize the complex nature of the territorial tithing system rather than painting it as a unidimensional framework simply used for the management of later medieval justice. The potential cash-raising abilities of the tithing are recognized together with its use as a mechanism for the exercise of certain rights and practices that are outside the manorial or land holding system.

INTERPRETING THE PATTERNS

Though the tithing units as recognized in the *Extenta Acrarum* documents undoubtedly expressed a real territorial framework, there is also a recognition that this framework should not be viewed simply. The actual function of the Cornish acre is not known, but an examination of the Cornish acre assessments reveals certain regularized lesser units manifested within the figures. The Cornish acre as an assessment appears to have been in use from at least Domesday, though the academic discussion of its origins and detailed nature has been inconclusive.[49] Examination of the assessments as portrayed throughout Cornwall in the *Extenta Acrarum* documents, however, tend to display a remarkable repetition of figures that are a function of three.

The 1345 *Extenta* records that thirty-one of the thirty-two tithings of the hundred of Kirrier are assessed at a figure that is divisible by 3.[50] An extension of this investigation is displayed in Figure 3, which shows the almost ubiquitous nature of the significance of the '3 Cornish acre' unit. Even in the private hundred of Penwith, almost half of the tithings are assessed at figures divisible by 3, and its exception is in line with its anomalous position in other respects. This hundred moved out of Crown control in the late eleventh century, which suggests that the root of the discrepancies in the Cornish acre assessments occurred following this 'privatisation'. The only other hundreds which demonstrate an assessment scheme that is at all out of line with the '3 Cornish acre phenomenon' are the two most eastern hundreds of Cornwall: East (Wivelshire) and Stratton, which are located along the border with Devonshire. When investigating the origins of the anomalous position of these hundreds, place name and other early evidence may provide the key. Preston-Jones and Rose[51] note the 'conspicuous absence' of Cornish place names between the Tamar and Lynher rivers.[52] They further note that in Stratton hundred over 90 per cent of the place names are of English origin, with particular concentration of *tún*, which they suggest may represent renamed Cornish settlements.[53] Wakelin also sees the Lynher river as an important ethnic, cultural and language frontier with the land to the east and in Stratton colonized by Saxons.[54] Although there is no evidence of the wide scale colonization and ethnic boundaries that Wakelin tends to allude to, the particular nature of the pre-Norman organization of this eastern strip should be recognized.

The six earliest charters that refer to land in Cornwall, including all the pre-tenth-century examples, are associated with land either in Stratton or the far south east, indicating a very early English interest in this area.[55] Although large scale population displacement and complete landscape reorganization seem very improbable, the very early English interest and involvement in this part of Cornwall provides an ex- planation for the apparent exceptionality of this most eastern zone. This is certainly so in terms of place-name distribution in the area, and may provide a context within which to view the apparently anomalous assessments of later years.

The existence of some significance surrounding the '3 Cornish acre'

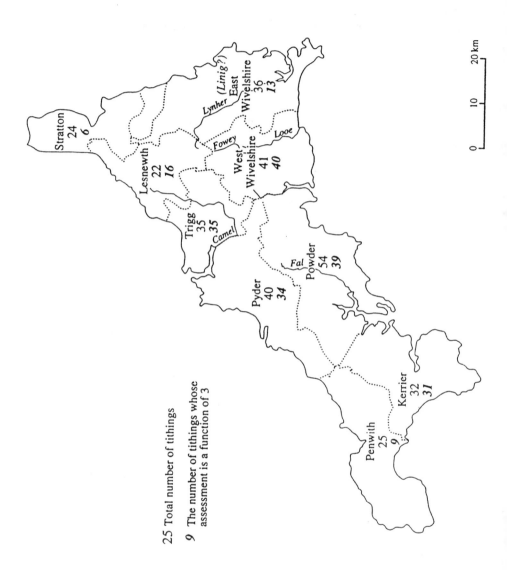

Figure 3: Three acres units in Cornwall hundreds
(From *Extenta Acrarum* (1345) which assesses tithings in Cornish Acres)

assessment strategy in the *Extenta Acrarum* documents is obvious, as is the peculiar and partially anomalous position of the hundreds of Penwith, Stratton and East. The nature of the Cornish acre, as implied in the *Extenta Acrarum* documents, certainly appears to be an artificial assessment, though bearing some relation to land area. By implication, therefore, the proposed '3 Cornish acre unit' appears to represent a certain level of status that was recognized in the assessment of the landscape administrative units. The tithings themselves, as displayed in the *Extenta Acrarum*, are territorial in nature and apparently made up of '3 Cornish acre units'. Some tithings are assessed at 3 Cornish acres, alluding to some reality in an actual '3 acre territory' though this may simply be a nominal assessment not related to a specific unit of actual land. It does seem, however, that the 3 Cornish acre unit is a building block of which the tithings are made up. In this respect, the emerging landscape organizational system of the tithings is represented by a developing territorial framework that is made up of 'building blocks' which, in the language of assessment at least, are reflected in the '3 Cornish acre unit'.[56]

The territorial tithings as illustrated in later medieval records represent much more than mere units for judicial convenience. Their assessment in Cornish acres is systematic and consistent, and seemingly independent of judicial consideration. The assessments themselves appear to reflect groups of lesser units in two ways. Firstly, and most obviously, the tithings are expressed as a group of Cornish acres; a term which is not sufficiently understood. Secondly, the records tend to imply the existence of a 3 Cornish acre unit, and tithings of 6, 9 or 12 Cornish acres seem especially common. The Cornish acre unit appears as some sort of building block: by nature, of economic association and by assessment, of exploitative consideration. The 3-acre label, therefore, appears to be a more nominal assessment related to status.

Although the later medieval tithings, as portrayed in judicial records, are assessed in Cornish acres, it is clear that in Penwith at least, the significance of the 3 Cornish acre unit was no longer recognized. The assessments of the *Extenta Acrarum* documents reflect a system of exploitation and administration, therefore, that did not give regard to such 3 acre significance. The question of what such supposed units actually meant in the landscape arises. They were building blocks of a system of landscape organization that appears to be related to the territorial framework that emerged in the form of later medieval tithings. This basic suggestion seems to be apparent throughout Cornwall and should perhaps be seen within the context of relatively early notions of landscape organization and exploitation. As with the place-name evidence, the apparent ubiquity of this regular assessment scheme breaks down slightly in far eastern areas of Cornwall. However, just as the relative lack of Cornish place names does not imply a complete overhaul of the settlement system, so the less regular Cornish acre assessments need not imply a total change in land organization.

Pool very strongly argues that the tithing system was 'based upon the earlier manorial system'.[57] Although there do appear to be very close and valid associations between the territories of the tithings and units of land holding, it may be more useful to suggest that the tithing framework was simply based upon an earlier scheme of land organization, and was institutionally unrelated to the medieval manor. The landscape was assessed in Cornish acres, groups of which were associated with a certain level of status. Later medieval material appears to suggest some significance of a unit of land, regularly assessed at 3 Cornish acres. This 3 acre unit acted as a building block for larger land units, some of which can be territorially associated with certain tithings and with aspects of land holding. The presence of such schemes of assessment reveals an expression of direct exploitation, and alludes to some earlier mechanism of landscape organization. The framework appears to be closely associated with the emerging pattern of land holding and hints at an earlier relationship with strategies of economic exploitation and political influence in the landscape.

CONCLUSION

This paper has extended Pool's earlier work in terms of its interpretation of meaning, origin and institutional relationships. This study has progressed from being a detailed description of the workings of the later medieval tithing system to examine the implications and significance of the territorial forms, assessments and relationships. This has allowed some useful conclusions to be made about the interpretation of such devices as the Cornish acre and has led to some meaningful impressions as to the origin of the Cornish tithing framework. The investigation of the origins and evolution of this framework has considered the territorial form with a view to understanding the social function and institutional construction of early mechanisms of landscape organization. In many respects, therefore, this study should be seen as a preliminary exploration into such territorial and social devices which may possibly have implications for a wide range of further research.

The suggestion of a complex and socially related assessment mechanism extends our understanding of the Cornish acre term and alludes to meaning or function connected with earlier landscape organisation. It appears, therefore, that the evolution of the Cornish acre assessment mechanism should be sought within a much earlier and longer temporal framework. The contemporary interpretation of this assessment seems to have itself transformed, and the identification of a supposed '3 Cornish acre' unit appears to be related to pre-Norman and even pre-Anglo-Saxon notions of landscape organization. A detailed description and intimate understanding of this system is not possible, but the interpretation of available records suggests that the assessments reflected aspects of social hierarchy and economic utility.

Further detailed work is required in order to explore possible connections with agricultural organization; for instance, with the implication of a large scale system of transhumance operating through the agency of Cornish acreage assessment. This work can act as a basis for further explorations by archaeologists, geographers, historians and the like, by providing a meaningful territorial context for their investigations. The association of institutional function to territorial form is crucial in an investigation of the relationship between society and landscape, with the understanding of early social hierarchy, status and the tribute taking place through the examination of their articulation in the landscape. In terms of landscape investigation and the analysis of later medieval institutions and practices, the crucial implication of this work is that later arrangements are dependent upon the reuse and reinterpretation of earlier arrangements. This continuity can be seen, not just in terms of territorial form and pattern but also in the persistence of traditions of assessment and function which are re-evaluated and interpreted according to newer principles of territorial order and exploitation that reflected the contemporary organization of society.

NOTES AND REFERENCES

1. For a more legally-based definition of the tithing see T.A. Critchley, *A History of Police in England and Wales, 900–1966*, London, 1967 pp. 2–3, or F. Pollock and F.W. Maitland, *History of English Law Before Edward I* (2 volumes), Cambridge, 1968, Vol. I, pp. 568–71.
2. C. Thomas, 'Settlement History in Early Cornwall; I, the Hundreds', *Cornish Archaeology*, no. 3, 1964, pp. 70–79 (p. 71) and W.A. Morris, *The Frankpledge System*, London, 1910, p. 38, among others, notes the existence of territorial tithings that elsewhere 'were called townships' right across Cornwall and the south western shires. Although territorial tithings appeared throughout the South West, it was Cornwall that contained the most systematic, developed and persistent of such territorial phenomena.
3. P.A.S. Pool, 'The Tithings of Cornwall', *Journal of the Royal Institution of Cornwall*, (new series), Vol. 8, 1981, pp. 275–337, (pp. 275–76).

4. Pool, 1981, p. 276.
5. Pool, 1981.
6. P.A.S. Pool, (ed.) 'The Penheleg Manuscript', (with extensive comment), *Journal of the Royal Institution of Cornwall*, (new series), Vol. 3, part 3, 1959, pp. 163–228, which was slightly amended in P.A.S. Pool, 'The Penheleg Manuscript; Some Errors', *Journal of the Royal Institution of Cornwall*, (new series), Vol. 3, part 4, 1960, pp. 284,
7. Pool, 1959, p. 215.
8. Pool, 1981, p. 278.
9. Indeed, Cornwall does not at all seem to be an area that can be described as typically representing a region of nucleated settlements, so the label of 'people living close to each other' simply does not fit.
10. W.L.D. Ravenhill and O.J. Padel, *Joel Gascoyne. A Map of the County of Cornwall*, Exeter, 1991, p. 6.
11. A basic 'checklist' of publicly recognized tithings can be gained from the two versions of the *Extenta Acrarum* (1284 and 1345). Further 'lists' of tithings are found in the Parliamentary Survey of the Duchy of Cornwall (1650), and, for Penwith, in the Penheleg manuscript of 1580 which formed the basis of Pool's reconstruction of Penwith tithings. A summary of these records is found in Pool, 1981, pp. 303-335.
12. These relate to the tithings of Tehidy in Penwith and those of Winnianton and Treleaver in Kirrier. These were abstracted by Pool, 1981, pp. 336–7 from Charles Henderson's manuscripts (MSS, HB/5/112 and MSS, HB/8/76) and the Penrose Estate manuscripts.
13. Roscroggan in Illogan parish is associated with Tehidy tithing in this document, thereby supporting the tithing extent of 1603. Trevaskis in Gwinear is placed within Connerton tithing, Mousehole is placed within the tithing of Alverton in two cases and Boswarva in Madron is placed within Binnerton tithing from this information. See G.D.G. Hall, (ed.), *Three Courts of the hundred of Penwith*, 1333, London, 1978.
14. See case 242, membrane 2, Assize Roll 1171, in D.M. Stenton, (ed.) *Pleas Before the King or his Justices 1198–1202*, 2 volumes, London, 1952.
15. In 1302 for instance, Gregory of Penzance was described as being in the tithing of Alverton, suggesting that Penzance was in Alverton. See case 19, in Pool's transcript of the Assize Rolls 1981, p. 282.
16. This was in St. Martins parish, where Rosemorder is mentioned as being both within the tithing of Treleaver and that of Trelowarren (Pool, 1981).
17. Thomas, 1964, p. 71.
18. Pool, 1981, p. 277.
19. M.S. Cartulary, f.175r–f.175v, case 445 in P.L. Hull (ed.), *The Cartulary of Launceston Priory*, Exeter, 1987.
20. This is especially so on the occasions that the reconstruction of the tithing framework is very dependent upon manorial records.
21. Pool, 1959, p. 215.
22. Pool, 1981.
23. A transcript of the session of Eyre is found in H.S. Toy, *The History of*

Helston, Oxford, 1936, p. 471. The borough was also exempt from toll, pontage, passage, stallage, lastage, soilage, pickage and quayage.

24. Tehidy covered much of eastern Penwith and is associated with the powerful manor of the same name. Treen seems to have comprised just a small part of the parish of Zennor and was manorially related to Hornwell. This tithing seems to disappear later in the record and Pool (1981) supposes that it was absorbed into the tithing of Hornwell.

25. The tithing extent of Winnianton for instance (Penrose Estate MSS. transcribed by Pool, 1981, p. 337) allocated varying amounts of smoke silver tax amongst its tenements. As the decayed, some powerful land holding bodies were able to affect the tithing form, though only after considerable effort. In a case already mentioned for instance, the Prior of Launceston went through a lengthy court challenge in 1357 so that his tenants did not have to serve as tithingmen (M.S. Cartulary, f.175r–f.175v, case 445 in Hull's edited transcript, 1987).

26. See for instance the detail of many cases mentioned in the 1333 hundredal court that has been transcribed by Hall (ed.), 1978.

27. Pool, 1981.

28. *Berbagium* appears several times in the Caption of Seisin record (1337). See P.L. Hull (ed.), *The Caption of Seisin of the Duchy of Cornwall, 1337*, Exeter, 1971. See work such as that by J.E.A. Jolliffe 'Northumbrian Institutions', *English Historical Review*, Vol. 41, 1926, pp. 1–42, or G.W.S. Barrow, *The Kingdom of the Scots*, London, 1973 for a further exploration of the meaning and interpretation of berbagium.

29. Pool, 1959, 1981.

30. Tin fines were noted by Pool (1981) as being organised around the tithing, and were also mentioned in the Caption of Seisin (1337). The Earldom Accounts of the Duchy of Cornwall (1296–1297) refer to this hundredal due as the *doublett de Kerrier* (Membrane 23, p. 248 in L.M. Midgley, (ed.) *Minister's Accounts of the Earldom of Cornwall, 1296/7* (2 volumes), London, 1945.

31. Pool, 1981, pages 178 and 299

32. Hull (ed.), 1971, pp. lix–lxii.

33. Pool, 1981, p. 288 for instance simply notes that the Cornish acre was 'a multiple' of the English acre.

34. Some of the small discrepancies will be discussed further, though many may simply reflect mistakes in the calculation, copying or interpretation.

35. Large tithings in terms of area do seem to have larger Cornish acreage than small tithings. The relationship will be discussed further however.

36. See Hall, 1978, p. 171 and Pool, 1959, pp. 165–171.

37. The nature of this 'common' relationship will be discussed in greater depth in the investigation into the origins of the tithing units and their Cornish acreage.

38. Pool, 1959.

39. The judicial and police function of the tithing of Kemyal for instance was

recognised in the Assize records of 1302 (Pool, 1981) and in the Penheleg Manuscript of 1580 (Pool 1959). However, it was not included in either version of the *Extenta Acrarum* suggesting that this document recognized a slightly different inclusion mechanism.

40. Almost every assessment is listed as a certain number of shillings and 1d. In Powder hundred almost every assessment lists a certain number of shillings and 8d. The other hundreds display a regularity in whole shillings. See the Parliamentary Survey summary in the appendix of Pool, 1981.
41. The parish of St Keverne appears to include the tithing centres of Treleaver, Traboe, Trenoweth, Trelan, Rosenithon and Rosuic tithings. See Figure 4.
42. This tithing is associated with the manor of Minster which itself was held by the powerful Episcopal manor of Penryn. See C. Henderson, 'The 109 ancient parishes of the four western hundreds of Cornwall, (Penwith, Kirrier, Powder and Pydar)' 1924, reprinted in the *Journal of the Royal Institution of Cornwall*, (in four parts), Vols. 2.3–3.3, 1955–1960, pp. 1–497.
43. Henderson, 1924, pp. 326–327.
44. Because these extra rights did not mean extra households or tenements, the smoke silver liability for the tithing of Minster was not especially increased thus.
45. Pool, 1981.
46. The Penheleg reference to the hundredal lord having certain rights to porpoises and the like may indicate a vestige of such rights.
47. Hundred Rolls I, 56 noted in the appendix of Pool (1981). The 'mare' part of this name is also suggestive of a strong relationship with the sea or to fishing.
48. The Penwith court records of 1333, transcribed by Hall 1978, show that Mousehole was within the bounds of Alverton tithing.
49. Padel, pers. comm. 1995.
50. This includes that of Kennall, whose assessment of one and a half Cornish acres is obviously half of 3.
51. A. Preston-Jones and P. Rose, 'Medieval Cornwall', *Cornish Archaeology*, Vol. 25, 1986, pp. 135–185.
52. These rivers are illustrated on figure 5. Preston-Jones and Rose do, however, rather overstate their case—placenames such as Trevollard, Trehan, Landulph, Tremoan, Polborder, Trewashford, Trefinnick, Tremollet, Halwinnick, Pengelly and Landreyne all lie between the Lynher and Tamar rivers and all exhibit obvious Cornish-language elements.
53. Preston-Jones and Rose, 1986, p. 142.
54. M.F. Wakelin, *Language and History of Cornwall*, Leicester, 1975, pp. 59–60.
55. For a list of charters, see H.P.R. Finberg, *The Early Charters of Devon and Cornwall*, Leicester 1953, items 16 and 72–77 inclusive. Item 73 of this list relates to a charter of King Ine (AD 705x712), that records the granting of 20 hides at Linig, which has been interpreted as the land between the Lynher and Tamar rivers.

56. The general theme of such land units representing a certain level of status seems closely related to the idea of the *terrae unius familiae* that is investigated in T.M. Charles-Edwards 'Kinship, Status and the Origins of the Hide', *Past and Present*, 1972, Vol. 56, pp. 3–33.
57. Pool, 1959, 1981.

TYRANNY IN *BEUNANS MERIASEK*

Lynette Olson

INTRODUCTION

The original contribution made by this article is to argue that the very different parts (outlined below) of the Middle Cornish play *Beunans Meriasek* (*The Life of [Saint] Meriasek*) are held together by a common theme of tyranny. While this will inevitably raise the question of the play's specific political relevance—whether, as Henry Jenner suggested, the Cornish scenes about the evil King Teudar represent 'a sly hit at Henry VII, who was not a *persona grata* with the Cornish'[1]—it is hoped that, however this question is answered, the essentially literary analysis of the play offered here can stand.

THREE PLAYS IN ONE

Beunans Meriasek is of especial interest in being a saint's play, a rare survival from medieval Britain.[2] It is even more interesting—and very Cornish (written in the Cornish language and set partly in Cornwall and in Brittany)—in that the saint is a relatively obscure regional rather than universal one, a bishop of Vannes with dedications in Brittany and one at Camborne in Cornwall.[3] Yet *Beunans Meriasek* is not only a saint's play, it is really three plays in one: the Life of St Meriasek proper, to which the title refers; the Life of St Sylvester, being the legend of the conversion to Christianity of the Roman emperor Constantine; and the Woman's Son, an example of the Miracles of the Virgin genre. These are interleaved in the following manner. First come scenes from the Life of Meriasek in which he leaves his noble home to become a monk, travels overseas to Cornwall but is driven out by the evil tyrant Teudar and returns to Brittany; then part of the Sylvester legend in which Constantine, stricken with leprosy, decides not to cure himself by bathing in the blood of slain infants and is baptized and cured by Pope Sylvester; then back to further adventures of Meriasek in Brittany and a second Cornish scene, wherein the saint is not present, in which bad King Teudar is defeated by the Duke of Cornwall—with this the first day of the play concluded. The second day's performance was introduced by Emperor Constantine, followed by more miracles of Meriasek and his consecration as bishop of Vannes (incidently his papal bulls for this are obtained from Constantine's Pope Sylvester); next comes the complete playlet of the Woman's Son; then a brief look at how Meriasek is getting on (fed by angels); then back to Constantine and Sylvester, who succeeds where pagan magicians fail at ridding Rome of a large dragon; and finally to the last miracles and death of St Meriasek. The construction is emphasized by using different-coloured pages for each of the three components in the modern English poetic translation published by Myrna Combellack, who edited the play as her doctoral thesis.[4] She considers the three plays to be thematically unrelated to each other, although cleverly, and appropriately in regard to some significant details, combined into a good two-day session worth people's while attending.[5]

Here I disagree, mainly because the evidence suggests that medieval people connected things together as much as possible. They held, after all, that God had created the world with the symbolism and allegory already built in. So I looked for a link between the three components of *Beunans Meriasek*, and found it in the theme of tyranny.[6]

Much of the Life of St Meriasek proper does not involve tyranny, but what does is highly significant. While King Conan, the Duke of Brittany and the Count of Rohan are distinctly cross about the noble youth Meriasek's decision to forsake his inheritance and obligations for a monastic life of spotless virginity, they take no action against him, and are given neither the name nor the attributes of tyrants. The king and the duke, who is Meriasek's father, are 'displeased' (*dysplesijs*), the count and other kin 'angered' (*serres/serris*), by him.[7] King Conan, having come expressly to offer an advantageous marriage to Meriasek, is understandably put out when the latter ascetically refuses it. His threat to give Meriasek's land to someone else is greeted joyfully by the aspiring saint. The cryptic stage direction *surrexit circa placeam* is intriguing, but essentially the king just takes himself and his entourage off, muttering 'Upon my soul, I shall forever like him the less while I live'.[8] Meriasek's parents let their son go with their blessing. Later the Count of Rohan puts his arguments to Meriasek, now an established holy man, but gives up easily ('I will not worry him'), and sensibly requests Meriasek to perform the socially beneficial miracle of ending outlawry in the district.[9] What the powerful could have done is intimated by the Bishop of Cornouailles' crozier-bearer's line just before Meriasek leaves Brittany for Cornwall, 'We really ought not to keep you against your will'.[10]

Teudar, self-styled 'reigning lord in Cornwall', 'prince', 'emperor', 'governor' and 'conqueror', is several times called 'tyrant' (*turant*) by the Duke of Cornwall.[11] Teudar is presented as a ranting Herod figure: the analogy is never made explicit, but the type was far too well-known (eventually giving rise to the line, 'it out-Herods Herod', in Shakespeare's *Hamlet*) to miss. His rages are foreshadowed by his threat, 'because when I come to get mad, the devil will come out of his pit before I relent, for certain'; however, this is immediately followed by, 'I am sorry, upon my soul, dear Meriasek, to do you other than good. Ah! Worship my beautiful gods.'[12] This mercurial temperament lends itself to comic presentation. He is a tricky and dangerous ruler whose servants treat him with a curious mixture of fear and apathy which gives further scope for comedy: it is in dealing with them that he flies completely off the handle. Teudar employs torturers, and invokes demons, the two being conveniently located next to one another in the north-west of this medieval Cornish theatre-in-the-round.[13]

TEUDAR AND TYRANNY

The nature of Teudar's tyranny needs to be explored. The Duke of Cornwall initially accosts him as '*Ty turant a thyscregyans*', literally 'You tyrant of unbelief', and that is significant. Teudar is a militant, persecuting pagan. It is because he had driven Meriasek out of Cornwall that the Duke of Cornwall has come after him in the first place. But there is more. The phrase just quoted is followed by: 'What is your right in this country? Obviously, you have no clear title or claim here on your mother's or father's side.'[14] There is a sustained portrayal of Teudar as a tyrant in the sense of 'illegitimate ruler', 'usurper'.[15] Thus, the Duke's self-proclamation, 'I am Duke of all Cornwall, as was my father', contrasts with his Chamberlain's statement that 'As you have heard, Teudar, an impious pagan, has landed in this country—and not long since'.[16] Teudar is twice called 'alien' (*alyon/allyon*).[17] Moreover, he had not originally amounted to much, according to the Duke of Cornwall. 'By my soul, you were a page to horses in your country, I have heard.'[18] 'Undoubtedly, I think, you were an evil wretch in your country.'[19] 'I did not know that you were born to a cantle of land in this world.'[20] Teudar himself responds to the first of these taunts by saying: 'Though my property was not large in my nation, I have certainly enlarged it. I am a conqueror, a proven personage, feared amongst lords.'[21] He is very much a tyrant as defined above in the sense of one who has seized power. Small wonder that the Duke of Cornwall again addresses him as *turant* in the next lines.

Although Teudar only takes part in two scenes out of many in the Meriasek component of the play, these are the only scenes in the entire play which are set in Cornwall, and as such (especially given the specific local references they contain)[22] would have been of greatest interest to the audience. Moreover, the defeat of the evil tyrant Teudar closed the first day of the play, and given that the second day would have had to finish with the glorious death of the saint, no more prominent place could have been provided for the former episode. In other words, the episodes of greatest interest to a Cornish audience concerning St Meriasek (the rest is bland by comparison) in the play show a tyrant at first apparently victorious, and then later getting his 'comeuppance'.

Between them we have Constantine, who is at first presented with the attributes of a tyrant.[23] He has torturers, whom he employs in persecution of Christians and then sends to collect the children to be slain. Indeed, his opening scene in which he summons them, coming as it does almost immediately after Meriasek's expulsion from Cornwall by Teudar and his men, would have recalled the latter to the audience.[24] 'There is current in the country a false belief, causing me the devil's own anger'[25] shows Constantine to be cast in the type of the furiously militant pagan ruler, although we never see him lose his temper. He is more in control than Teudar, but more lethal. Christians are martyred, and the scene is set for a repetition of Herod's massacre of the innocents, a connection which, although not made explicit, would not have been missed given the notoriety of the biblical episode in song and story.

But Constantine is not without private and public scruples: actually confronted by the infants and mothers, he feels pity and reflects, 'The honour of the royal blood in Rome is, as our law records: whoever shall slay a child in battle shall be held a cruel man'.[26] To kill 3,000 such so that he can be cured of leprosy would be wrong. So Constantine turns from tyranny. He does not invoke demons, but instead receives a vision of St Peter and St Paul. His conversion and cure follow, and after that he is a reformed character.

The third component of *Beunans Meriasek*, the Woman's Son miracle of the Virgin, is entirely concerned with tyranny. The son is imprisoned by an evil tyrant, the mother not only prays to the Virgin but even takes the Christ Child away from her statue: in effect, 'I'll give you back your son when you've returned mine!'. Mary enters the prison cell and releases the Woman's Son. Yet the *Legenda Aurea*, the likely source of this episode, says only that the son was captured by enemies and imprisoned, without any mention of rulers, tyrannical or otherwise.[27] Thus, in contrast to the Constantine episodes, which may also have been extracted from the *Legenda Aurea* 'Life of Sylvester', the material to be analysed here represents a considerable addition to the putative original.[28]

In the play, the Son takes himself off to serve good King Massen.[29] Soon they encounter the Tyrant, who is true to type. 'When I am mad and violent, there is none born in the world to oppose me.'[30] His torturers are less obedient than Teudar's, holding out for better wages until the Drudge turns the tables on them nicely by pointing this out to the consequently enraged Tyrant, to good comic effect.[31] He and his crew fortify themselves for battle with the King by sacrificing to demons.[32] Their dispute is over hunting grounds, and the pre-battle taunts begin with the Tyrant's right to these being questioned: 'Never yet was a son of your mother born to this inheritance',[33] but mainly focus on his unbelief. Yet the parallels with the struggle between Teudar and the Duke of Cornwall end when King Massen is defeated. The Son is captured by the Tyrant and threatened with death if he does not renounce his Christian faith. It is here that the Virgin intercedes.

This is the shortest of the three components of the play, and, as stated above, is performed all in one section, unlike the others. What I find striking is its abstract nature: the woman is just called the Woman, the son, the Son, and the tyrant is called the Tyrant by everyone, including himself: 'I am a tyrant without equal, a prince under the sun'.[34] It is almost a tableau, in which the theme of tyranny is presented in abstract terms for maximum focus and clarity.

CONCLUSION

To sum up, the theme of tyranny crushed, rejected or thwarted links the three components of *Beunans Meriasek*. Indeed, it is present so significantly in all of them as to suggest even that they were deliberately combined to emphasize it. As a whole or in parts, the *Meriasek* play is certainly not a political play but a religious one, sincerely meant and sincerely taken, with a good deal of fun and entertainment in the process.

This is not, however, to deny the play's political context. As Murdoch has argued, in the sixteenth century *Beunans Meriasek* would have appeared increasingly subversive in Protestant eyes, probably an important reason why the play fell into disuse. Moreover, the existence of an edited performance version of the play dated 1508 suggests strongly that *Beunans Meriasek* was performed in the aftermath of the 1497 rebellions in Cornwall. The theme of tyranny and the defeat of the evil King Teudar (namesake of Henry Tudor) at the hands of the good Duke of Cornwall would have raised more than a wry smile in post-1497 Cornwall, while the celebration of an overtly Cornish/Breton saint and the medium of the Cornish language could have been construed as a statement of Cornish sentiment[35].

NOTES AND REFERENCES

1. H. Jenner, 'King Teudar', *Tre Pol and Pen*, London, 1928, p. 33. Cf. P. Payton, ' "a . . . concealed envy against the English": A Note on the Aftermath of the 1497 Rebellions in Cornwall', in Philip Payton (ed.), *Cornish Studies: One*, Exeter, 1993, pp. 4–13.
2. For the full European context of the genre, see B. Murdoch, *Cornish Literature*, Cambridge, 1993, pp. 103–4.
3. G. Doble, *Saint Meriadoc, Bishop and Confessor*, Truro, 1935.
4. M. Combellack (trans.), *The Camborne Play*, Redruth, 1988; M. Combellack- Harris, 'A Critical Edition of *Beunans Meriasek*', unpublished Ph.D. thesis, University of Exeter, 1985, used for Cornish text and English translation in this article.
5. Combellack, 1988, p. ix; Combellack-Harris, 1985, pp. 4, 79 (n. 3), 25–57.
6. Not the only theme; Murdoch (p. 102) lists several: 'the relations between Church and State, the combatting of evil and the conversion of unbelievers, healing in the physical and soteriological sense, and the role of saints (and the clergy) as intercessors, with special emphasis on the Virgin'.
7. Lines 490-1, 1943 and 1955, respectively.
8. '*the lee nefra/war ov ena/me an car in ov bevnans*' (lines 481–83). The Latin comes before line 456.
9. '*Ny vannef y annye*' (line 2054 [ff]).
10. '*erbyn the voth : thynny ny goth : sur the lettya*' (lines 584–6).
11. '*arluth regnijs in Kernov*' (line 760), the others are all English loanwords in lines 924, 930–2 and 2403; the references to 'tyrant' are in lines 2280, 2369, 2407 and 2494, see further discussion below.
12. *Trag pan deffen ha moys fol/an Iovle a thue mes ay dol/kyns es ov ruthy purguir/Drok yv gena/war ov ena/Meryasek wek/gul dis mas da/ha gorthyans grua/thum dewow tek* (lines 906–14).
13. Lines 950–82, 1017–65, 2310–56 for the torturers, who are particularly at the receiving end of Teudar's anger in 950 ff and 1054 ff; 2326–56 for the demons; the diagrams for staging the first and second days' performances are found on pp. 98 and 180 of the sole manuscript Peniarth 105 in which the play survives.
14. '*pendryv the kerth in povma/tytel na chalyng dyblans : aberth mam na tas oma/purguir nyth us*' (with the above, lines 2369–73).
15. This was its pre-eminent meaning by the later Roman Empire; and is the first one given in *The Oxford English Dictionary*, 2nd ed., Oxford, 1989, XVIII.795, with the parenthesis, 'Chiefly in reference to ancient rulers, and in early use with suggestion of sense 3', which is 'A king or

ruler who exercises his power in an oppressive, unjust or cruel manner; a despot'.

16. '*Me yv duk in oll Kernov : indella ytho ov thays*' (lines 2205–6) and '*Tevdar pagan ongrassyas/in povma eff re dyrhays/del glovsugh ha nynsyv pel*' (lines 2242–44); both the Duke and his Steward subsequently refer to Teudar's coming to the country—'and without my leave' ('*heb ov lessyans in certan*'), says the Duke (2265–6 and 2273–5); when the Duke is about to confront Teudar, the Steward asks, 'Do you wish to speak with him and ask him what he really wants in this country?' (*covse ganso a vynnogh wy/ha govyn orto defry/in povma pendra wyla*' [lines 2360–2]).

17. In lines 2415 and 2451.

18. '*pagya mergh es by my sovle/me a glowes in ze pov*' (lines 2393–4); Combellack-Harris, 1985, pp. 473 and 475 (nn. 14–15), translates the English oath into Cornish to keep it in a foreign language and includes R. Morton Nance's 'ostler's boy' to clarify the literal translation. Later (in line 2458) Teudar is called *grome*, an English loanword which as she points out may have had the broader meanings of 'boy' or 'servant' but in view of the earlier *pagya mergh* probably had the narrower meaning which survives for modern 'groom' as 'one who cares for horses' (p. 484 [n. 7]).

19. '*predery a raff heb fal/in the pov ythesta gal*' (lines 2411–12). The implications of Teudar's being called '*tebel genesek*', translated 'ill-born', where *tebel* is literally 'evil', are unclear to me but are clearly not good (line 2287, cf. Combellack-Harris, 1985, p. 465 [n. 6]).

20. '*me ny won the voys genys/in bysma the pastel dyr*' (lines 2449–50). A reference to 'my inheritance' ('*ov hertons*') follows in the same speech by the Duke.

21. '*kyn nag o ov poscessyon/bras in meske sur ov nascyon/me ren moghheys eredy/conquerrour off/corff da in proff/dovtijs in meske arlythy*' (lines 2400–5).

22. See C. Thomas, *Christian Antiquities of Camborne*, St Austell, 1967, ch. 2.

23. No one ever calls him a tyrant. He introduces himself as 'a personage without equal, and feared by the people', which is similar to what Teudar says as quoted just above but later in the play, and 'noble emperor, son of Queen Helen, head of all his tribe, as many a one has heard', which is equivocal about his right to rule even if it does mention a significant name in British tradition. The whole passage is: '*Drefen ov boys corff hep par : ha dovtijs gans an bobil/ov hanov in guire heb mar : yv Costyntyn the nobil/emperour worthy/map then vyternes Helen/neb yv pen ol y ehen/del glowas lues huny* (lines 1153–1160). In reality the grounds for Constantine's imperial legitimacy were complex, but probably unknown to the author, who does however know enough to have him swear by Sol.

24. Constantine's 'Torturers, wake up!' ('*tormentoris dufunugh*') at their later summons would have done so as well (line 1526; cf. lines 950–961). Both rulers employ three torturers and a drudge (calo), as does the Tyrant in the third component of the play.

25. '*Yma in pov falge cregyans : ov cul dym angyr an Iovle*' (lines 1161–62).
26. '*Dynyte an goys ryel/yv in Rome pur thyhogel/del recorde agen latha/neb a lath flogh in batel/sensys y feth den cruel*' (lines 1627–31); the *Legenda Aurea* is closely followed here (see below); see also lines 1653–66 which are summarised by my next sentence above.
27. *Jacobi a Voragine Legenda Aurea vulgo historia lombardica dicta*, ed. T. Graesse, 3rd ed., 1890, rpt Osnabrück, 1969, pp. 591–2.
28. Cf. pp. 70–9 in the edition previously cited; note that the Constantine component of the play represents a considerable subtraction from that original.
29. Another significant name in British tradition, this is Magnus Maximus, who at least lived in the same century as Constantine but was actually a usurper, indeed one of Gildas' tyrants *(De Excidio Britonum*, 13, ed. and trans. M. Winterbottom, London and Chichester, 1978, pp. 93 and 20–1).
30. '*pan veua fol ha garov: nynsus in beys genesyk/thym asetya*' (lines 3210–12).
31. Lines 3245–3368.
32. Lines 3369–3443; cf. lines 2326–56 before Teudar fights the Duke of Cornwall.
33. '*bythqueth ny vue map the vam/genys wath then eretons*' (lines 3468–69). The King also says he has been 'lord of this ground this twenty years' ('*me yv prest arluth an gront/nansyv blethynnyov vgons*') and denies that he is the Tyrant's vassal (lines 3471–2 and 3482–4, respectively).
34. '*Me yv turant heb parov : in dan an hovle pensevyk* (lines 3208–9); also by King Massen (lines 3206 ['there is an evil tyrant in the country' 'yma drok turant in pov'], 3452, 3467), the King's Second Hunter (lines 3239 and 3444), the First Torturer (line 3246), the Second Torturer (line 3270), the Drudge (lines 3284 and 3296 ['*ser turant floyr*']), the First Demon (line 3383), the Third Soldier of the Tyrant (line 3548), the Gaoler (lines 3567 and 3723), his Boy (lines 3720 and 3737), the Messenger (line 3582) and whoever labelled the parts (*passim*; Tyrannus Imperator is just west of Imperator Constantinus at the bottom (south) of the staging diagram for the second day's performance on p. 180 of the manuscript).
35. See P. Payton, *Cornwall*, Fowey, 1996, pp. 132–136.

PROTO-INDUSTRIALIZATION AND POTATOES: A REVISED NARRATIVE FOR NINETEENTH-CENTURY CORNWALL

Bernard Deacon

INTRODUCTION

The turning point of the 1860s is an accepted part of Cornish historiography. In 1866 copper prices collapsed and triggered Cornwall's long descent into de-industrialization. This process then involved both economic restructuring and cultural repositioning as a 'semantic space' opened up and romantic images of Cornwall finally colonized the popular imagination.[1] Such a narrative framework, with a sharp divide in the late 1860s/early 1870s, has not been challenged since Rowe placed the end of his work on *Cornwall in the Age of the Industrial Revolution* firmly in the 1870s. The years of 'decline and diaspora', centred on the 1870s, are also used by Payton as one hinge of his history of modern Cornwall, the transition from 'Cornubia triumphant' to 'the great paralysis'.[2]

It is not difficult to find various economic and demographic indicators to support the view that the decade of the 1860s was a major watershed. The fall in copper ore production is too well known to need repeating here.[3] However, we might turn to another pattern in order to demonstrate Cornwall's divergent pattern after the 1860s. Southall and Gilbert have discovered that marriage statistics were the most sensitive indicator of the state of the economy in nineteenth-century Britain, showing a 'remarkable' relationship with the ups and downs of the trade cycles.[4] If the numbers of marriages for England and Wales and for Cornwall are compared, using 1800 as a base, the 1860s watershed becomes strikingly clear. Figure 1 shows that, while the trend in numbers of marriages in Cornwall closely mirrored that of England

and Wales to the mid-1850s it fell away markedly after the mid-1860s, reflecting Cornwall's demographic stagnation of the later nineteenth century and dramatically reinforcing the notion of the 1860s as turning point.[5]

Nevertheless, such data do not tell the whole story. The dominant narrative, with its emphasis on the 1860s/1870s disjunction, tends to underplay the continuities carried over from Cornwall's industrial into its de-industrializing period. At its worst this telescopes longer processes of change; thus Berg simplifies the history of late nineteenth-century Cornwall in the words 'the region was rapidly transformed into a holiday resort'.[6] At the same time it underestimates the structural changes that occurred earlier in the century.

It is these earlier processes of change that this article seeks to uncover. In doing so a revised narrative framework is put forward for understanding nineteenth-century Cornwall, one that views the 1840s as a major structural turning point rather than the 1860s. In this we are building on Payton's suggestion that 'while changes in the international copper market in the 1860s did precipitate a new era of mass movement, emigration from Cornwall had been noticeable by the 1820s and was already a significant phenomenon by the 1840s'.[7] But this hypothesis, restricted to the emigration trade, may be applied more widely to Cornish society as a whole. In suggesting a revised framework for the social history of Cornwall we will also put industrial Cornwall into a wider context as an industrial region with a unique pattern. It will be argued that in Cornwall a particular form of industrial society had been produced by the 1830s but that this was being subjected to increasing tensions. In the 1840s these tensions upset the balances constructed over the previous 100 years and pitched Cornwall into a more superficially convergent path with other industrial regions. This apparent convergence was in turn, however, shattered by shifts in the global metal markets in the late 1860s and early 1870s.

INDUSTRIAL ECONOMY, PROTO-INDUSTRIAL SOCIETY: CORNWALL BEFORE THE 1840s

By the 1830s a hundred years of industrialization in Cornwall had created a region where a capitalist economy accompanied a proto-industrial society. Burt was the first to suggest that Cornwall's early modern mining sector might be viewed as a proto-industrial industry;

> the essence of the proto-industrial model is that labour was the principal cost item in the manufacture of certain industrial goods, particularly textiles. Where such manufacturing could be combined

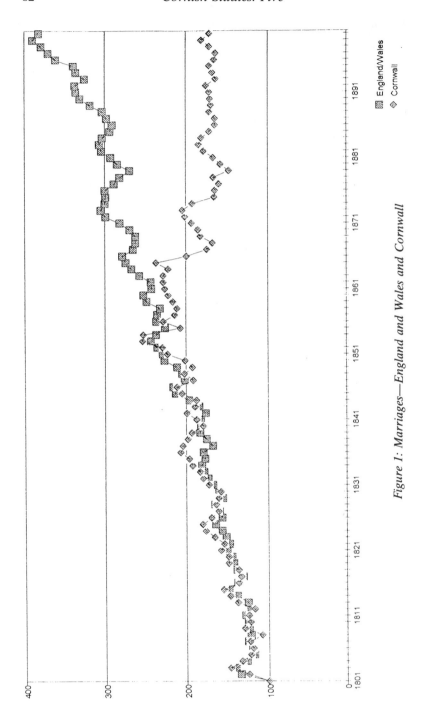

Figure 1: Marriages—England and Wales and Cornwall

England/Wales

◇ Cornwall

with other income producing activities, such as farming, the manufacturing costs were effectively subsidized by those other activities . . . Substitute metal mining for manufacturing, and here we also have the story of the survival of the Cornish tin industry.[8]

Cullum, however, has questioned this, noting that 'the term "proto-industry" implies more than just dual employment, but is concerned also with fundamental organisational and attitudinal developments', such as a wage economy and a more sophisticated division of labour. He sees the early modern miner-farmer in Cornwall as more of 'venture capitalist, than . . . proto-industrial worker'.[9] Nevertheless, through the eighteenth century, with the expansion of deep copper mining, the Cornish mine worker became at least partly proletarianized so the notion of proto-industrial workers becomes more applicable as long as dual employment remained.

However, as we shall see below, some have questioned the continuation of large scale dual employment into the nineteenth century, although if we turn our attention to the scale of the family rather than the individual the outlines of a dual economy might still be recognized. But in addition our mineworker was now more likely to work for a large integrated mining operation rather than the small-scale family-bound production units familiar to the classic proto-industrial woollen textile regions. But the concept of proto-industrialization seems to be used in an eclectic fashion so, instead of focusing on the economic criteria of proto-industrialization, debatable in their application to Cornwall, we might adopt the usage of Koditschek in his study of Bradford. For him proto-industrialization in the Bradford district in the late eighteenth century had resulted in a class system of an entrepreneurial elite of landowners and merchant capitalists together with proletarianized workers. The latter lived in 'traditional' households, relatively dispersed village communities and were engaged in a handicraft mode of production. Proto-industrialisation refers more to a social formation marked by strongly 'traditional' aspects than to a particular division of labour.[11] It is this pre-urban society in the West Riding which bears many striking similarities with Cornwall before the 1840s.

As the reference to Bradford implies, in containing a mix of the 'modern' and the 'traditional', Cornwall was by no means unusual. We now know that early nineteenth-century society was a complex combination of change and continuity. Whereas earlier social and economic historians privileged change, the industrial revolution, the making of the working class, the victory of an entrepreneurial ideal, more recently the focus has been on continuity and the resilience and continuation of traditional structures into the nineteenth century.[12] Perhaps both traditional and revisionist historiographies overplay their hands. It is possible to identify both change and continuity in the early nineteenth century. But this balance of change and continuity was itself geographically uneven, with different regions displaying differing patterns of accommodation between the new and the old, the modern and the pre-modern.

Furthermore, there is a danger that concepts of change and continuity to some extent over-simplify the situation. Despite the binary opposition implied by these linked concepts there was no clear boundary between the new and the old. New practices would be clothed in the language of tradition and apparently traditional forms might in fact be relatively new. The notion of 'tradition' itself was constantly being contested, renegotiated and recreated and could be interpreted in different ways by differing groups. Nevertheless, keeping this qualification in mind, the contrast between the modern and the traditional is still a useful device for making sense of early nineteenth-century Cornwall.

THE ECONOMIC SPHERE—AN EARLY EUROPEAN INDUSTRIAL REGION

The wage earner of the late eighteenth and early nineteenth centuries would appeal to 'customary practice and claimed rights' to try to restrain market forces. It was this cultural appeal to a 'moral economy' that underlay food riots, with their elements of ritual and ceremony. In regions like Cornwall, where such forms of protest continued well into the nineteenth century, the implication is, therefore, that the role of customary as opposed to market relations lingered longest.[14] Yet it would be a mistake to assume that Cornwall had always been a customary society, at least in a relative sense. Indeed, the picture of the pre-modern economy in Cornwall is one of a lack of customary relationships and an early penetration of market and even capitalist relations.

According to Hatcher, the medieval Cornish economy was 'fundamentally different from the economies of many other English counties; it was complex and diverse, with a high industrial and commercial content'. Seine fishing was already a capitalist industry with a distinction between those who owned the seine boats and those who worked them appearing early. And the seven year conventionary tenancies of Cornish manors in the same century suggest an early and vigorous land market. Burt points out how tin mining became a capitalist operation during the late sixteenth and early seventeenth centuries.[15] This paved the way for the expansion of copper mining in the eighteenth century. Mining then became the leading sector of Cornwall's industrial revolution. Focusing on the four aspects of growth, capitalization, technology and specialization will allow us to put this briefly into context.

If we compare the growth of copper output with overall industrial growth rates for the British economy we find that copper output rose considerably faster in the eighteenth century. Table 1 shows the comparison with three estimates of British industrial production.

TABLE 1
Growth of industrial production [% per annum]

	Crafts (1985)	Britain CLM (1989)	Jackson (1992)	Cornish copper
1700–60	0.7	0.8	—	2.0
1760–80	1.5	0.9	1.3	2.2
1780–1801	2.1	1.9	2.1	2.8
1801–31	3.0	2.7	3.0	2.7

While there is room for debate between the three estimates for total industrial production even the highest one fails to match the rate of growth of Cornish copper before 1801. Only in the nineteenth century did the growth rate of British industry in general begin to overtake that of copper mining in Cornwall. Even then the 1810s and 20s saw *per annum* Cornish copper growth rates of around 3.4 per cent; it was only the depressed decade of the 1800s that temporarily held back the copper growth rate. When copper mining is compared with other industrial sectors we find that it kept pace with most of them before the 1830s in all decades except the 1770s and 1800s. The unsurprising exceptions were cotton textiles and iron. And before 1770 the growth rate of Cornish copper surpassed even these.[17]

Turning to capitalization Rule points out how, in terms of organization, Cornish mines were among the biggest employers in the British economy in the late eighteenth century. Burt reinforces this; by the 1810s Consols mine in Gwennap was an 'enterprise which compared in scale and turnover with the largest in any sector of industry and commerce'. These large enterprises involved 'capital investment of tens of thousands of pounds'. Mathias concludes that Cornish mines in the mid nineteenth century were as capitalised as coal mines in North East England and Pollard sums up pre-1840 Cornwall as being 'one of the most advanced engineering centres in the world . . . a complex industrial society exhibiting early developments of banking and risk-sharing to deal with the particular needs of local industry as well as a remarkable attempt to cartelize copper in the 1780s.'[18]

High levels of capitalization were reflected in early and widespread investment in steam engine technology. Between 1734 and 1780 only the Northumberland and Durham coalfield saw more engines erected. At the same time as Cornwall was becoming a major centre of steam engine technology, William Murdoch was inventing gas lighting in Redruth in 1794 and Thomas Macadam was theorizing about new technologies of road building a few miles away at Flushing. Cornwall was a leading technological region in the late eighteenth century, according to one view 'the powerhouse of the English industrial revolution'.[19]

Finally, Cornwall's industrialization was marked, as in other industrial regions, by specialization. By 1851 29 per cent of Cornish men were directly employed in mining and quarrying, This compares with the 27 per cent directly employed in cotton textiles in Lancashire and Cheshire and the 25 per cent in coal mining in South Wales.[20] Cornwall had, over the eighteenth century, become an industrial region specializing in metal mining, relying on the production of an export commodity for its economic well-being.

Nevertheless, these aspects of industrial change co-existed, as elsewhere, with other, less 'modern', elements of social continuity. For example, in terms of production Cornwall was still in an era of handicraft relations. Marx distinguishes between 'formal' and 'real' control of a workforce. In conditions of formal control the means of production are owned by a capitalist class but the technologies of production remain extensions of the human hand. In conditions of real control, for Marx the point at which capitalism subordinates labour, workers become extensions of the machine, working to its rhythm. In the former conditions labour retained some control over the production process but in the latter this control was lost.[21] Cornish mineworkers, both below and above ground, were only formally controlled and before the 1840s retained some control over the pace of their labour, with most discretion being given to those on tribute contracts.[22]

THE SOCIAL SPHERE: MERCHANTS AND PROTO-PROLETARIANS

We can add to this relative autonomy of the labour process in Cornwall the fragmentation of capitalist ownership and the early division between ownership and management in the mining industry. The majority of mines were owned by a number of adventurers rather than single owners and these investors in turn spread their holdings over several production units.[23] This produced no visible employer class. In any case, real power in Cornish mining by the early nineteenth century resided with a smaller group of bankers, merchants and smelters, the new merchant bourgeoisie who controlled the trade in metals. As in late eighteenth-century Bradford, this merchant bourgeoisie, families such as the Williamses, Bolithos or Daveys, were fusing with the landed class by the 1830s. There was nothing particularly new about this in Cornwall. Social mobility into the gentry via riches made in mining was an established route by the seventeenth and eighteenth centuries, as the Lemon and Carlyon families had demonstrated. Chesher concludes that, in the first half of the eighteenth century, there were 'probably more *nouveau riche* . . . than in almost any other county'.[24]

The merchant bourgeoisie were content to cede social and political power to the landed gentry. Despite their economic power—Cornish tin smelters in particular were, by the 1800s, 'completely controlling the smelting, financing and purchasing of tin'[25]—the merchant bourgeoisie in Cornwall were slow to take their places in the institutions of political power. In contrast, after 1832 cotton merchants in Lancashire were increasingly represented as JPs. In some places this process began even earlier. For example, in South Wales and Gloucestershire merchants could be found on the bench as early as the 1780s. However, by the mid- nineteenth century it was more usual for about 10 per cent of county magistrates to be merchants or others still active in trade.[26] But in Cornwall, despite industrialization, it was not even that high. In 1856 only eleven, or 8 per cent, of the county magistrates were from outside the ranks of the landed or clerical gentry.[27] This trade-off, economic wealth and social fusion in return for ceding political power to the gentry, gave the appearance of hierarchy and deference in early nineteenth-century Cornwall. But other aspects seemed to belie this appearance of deference.

For the most important of these aspects we can return to the relatively autonomous labour process in Cornish mining, which was underpinned by the tribute and tutwork systems of wage payment. These, formalized during the eighteenth century, had solved the problems associated with capitalization of deep mining—the need for a more sophisticated division of labour and better labour discipline. Tying wages to the price of ore tribute and tutwork contracts avoided the need for collective wage negotiations and resulted in the underground worker to some extent policing himself. This was, of course, reinforced by the emergence of a category of mine captains and managers who used paternalist relations and hierarchical controls to support the disciplines of the market. But the important point to note here is that tribute and tutwork also institutionalized cultural ideas of independence. Outside observers represented this wage system in the early nineteenth century as producing 'a degree of intelligence and independence, which raises the condition of the Cornish miners, far above that of the generality of the labouring class'.[28] Meanwhile, the early nineteenth-century miner too could still imagine himself as 'independent', even though the reality of that independence was circumscribed by fines and other forms of labour discipline and was very different from the 'independent tinner' of the pre-modern period. In doing this, moreover, the world of work intersected with and was underpinned by the world of custom.

THE CULTURAL SPHERE: CUSTOM AND COLLATERAL AIDS

Autonomy at work was reinforced by that other sign of the proto-industrial worker, access to non-commodity production, what one contemporary termed 'collateral aids'.[29] Rose points out that

> The commonly-held *image* of the mid-nineteenth century Cornish miner, then, is one of an owner-peasant, making part of his living through mining, part through the work of his family in subsistence farming, and perhaps in seasonal work fishing—and only partially integrated into the processes of industrial capitalist development.

She suggests that access to land in the form of renting and owning smallholdings was 'the norm in rural areas' in eighteenth-century Cornwall, lowering dependence on wages through the production of houses and food in non-commodity forms. Rowe also notes that in the eighteenth century the number of smallholders in Cornwall grew at a time when this class was under pressure elsewhere. However, others have suggested that access to smallholdings was becoming less frequent by the end of the eighteenth century as specialization increased and hours of work for underground miners, while still relatively low, nevertheless rose as intensity of labour deepened. For instance the implication of Burt's observation that 'down to the late eighteenth century most mining families in most districts continued to supplement their income from a wide range of activities' is that a change took place at the end of the eighteenth century as wage relations ousted the customary relations of non-commodity production.[30]

How far was the image of the mid-nineteenth century Cornish miner as worker-peasant a myth? We are fortunate in having two reports, published in the early 1840s, that provide contemporary evidence of the extent of access to land in Cornwall. Tremenheere, in his report on the *State of Education in the Mining Districts of Cornwall*, found that just under a quarter of the 685 miners in his three districts of St Blazey, Redruth and St Just had cottages built by themselves on smallholdings usually held on a three life lease.[31] So, by 1840, while still significant for a minority, such access was no longer 'the norm'. Barham, in his report on children's employment, published two years later, focused on the situation in St Just. Here 'in the extreme western district the different collateral aids which contribute to the comfort of the miner are perhaps more concentrated than in any other'. But Barham makes no mention of smallholdings in St Just, just the practice of taking shares in boats and in cows. In fact, he notes that 'the attempt to combine the cultivation of a farm of several acres with regular mining engagements is seldom successful'. In addition, 'men so situated are also considered by the agents less eligible for employment'.[32]

In order to check the degree of access to land in St Just parish we might focus in more detail on Pendeen. Here, a nominal record linkage of the 1841 Census and the 1841 Tithe Assessment in the two adjoining manors of Trewellard and Boscaswell reveals that, while over a fifth of households in Boscaswell had access to small holdings, this proportion was much lower in Trewellard, the difference being in exactly those very small holdings that would be let out to miners rather than to full-time or virtually full-time small farmers.

TABLE 2
% of total households occupying land; 1841

	1/4 to 5 acres	*5—20 acres*	*total*
Trewellard	2.7	6.4	9.1
Boscaswell	15.0	5.6	20.6

The marked difference between the two enumeration districts would appear to be a function of their landholding history, different manors and different landowners having evolved different practices. In both districts landholding was complex, with the Tithe Apportionment noting a large degree of subletting. It is possible that even those holdings of the occupiers according to the Tithe Apportionment were further subdivided, resulting in an underenumeration of smallholders by this source. However, we do not have to resort to this in order to combine an access to non-commodity food greater than the bare figures above imply.

Tremenheere in 1840 does not highlight the lease of a few acres of land, which is clearly the privilege only of the successful tributer, but nevertheless he does foreground 'resources in the use of land to a greater or lesser extent'. For there was another collateral aid open to the miners by the late 1830s, one given prominence by Tremenheere. He explains further:

> Among the most important is the opportunity of cultivating potatoes in the fields of neighbouring farmers. A natural allotment system has thus sprung up, which proves beneficial to both parties. The miner obtains a stock of potatoes, without, in general, any money-payment; the farmer in that case allotting a perch of land for each load of household manure furnished by the miner. The latter plants and draws the crop, the farmer preparing the land and carting the manure, of which he has the benefit for the corn crop of the following year. The number of perches which a miner can thus secure depends usually upon the quantity of manure he can collect; and this again greatly depends on his facilities for cutting turf or furze for fuel, of which the ashes form the staple of the manure.[33]

With care, he adds, this can supply the family for some months as well as feed a pig or even two. Such a system, one invisible in the tithe apportionments, was also given pride of place by Barham. 'It is a common and growing practice for the farmer to allot and prepare as potato ground for the miner as much land as the latter can supply with adequate dressing for the subsequent tillage of corn.'[34] This, it appears, was the mechanism through which families in rural- industrial Cornwall maintained access to land even if they could not aspire to the actual lease of a few acres.

There was also clearly a relationship between possibility of leases, potato allotments and population change. The population of the mining districts had continued to grow rapidly over the first four decades of the nineteenth century. Lawton suggests that Cornwall, in the late eighteenth century, was a region of relatively high population increase, along with other industrial regions such as North West and North East England or South Wales.[35] Population continued to grow to 1841, the increase of 78 per cent between 1801 and 1841 being slightly in excess of the 73 per cent for the population of England. In Cornwall's mining districts this growth was much faster, 154 per cent in St Just, 137 per cent in Breage/Germoe and 120 per cent in the central mining district.[36] In some areas, with stocks of unenclosed land, such as St.Agnes, there were clearly still possibilities for new three life leases into the 1830s or even later. But in the older mining districts, around Camborne-Redruth and also in St Just:

those parts in which many large mines have been long worked, towns and villages have sprung up, and the greater number of miners are unprovided even with a garden. In such neighbourhoods the land is also of course generally cultivated. Where the mines are more dispersed, and the wastes more extensive, no other difficulty but the disinclination of some landlords presents itself to the establishment of the miner on his little farm.[38]

As the data for Trewellard suggest, in some areas these 'little farms' were not common, something noted by Barham who links renting cows to the fact that 'the quantity of land occupied by each is small'. But this also suggests that, as opportunities of direct access to land through leases were being squeezed by increasing population other possibilities were emerging, at least in the rural mining areas. This all adds up to a continuing access to non-commodity food supplies on the part of the Cornish working people, though the exact mechanism was changing as population rises put pressure on the finite resource of land supply.

The really important collateral aid by the 1840s had therefore become the informal potato patch. This allotment system was widespread, even outside the mining areas. For example, it was found in the Lizard peninsula at Cury, the beneficiaries being local labouring families and even 'townspeople living some distance away' in Helston.[39] So non-commodity production of food continued but in the form of allotments, increasingly underpinned by customary rights to fuel and grazing rather than formal three life leases. These insulated at least a section of the working class from trade cycles (even in the growing towns of Camborne and Redruth rows of cottages were built with long gardens, perhaps reflecting this customary access).

However, three life leases and the informal potato allotments might be interpreted in very different ways, as indicators of dependence or its opposite, of independence. Archer has recently argued that the role of allotments has to be understood in the context of the social relations underlying them. In East Anglia allotments were used as a form of social control by landowners after the 1830s, the result of a 'new paternalism' that saw allotments as a weapon in a 'social and economic power struggle between landowner and farmer'.[40] Some have viewed the Cornish three life leases in a similar light. Rule points to how the granting of such leases by landlords like the Bassets 'began' in the eighteenth century and helped maintain the humane, benevolent image of these lords at a time of social change. Smallholdings linked the lord to the miner and helped to weave a 'web of dependence and deference'. But Rose, in contrast, sees 'customary rights of access' and 'very cheap leaseholding' as reinforcing the 'partial independence that the skilled miner still had in the labour process'.[41]

Whatever the case with the formal leases of land in the eighteenth century, and these do look more like aspects of paternalism, the later informal potato allotments occurred in a social context which had certain distinguishing characteristics. First, the allotment bargain itself was informal, no money changing hands. Second, it was the result of an agreement between labouring miner and farmer, not landlord. Landlords and clergy instituted allotments in 'one or two parishes' in Cornwall but this was unusual.[42] In non-industrial regions it seems that farmers were much more reluctant to provide allotments.[43] In West Cornwall potato allotments may have served as a low cost method of preparing ground for a grain crop in the context of reliance on family labour and relatively higher wages for agricultural labourers when compared with rural areas to the east. The provision of allotments may also have been eased by the narrower social gulf between miner and farmer in a region of small farms. Finally, even if three-life leases began to weave a 'web of deference', the social control of landlords tended to be limited to the one area of access to land. Unlike in the agricultural regions, the influence of Cornish landlords did not in the early nineteenth century penetrate to the heart of local popular culture.

POPULAR METHODISM: A STRUCTURE OF INDEPENDENCE

A powerful force insulating Cornish workers from structures of dependence was their religious affiliation. In the period from the 1780s to the 1820s Methodism won for itself a hegemonic position in Cornish popular culture. By rooting itself in communities and cottages Methodism was inserted into the heart of industrial communities and provided them with a badge of identity. Luker argues that, in doing this, Methodism provided a bridge between the pre-modern and the modern. Cornish Methodism in particular was marked by the active control of the chapels by local communities. From the 1780s the most spectacular form of this local self-management was the mass revivalism that sporadically flamed through Cornish communities, winning converts to the chapel. While frowned upon by the Wesleyan Conference, which preferred steadier and more administratively manageable forms of expansion, this continued to be the main form of recruitment to Cornish Methodism into the 1840s.[45]

Rule has suggested that in early nineteenth-century Cornwall there was a 'configuration of quietism' as various structural factors, such as the tribute wage payment system, the organization of mining with no visible employer class, paternalism and Methodism combined to prevent workers from engaging in the forms of collective activity more usually associated with modernizing regions, notably trade unions, strike action and political radicalism.[46] Yet the proto-industrial society so far outlined seems to be more than just quietist. A labour process which retained some elements of autonomy and control over the pace of production combined with continuing access to forms of collateral aid, and these meshed into a framework of custom and culture that was decentralized, non-deferential and self-managed. 'Tradition' here, as elsewhere, was hardly unchanging and had mutated over the years into different forms. Nevertheless, the appeal to tradition and custom was itself the element of continuity and, together with the role of the self-managed Methodist chapel, helped provide the resources necessary for working-class families actively to evolve strategies that had succeeded in coping with the pressures of an industrializing economy without the intensified social conflicts of some other industrial regions.

THE 1840S: DECADE OF CHANGE

However, this balance of industrialization and tradition, modernity and custom was to emerge from the 1840s radically altered. A number of pressures combined to ensure that older survival strategies became less applicable and the appeal to custom and tradition a less rational or relevant strategy. As a consequence Cornish society entered a recognizably more 'modern' phase.

Rule points out how potatoes were the key to working class living standards in many parts of southern Britain by the 1840s. But they had been adopted early in Cornwall, becoming 'the usual fare of Cornwall's labouring population' by the end of the eighteenth century.[47] Consequently, the blight that hit Cornwall particularly badly in 1845–7 was a disaster. In 1846 the potato harvest in East Cornwall was described as 'not one hundredth part of a crop, and so wretchedly poor that many will say they are unfit to use'. Payton has already alerted us to the neglected role of this contingent event in the history of Cornish emigration. In the context of the argument here, the potato blight's effect was even more profound. In the short run it made the allotment system unworkable and threw labouring families back onto a reliance on bread. As the editorial of the *Royal Cornwall Gazette* put it in early 1847:

> In past seasons, the industrious cottager or miner could rely on his potato crop in aid of his wages. With store of potatoes, the pig fed with the refuse of the crop, and a few hundreds of fish salted by in the Autumn, his winter comforts were secured; but his crops have

failed, and he has nothing but his wages to rely on, with bread nearly double its usual price.[48]

The inevitable result was widespread food rioting in 1847 as mining communities adopted their traditional resort to the moral economy. Yet this episode of rioting was to be the last of its kind, the final spasm of the traditional customary way of life. For in the medium to long run the reliance on potato allotments, involving a socially symbiotic relationship between farmer and industrial worker, was not to return. The attractions of more commercialized farming and perhaps yet to be identified changes in social relations between industrial workers and farmers or changes in the micro-structures of the family wage economy and the labour process in Cornish mining resulted in its demise. The *Morning Chronicle* reports of 1849 emphasized how, in Cornwall, 'so long as the potato succeeded, the spare time of the miner was, in perhaps the majority of instances, well employed' but 'the loss of the potato has . . . been a great blow to the miner'.[49]

Another longer-term factor associated with the demise of the allotment system may have been the pressure imposed on customary rights (to fuel and grazing) by continuous population growth in the mining districts since the early 1700s. Whether or not that was the case, generalized population growth had resulted in the expansion of Cornwall's small towns. The growing confidence of small-town society was accompanied by the formation of literary institutes, of both the 'county' type, like the Royal Cornwall Geological Society, the Royal Institution of Cornwall and the Royal Cornwall Polytechnic Society, and more local institutions such as that at Camborne, formed in 1829. Bolstered by the onset of a wider male ratepayers' democracy after the 1835 Municipal Corporations Act, the urban middle and professional classes provided the antithesis for the traditional customary society of Cornwall's essentially rural industrialization. This had its cultural consequences. In 1845 the disquiet felt by the urban Wesleyan middle classes at Truro and Penzance for the revivalist popular religion of their circuits and their desire to 'demonstrate their own credentials, both as middle class citizens and as Methodists, on the national stage' was the trigger for Conference to send travelling ministers into Cornwall who were determined to re-establish the authority of Conference.[50] On this reading, the popularity of teetotalism in the early 1840s in Cornwall is seen as a 'rearguard action' by indigenous Methodism, as it fought an ultimately unsuccessful battle against connexional orthodoxy.

The decade of the 1840s also marks the visible onset of a moral campaign against another local group of independent labourers. With the expansion of mining, the number of women and girls employed on surface works had risen to over 3,000 by 1841, almost 13 per cent of females in paid work. These bal maidens, predominantly young and unmarried, have been described as demonstrating an 'independence—a lack of subservience and a pride in self'.[51] Work as a bal maiden offered a role model of independence for single young women in the mining districts. However, already by the 1840s there is evidence that some labouring men felt differently, Rule citing the miner who, in 1842, said that 'if he had fifty daughters he would not send them to the mine to be "corrupted by bad conversation"'. The moral arguments about the 'evil' caused by 'the continual association' of the two sexes at the surface works and the condemnation of the bal maidens' 'spirit of rivalry in dress' were repeated by the Cornish mining journalist George Henwood in the later 1850s who continued the ideological attack on this particular display of independence.[52]

Finally, the contingent events of potato blight, along with underlying processes of demographic and cultural change, were paralleled by a more global change. By the 1840s, as Payton notes, a global labour market had emerged for mine labour.[53] In the 1840s emigration to Canada, Australia and the United States became, for the first time, a mass movement, reflected in the sudden slow-down in population growth, from the 13.6 per cent of the 1830s to a mere 3.9 per cent in the 1840s. Emigration was providing Cornish families with a new strategy. Given the pressure on collateral aids posed by a rising population, it was a rational response to ease the pressure by departing. By the 1840s, Cornwall's insertion in the global metal mining economy and its position as a leading mining region ensured that the conditions were right for Cornish labour to meet the demand for skilled miners overseas.[54] And, as migration chains became established, not just miners but others were quick to join the emigration stream.

THE 1850S AND 1860S: ON THE PATH TO MODERNITY
The two decades between the crisis of 1845–47 and the onset of major de-industrialization in the late 1860s and early 1870s tend to be lost from sight. With the advantage of hindsight historians have seen these years as 'but the brief and illusory Indian Summer of the Cornish copper mining industry' or a period when Cornwall teetered on the inevitable abyss of marginalization and 'second peripheralism'.[55] It is the argument here, however, that mid-century Cornwall needs to be re-assessed. In many ways it can be seen as a short-lived period when Cornwall, shedding the proto-industrial social conditions of the period before the 1840s, took on some of the trappings associated with other

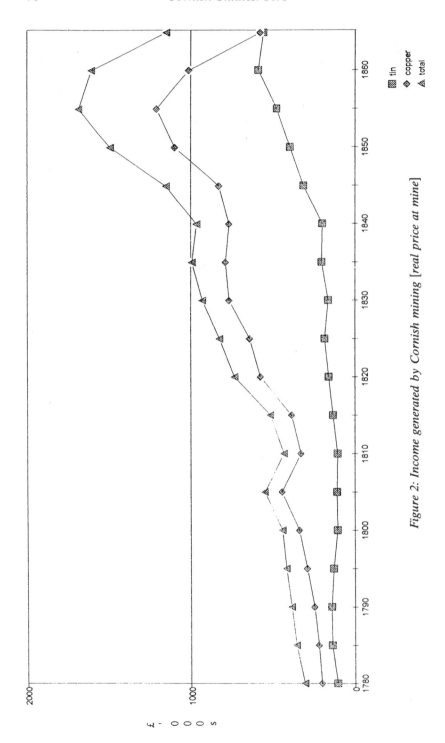

Figure 2: Income generated by Cornish mining [real price at mine]

industrial regions and seemed to have set out on a path to modernity.

We have already seen how the loss of collateral aids in the 1840s had the longer-term effect of making labouring families more dependent on wages and commodity markets for their food consumption. At the same time, the role of popular revivalism was becoming increasingly confined to village communities as the bureaucratization of Methodism proceeded apace. To these twin processes of the commodification of the customary economy and the formalization (and commercialization) of customary culture,[56] we might add three other elements that illustrate the modernization of Cornish society in these decades.

Economically, the late 1840s and 1850s were years of economic growth. The real income generated by Cornish mining, illustrated in Figure 2, began to rise sharply in the second half of the 1840s to peak in the late 1850s at levels perhaps 50 per cent above those of the 1830s and early 1840s.[57] This marked rise in the income generated by Cornish mining must have meant rising per capita income, something perhaps reflected in the relative increase in assessed income tax in Cornwall between 1848 and 1858 when compared with the English norm.[58] It may also go some way towards explaining the 'very curious anomalies' that Rubinstein discovered when calculating the proportion of income tax payers in the parliamentary boroughs of Britain for 1859–60. 'Cornish boroughs like Helston and Bodmin' appeared in his list of borough seats with 'markedly higher [than average] middle class percentages'.[59] Was this, perhaps, the Indian Summer of the Cornish petty bourgeoisie, fuelled by wealth generated from the 1850s boom in mining?

Rising middle class incomes were associated with the emergence of a new sense of territorial identity, clearly penetrating further than the county patriotism of the gentry.[60] The emerging local press of the 1850s helped to reproduce a robust and literate territorial identity. The press carried news of the literary and mutual improvement societies where lectures on the Cornish dialect were becoming increasingly popular. J.T. Tregellas, who died in 1863, had in this period become 'well known throughout the whole of the West of England, a lecturer on the idioms of the Cornish dialect which with his numerous poetical effusions relating to the mining population of the county, and their eccentricities'. Tregellas' papers 'drew more crowded audiences than almost any others at the numerous Scientific and Literary Institutions of the County'.[61] Netherton's *Cornish Almanack*, first published in 1854, with its mixture of information on local politics, business and finance, dialect stories and pieces about the Cornish language, was also indicative of a new form of literate, articulate, self-conscious and middle-class regional identity, one that had a lot in common with the regional identities that had accompanied the rise of industrial regions elsewhere in Britain.[62]

While the Cornish middle classes adopted a self-confident provincial identity typical of industrial regions, the Cornish working classes began to experiment with collective strategies to improve their lot. Despite the myth of the strike-free Cornish mining industry, there are some documented instances of strike action among miners in this period. Strikes occurred at Consolidated Mines, Gwennap, in 1842, amongst St Just miners in 1853, with further industrial action taken by miners at Balleswidden mine in St Just in the late 1850s. While this is not a long list, in 1866 there was generalized strike action in East Cornwall, at the Caradon mines and in the Calstock/Tavistock areas, and in 1872–4 mine workers in at least 18 mines, from St Just in the west to Caradon in the east, took strike action.[63] Clearly, the strike weapon was not one unknown to Cornish miners by the third quarter of the nineteenth century.

Turning our attention away from the miners for a moment, we find that trade unionism was increasingly resorted to by skilled workers in Cornwall after 1840. For example, the quarrymen, who had already organized themselves into branches of the Operative Stonemasons at St Blazey, Luxulyan and Bodmin in the 1830s, moved in 1840 to the western granite quarrying district, with branches formed at Truro, Penryn, Constantine and Penzance in 1840 or soon after. The Penryn branch even took on an employer over wage rates in 1854 and won the dispute. Similarly, boot and shoe makers and bookbinders seem to be organized at Truro in the 1840s and in 1858 there was a branch of the Amalgamated Society of Engineers at Hayle. Building workers and pilchard seiners too were involved in strike action in the 1850s. Even unskilled workers at the fast growing clay works in mid-Cornwall took strike action in 1845 and 1853 and, like the miners, attempted to unionize in the 1870s.[64]

Rather than the desert of working class collectivism that it is often portrayed to be, in mid-century Cornwall strikes and trade unions were perhaps more common than some of the literature would suggest. The example of another working class institution, co-operative societies, also shows that Cornwall was not particularly exceptional. The first major surge of co-operative society formation in England and Wales outside Lancashire took place in the early 1860s and in this wave societies were formed at Truro and St Ive near Liskeard. In the later 1860s and first years of the 1870s, other societies were formed, or attempted, at Penryn, Falmouth, St Austell, Liskeard, St Cleer, Menheniot, Camborne and Upton Cross. There may well be other unrecorded early examples. In fact, in 1872 the geography of co-operative societies shows more societies in Cornwall than in neighbouring (and larger) Devon.[65]

CONCLUSION

Table 1 summarizes these associated changes in economic, social and cultural spheres in the 1850s and early 1860s that appeared to put Cornwall on a path of convergence with other industrial regions.

TABLE 1
Socio-economic and cultural change

	1740s–1830s	*1840s–1860s*
Economic	capitalist accumulation	capitalist accumulation
Social	semi-proletarianization collateral aids mobile merchant bourgeoisie	some w/class institutions pressure on collateral aids coalition of MB and landed class rise of small town middle class
Cultural	popular Methodist hegemony established customary 'traditional' culture	institutionalization of Methodism moral panic about bal maidens 'respectable' leisure pursuits articulated regional identity
Demographic	population rise	population slow down mass emigration

A provincial industrial society was emerging, reminiscent in many respects of other industrial regions. And yet there remained one crucial difference. Cornwall was the only industrial region which was experiencing a major outflow of people. Mass emigration coinciding with continued economic expansion made Cornwall a unique case. In the short run it helped to keep wages up, by removing a surplus supply of labour, but in the long term it reduced still further the chances that the Cornish industrial region would meet the 'critical mass' necessary for a consumer goods market to flourish and for a more diversified economic structure to appear. In fact, as we know, the limited diversification of the Cornish economy was insufficient to weather the restructuring storms of the 1870s to 1890s. As a result Cornwall's mid-century modernization was arrested in mid-development.

The events of the generation after the late 1860s were clearly more catastrophic but the underlying structures of Cornish society changed less than they had done in the 1840s. The pattern of late nineteenth- and early twentieth-century Cornwall was one established in the 1840s, the decade when Cornwall decisively moved from a proto-industrial to an industrial society. That partially urbanized, partially industrial society, with a territorial identity delineated by the symbols and icons of its industrial experience and a popular culture dominated by the institution of the chapel, one where emigration was the preferred working-class survival strategy, was the society created by a combination of the events of the 1840s and the 1860s and 1870s. The events of the later period marked the beginning of the end of mining's dominance of the economy. But it was not these events that, as Burke proposes, 'dissolved old networks of custom, tradition and reciprocity'.[66] The social and cultural glues for these were already being dissolved before the catastrophes of the 1860s and 1870s. Some of the old practices, in the form of tributing, cost book financing, three life leases and indigenous Methodism, remained superficially in place, but it was a society fundamentally changed at the core after the 1840s.

NOTES AND REFERENCES

1. For the notion of a 'semantic space' in the late nineteenth-century Cornwall see Jane Korey, 'As We Belong to be: The Ethnic Movement in Cornwall England', unpub. Ph.D. Brandeis University, 1992, p. 148. For the cultural repositioning see Philip Payton, 'Paralysis and Revival: the reconstruction of Celtic-Catholic Cornwall 1890–1945', in Ella Westland (ed.), *Cornwall: The Cultural Construction of Place*, Penzance, 1997, pp. 25–39.

2. John Rowe, *Cornwall in the Age of the Industrial Revolution*, Liverpool, 1953; Philip Payton, *The Making of Modern Cornwall*, Redruth, 1992, pp. 99–114.

3. See Roger Burt, Peter Waite and Ray Burnley, *Cornish Mines*, Exeter, 1987, p. xli and Rowe, 1953, pp. 315–26.

4. Humphrey Southall and David Gilbert, 'A Good Time to Wed?: Marriage and Economic Distress in England and Wales, 1839–1914', *Economic History Review*, 49, 1996, pp. 35–57.

5. Data from Annual Reports of the Registrar-General. Summary tables in 8th Report, 1847–1848, pp. 40–46; 13th Report, 1950, pp. 170–93; 23rd report, 1860, pp. 174–95; 33rd Report BPP 1872, p. xvii and Annual Reports, BPPs 1873–1900.

6. Maxine Berg, *The Age of Manufactures 1700–1820*, London, 1985, p. 125.

7. Philip Payton, ' "Reforming Thirties" and "Hungry Forties"—The Genesis of Cornwall's Emigration Trade', in Philip Payton (ed.), *Cornish Studies: Four*, Exeter, 1996, p. 108.

8. Roger Burt, 'The International Diffusion of Technology in the Early Modern Period: The Case of the British Non-ferrous Mining Industry', *Economic History Review*, 44, 1991, p. 269.

9. David Callum, 'Society and Economy in Wet Cornwall c1588–1750', unpub. PhD, University of Exeter, 1993, p. 283.

10. Pat Hudson, 'Proto-industrialization in England', in Sheilagh Ogilvie and Markus Cerman (eds), *European Proto-industrialization*, Cambridge, 1996, pp. 49–66.

11. Theodore Kositschek, *Class Formation and Urban Industrial Society: Bradford 1750–1850*, Cambridge, 1990, pp. 40–47.

12. For an overview of this changing historiography see Richard Price, 'Historiography, Narrative and the Nineteenth Century', *Journal of British Studies*, 35, 1996, pp. 200-256.

13. John Rule, 'Review Essay: Proto-Unions?', *Historical Studies in Industrial Relations*, 2, 1996, p. 144.

14. John Stevenson, *Popular Disturbances in England 1700–1832*, Harlow, 1992, p. 130.

15. John Hatcher, *Rural Economy and Society in the Duchy of Cornwall 1300–1500*, Cambridge, 1970, p. 35; Rowe, 1953, p. 290 and John Scantlebury, 'Development of the Export Trade in Pilchards from Cornwall during the 16th century', *Journal of the Royal Institution of Cornwall*, NS10, 1989, pp. 330–359; Hatcher, 'Non-manorialism in Medieval Cornwall', *Agricultural History Review*, 18, 1970, pp. 1–16; Burt, 1991, p. 265.

16. R.V. Jackson, 'Rates of Industrial Growth during the Industrial Revolution', *Economic History Review*, 45, 1992, pp. 2 and 19. Copper statistics calculated from production figures in J.B. Hill and D.A. Macalister, *Memoirs of the Geological Survey; The Geology of Falmouth and Truro and the Mining District of Camborne and Redruth*, London, 1906, pp. 310–12.

17. Cf. Pat Hudson, *The Industrial Revolution*, London, 1992, p. 43.

18. John Rule, *The Vital Century: England's Developing Economy 1714–1815*, Harlow, 1992; Roger Burt, *John Taylor: Mining Entrepreneur and Engineer 1779–1863*, Buxton, 1977, p. 29; Peter Mathias, *The First Industrial Nation: An Economic History of Britain 1700–1914*, London, 1983, p. 248; Sidney Pollard, *Peaceful Conquest: The Industrialisation of Europe 1760–1970*, Oxford, 1981, p. 14.

19. John Kanefsky and John Robey, 'Steam Engines in 18th century Britain',

Technology and Culture, 21, 1980, pp. 176–77; John Griffiths, *The Third Man: The Life and Times of William Murdoch 1754–1839*, London, 1992; Alan Buckley, *The Cornish Mining Industry: A Brief History*, Penryn, 1992, p. 15.

20. Calculated from C.H. Lee, *British Employment Statistics 1841–1971*, Cambridge, 1979.
21. Gareth Stedman Jones, *Languages of Class: Studies in English Working Class History 1832–1982*, Cambridge, 1983, p. 13.
22. P.E. Razzell and R.W. Wainwright (eds), *The Victorian Working Class: Selections from Letters to the Morning Chronicle*, London, 1973, p. 23. And see Gill Burke, 'The Cornish Miner and the Cornish Mining Industry 1870–1921', unpub. PhD, University of London, 1981, p. 30.
23. See the evidence on ownership given to the *Report on the Copper Trade from the Committee appointed to inquire into the state of the copper mines and copper trade of this kingdom*, BPP, 1799, pp. 159–61.
24. Veronica Chesher, 'Some Cornish Landowners 1690–1760; A Social and Economic Study', unpub. MA, University of Oxford, 1957, p. 11.
25. Burke, 1981, p. 37.
26. John Beckett, *The Aristocracy in England 1660–1914*, Oxrford, 1986, pp. 122–26.
27. *Kelly's Directory*, 1856.
28. J.D. Tuckett, *A History of the Past and Present State of the Labouring Population*, London, 1846, p. 536.
29. Charles Barham, *Evidence to the Childrens Employment Commission*, BPP, 1842, p. 754.
30. Damaris Rose, 'Home Ownership, Subsistence and Historical Change: the Mining District of West Cornwall in the Late Nineteenth Century', in Nigel Thrift and Peter Williams (eds), *Class and Space: The Making of an Urban Society*, London, 1987, pp. 120 and 113; Rowe, 1953, pp. 225-26; John Rule, 'Some Social Aspects of the Cornish Industrial Revolution', in Roger Burt (ed.), *Industry and Society in the South West*, Exeter, 1970, pp. 72–79; Burt, 1991, p. 267. And see Rule, 'The Labouring Miner in Cornwall c1740–1870, PhD, unpub. University of Warwick, p. 99.
31. Seymour Tremenheere, *The State of Education in the Mining Districts of Cornwall*, BPP, 1840, p. 84.
32. Barham, 1842, pp. 753–54.
33. Tremenheere, 1840, p. 88.
34. Barham, 1842, p. 754.
35. Richard Lawton, 'Population and Society 1730–1914', in R.A. Dodgshon and R. A. Butlin (eds), *An Historical Geography of England and Wales*, London, 1990, pp. 297.
36. Calculated from published Census reports.
37. Barham, 1842, p. 830.
38. Barham, 1842, p. 754.
39. John Rowe, *Changing Times and Fortunes: A Cornish farmer's Life 1828–1904*, St Austell, 1996, pp. 71–72.

40. John Archer, 'The Nineteenth-century Allotment: Half an Acre and a Row', *Economic History Rview*, 50, 1997, pp. 2–36.
41. John Rule, *The Labouring Classes in Early Industrial England 1750– 1850*, Harlow, 1986, p. 84 and 'A Configuration of Quietism? Attitudes towards Trade Unionism and Chartism among the Cornish miners', *Tijdschrift voor Sociale Geschiedenis*, 2/3, 1992, pp. 255–57; Rose, 1987, p. 149.
42. Rowe, 1953, pp. 238–39.
43. Archer, 1997, pp. 21–22.
44. E.H. Hunt *Regional Wage Variations in Britain, 1850–1914*, Oxford, 1973, p. 14.
45. David Luker, 'Cornish Methodism, Revivalism and Popular Belief, c. 1780– 1870', unpub. PhD, University of Oxford, 1987, pp. 381–410 and 'Revivalism in Theory and Practice: the case of Cornish Methodism', *Journal of Ecclesiastical History*, 37, 1986, pp. 603–19.
46. Rule, *Configuration of Quietism*, 1992, pp. 248–49.
47. Rule, 1986, p. 53.
48. *Royal Cornwall Gazette*, 1 January 1847; Payton, 1996, pp. 110–11; *Royal Cornwall Gazette*, 22 January 1847.
49. Razzell and Wainwright, 1973, p. 28.
50. Luker, 1987, p. 356.
51. Gill Burke, 'The Decline of the Independent Bal Maiden: The Impact of Change in the Cornish Mining Industry', in Angela John (ed.), *Unequal Opportunities: Womens' Employment in England 1800–1918*, Oxford, 1986, p. 180.
52. Rule, 1986, p. 186; Roger Burt (ed.), *Cornwall's Mines and Miners*, Truro, 1972, pp. 118–20.
53. Payton, 1996, pp. 112–13.
54. See also Gill Burke, 'The Cornish Diaspora of the Nineteenth Century', in Shula Marks and Peter Richardson (eds), *International Labour Migration: Historical Perspectives*, London, 1984, pp. 65–75.
55. Rowe, 1953, p. 164; Payton, 1992, pp. 99–103.
56. By 1850 wrestling competitions at Truro were attracting large crowds and competitors from across Cornwall, from St Just in the west to Callington in the east, lured by prizes equivalent to half a year's wages (*West Briton*, 26 July 1850).
57. Output and income calculated from Hill and MaAlister, 1906, pp. 310–12. Price adjustments calculated from N.J. Silverberg, 'British Prices and Business Cycles, 1779–1850', *Review of Economic Statistics*, 1923, p. 235 and E. M. Carus-Wilson (ed.), *Essays in Economic History*, Vol. 1962, pp. 142–43 and 250.
58. Calculated from statistics in W.D. Rubinstein, *Elites and the Wealthy in Modern British History*, Brighton, 1987, pp. 92–93.
59. W.D. Rubinstein, 'The Size and Distribution of the English Middle Classes in 1860', *Historical Research*, 61, 1988, p. 79.
60. This was part of what Payton describes as a 'new Cornishness' that emerged in the mid-nineteenth century (Payton, 1992, p. 82).

61. *West Briton*, 20 March 1863 and anon., *Journal of the Royal Institution of Cornwall*, 1, 1865, p. 55.
62. See John Langton, 'The Industrial Revolution and the Regional Geography of England', *Transactions of the Institute of British Geographers*, NS 9, 1984, pp. 145-67.
63. *West Briton*, 1 April 1842, 25 March 1853, 18 July 1856; *Royal Cornwall Gazette*, 4 March 1859; Bernard Deacon, 'Attempts at Unionism by Cornish Metal Miners in 1866', *Cornish Studies*, 10, 1982, pp. 27–36 and 'Heroic Individualists? The Cornish Miners and the five-week month 1872– 74', *Cornish Studies* 14, 1986, pp. 39–52.
64. Alf Jenkin, 'The Operative Masons of Luxulyan', *Cornish Association of Local Historians News Magazine*, 8, 1984, pp. 6–7; Rule, 1986, p. 318; Alf Jenkin, 'The Cornish Chartists', *Journal of the Royal Institution of Cornwall*, NS9, 1982, pp. 53–80; *West Briton*, 1 April 1853, 12 November 1858, 8 September 1848, 14 October 1859, 3 October 1845; Jack Ravensdale, 'The China Clay Labourers Union', *History Studies*, 1, 1968, pp. 51–62.
65. *The Co-operator*, August and December, 1865, April 1867; *Royal Cornwall Gazette*, 13 February 1868, 12 November 1868; *West Briton*, 27 December 1867; *Royal Cornwall Gazette*, 10 May 1873; *Cornish Times*, 16 August 1873; *Royal Cornwall Gazette*, 19 July 1873; *Cornish Times*, 8 March 1873; Martin Purvis, 'Popular Institutions', in John Langton and R.J. Morris (eds), *Atlas of Industrialising Britain*, London, 1986, p. 195.
66. Gill Burke, 'The Impact of Industrial Change on Working Class Family Life in the Mining Districts of Nineteenth-century Cornwall', *Bulletin of the Society for the Study of Labour History*, 48, 1984, p. 14.

ACKNOWLEDGEMENT

The author gratefully acknowledges the support of the Open University Faculty of Social Sciences in part-funding the research upon which this article is based.

RETHINKING CELTIC CORNWALL: AN ETHNOGRAPHIC APPROACH

Amy Hale

INTRODUCTION

In studying the Celtic Revival in Cornwall one thing stands out: throughout the course of the Revival too much time and energy has been spent justifying Cornwall's 'Celticity'. Practically every public address Henry Jenner ever made, from 1903 onwards, dealt with the subject, and even Charles Thomas' address to the Celtic Congress over seventy years after Jenner's initial triumph seemed intent on rehearsing the case once more.[1] One asks, why there was ever any doubt?

If we look back at how the term 'Celtic' has developed in the past 300 years, Cornwall has always been included in definitions and explanations, but it seems that as time went on, at least some observers lost sight of this. Perhaps this was because certain 'Celtic characteristics' began to take precedent over others in the evaluation of a particular culture's 'right' to call itself Celtic. As in most measures of 'Celticity', Cornwall has been evaluated in terms of the past—in language (or as in Thomas' case, material culture), the language issue in particular giving activists in other Celtic areas an axe to grind (if Cornwall has 'lost' its language, then is it still to be considered Celtic?). Sometimes, however, other cross-cultural factors have been considered, such as the interest in those saints' lives that provide evidence for greater 'Celtic' links, diffusion, or a common cultural inheritance. Yet none of these factors seems satisfactory in explaining the phenomenon of contemporary Celtic identities (in Cornwall or elsewhere), or indeed the explosion of 'Celtic styles' in popular culture. Many of these forms of Celticity have a basis in experience, aside from language, or in other expressions of cultural inheritance. Thus it may be more relevant to re-examine Celtic Cornwall through concepts like style and meaning, sometimes relating it to a broader network of contemporary Celtic expressions, situating it as a phenomenon that is culturally relevant and ethnographically real. In so doing there is an opportunity to re-evaluate such concepts such as 'tradition' and 'authenticity', to see how these notions function in situations of cultural revival and the construction of social visions. The project is not to justify or judge, like so many others before, but potentially to give voice to those for whom Celtic identities are meaningful, and to examine Cornwall's role in a wider Celtic network.

HISTORICAL ORIGINS
First, however, it is important to contemplate the historical usages of the term 'Celtic', and to understand how the concept has evolved. That a language or a group of people can be 'Celtic' *appears* to denote a closed category, a set with particular distinguishing characteristics that can be recognized and classified. This is how we determine that something either is, or is not, 'Celtic'. Probably due as much to the development of the social sciences as anything else, cultural categories have a sense of being 'natural', organic in their development.[2] Cultural traits are thought of as being owned, and inherited. But Celtic, like other cultural categories, has a history all its own—a history shaped by politics, fashions and intellectual trends. Inevitably, this has affected how we might define who and what is Celtic.

However, Celtic categorizing has always been messy . The Greek ethnographies of the fifth century BC employed the word *keltoi* (Celts, Celtic) to describe the various barbarian groups to the north and west of Greece. Later, Romans wrote of the people in this area of Europe using the term *galli*, which they equated to the Greek *keltoi*. The Celts feature in many geographies of the classical world, Tacitus and Posidonius being two of the most well-known chroniclers. Probably one of the best known accounts is from Caesar's reports of his conquest of Gaul, which describes Celtic military tactics and includes some telling ethnographic musings about the Druids. Since these various peoples known to the ancient world as Celts did not use writing to record their history, classical accounts form the basis of what we know about Iron Age Celtic society, written by their contemporaries rather than themselves. Malcolm Chapman, therefore, postulates the controversial view that these records tell us nothing of 'The Celts', since there is no evidence that the term was ever self-ascribed.[3] He believes that there is strong evidence to suggest that the Greek *keltoi* was merely a generic term used by Greeks to denote the vague barbarian groupings at a point relative to the Greek centre, and that the term never described an actual or 'real' group of people.

What is significant, however, is that observers do not start writing or talking about 'The Celts' again until the Middle Ages, when the classics were starting to be rediscovered by the European intelligentsia.[4] One of the earliest accounts we have of the term resurfacing is that by Annius of Viterbo in a piece from 1498 in which he constructs a false pedigree for the early peoples of Europe using Biblical patriarchs and bad philology. In this context, the Celts, being somehow related to Noah, were one of the first people to inhabit Europe. This is a very common context in which to find 'The Celts' and this practice continues well into the eighteenth century where we see the Welsh (Cymry) being descended from Gomer, son of Japhet. It is not until the very late seventeenth century that the term Celtic is being used to describe living populations, yet it is still not a term that is self-ascribed. It is at this time that the first major comparative work on language families was being done. Edward Lhuyd, the groundbreaking linguist, is credited with being the first in the eighteenth century to label the linguistic groupings of Irish, Cornish, Welsh, Breton, and Scots Gaelic as 'Celtic', although they had been arranged into a 'language family' by George Buchanan as early as 1584. Since the languages were held to be similar, the peoples who spoke them were also thought to have common roots, and be derived from a single culture.

Linguists and antiquarians saw Celtic subjects as fit material for research, since they were on the outskirts of the Empire yet conveniently close to home, exotic, perceived as barbaric, and conquered. As Chapman and others note, the fact that they were seen as fit subjects for early ethnographers implies something about how these people were conceived.[5] Within the several early models of cultural evolution of that time, the Celts were somewhere between 'savage' and 'peasant', but definitely an inferior Other, with all that that implied. In a tandem development, in the late eighteenth century, Johann Herder promoted the belief that the unique folk soul of a people was most present in its folklore. By the next century this line of thought had become the inspiration for emerging principles of ethnographic inquiry, and the springboard for a whole series of cultural nationalist movements seeking to cultivate their distinctive folk souls.[6]

As in the German and various Scandinavian nationalist movements, activism and scholarship fused Celtic cultures.[7] As the 'noble savage' and 'enlightened peasant' became more popular in the estimation of establishment European culture, scholars from the Celtic-speaking areas began producing their own research within a new, comparative framework. Early Celtic activists, many of whom were also scholars, could use this perceived exoticism to advantage while studying and codifying their distinctive cultural traits. The Welsh scholar and inventor of the Gorsedd, Iolo Morganwg, and later Irish activists such as W.B. Yeats and Douglas Hyde, are prime examples of the interface of Celtic scholar and cultural entrepreneur. This process prompted a more self-conscious usage of the term Celtic, especially as it related to both a wider network of various peoples and the relationship with a more dominant culture.

THE EMERGENCE OF 'CELTIC CORNWALL'

So where does Cornwall fit into this history? Ever since 'Celtic' has been on the lips of interested researchers, Cornwall has been considered a worthy subject. The two predominantly 'Celtic' features of interest to early researchers were, of course, the Cornish language and the megalithic monuments, and the resultant studies contributed greatly to Cornwall's emerging 'Celticity'. Indeed, Edward Lhuyd researched Cornish in 1700 as part of his inquiries into Celtic linguistics. Although concerned solely with language, this study suggested Cornwall's connections to other 'Celtic' regions, and was to form the cornerstone for further antiquarian inquiries that were to make similar, comparative ethnographic suggestions and assumptions.

Almost simultaneously adding to Cornwall's emergent 'Celticity' was the proliferation of interest in the various types of ancient stone structures (of which Cornwall has many), a preoccupation that fuelled seventeenth and eighteenth-century speculation about ancient Druidic rites. Although it is now known that the late Bronze and Iron Age Celts did not build these megalithic monuments, this fact is of little relevance in the history of people's perceptions of 'Celticity'. What is important is that for centuries people thought these stones *were* Celtic, a powerful misconception that continues to pervade the popular imagination and iconography of Celtic Cornwall. Oddly enough, early studies of Cornish megaliths were often combined with statements and assumptions about the 'primitive' and 'backward' nature of the native Cornish population, which in turn became crucial factors in creating a contemporary sense of Celtic ethnicity. Borlase's *Antiquities Historical and Monumental of the County of Cornwall* of 1754, with a revised and enlarged edition in 1769 in which he connected the religion of the ancient Celts to the stone monuments of Cornwall, was an important early contribution. The first section of this massive tome was dedicated to the history and religion of the Druids, which Borlase felt was an institution native to Britain and most heavily concentrated in Cornwall, as evidenced by the great number of stone monuments.[8] Borlase seemed quite certain that the contemporary inhabitants of Cornwall were the remains of the original Celtic population of Britain. As well as the evidence of the Cornish language, the Cornish (Borlase argued) were like the Welsh and Hebridean Scots in that they still carried out the remains of Druidic worship in their folk beliefs and practices.[9] None of this was considered absurd reasoning for the time, yet one wonders what was the cultural impact, if any, upon the identity of the 'common' or 'vulgar' Cornish people (as Borlase called them) as a result of being linked with 'Ancient Britons' and Druidic rites.

The great-great grandson of William Borlase, William Copeland Borlase, maintained the family tradition with a scholarly interest in the earthworks and folklore of Cornwall. He argued that the Druids had no connection with the Cornish stone sites, yet the enduring influence of the elder Borlase's work perpetuated this idea for many years among the native population.[10] In William Copeland Borlase's 1893 ethnographic description of the Cornish, writing over 100 years after his great-great grandfather, he does not use the term 'Celt' but nonetheless draws numerous physical comparisons with the populations of other 'Celtic' areas, usually indicating that these people are of a lesser, inferior stock than the later Germanic inhabitants. He considered that the native population of Cornwall was the remnant of an earlier race that had settled Britain, those who had built the stone structures. He thought that they were the 'Short, dark dwarfish people who imparted superstitions' to the 'tall, fair Germanic types' who later invaded.[11] He added that the Cornish showed a 'marked nigrescence . . . only equalled in Southern, Western and North Western Ireland, and the Western counties of Scotland'.[12] Borlase also used the term 'Mongoloid' to describe the Cornish and Welsh, and compared the physical type to the Japanese, implying that these shared physical attributes might have been a factor in the development of both Celtic and Shinto practices of ancestor worship.[13] That Borlase considered the aboriginal inhabitants of Cornwall inferior is clear from his description of the 'invaders':

> From remains found, however, in other parts of Britain, we know what manner of man the 'round barrow' man was. He was tall in stature, powerful in limb, his head broad and of rugged outline, and his hair probably light. His race we believe, represents the first of the ingressive and dominant races of Britain.[14]

Again, Borlase does not refer to Celts anywhere in his ethnographic musings, yet his theories exemplify some of the important social assumptions about the people he had categorically lumped together, those whom others of the same period were calling 'Celts', inferring that they were somehow similar, probably related, and inferior. By contrast, Robert Hunt, in a slightly earlier publication, does call the Cornish 'Celts', and in his work he wants to celebrate their folklore and their cultural 'difference'. However, the way that he conceptualizes the Cornish as Celts is consistent with a broader pattern, and in substance not all that different from the latter Borlase.

In the work of Robert Hunt we may find the earliest bold assertion of the contemporary Cornish as living Celts, an assertion that was to have a major impact for those in the later Celtic-Cornish Revival. Robert Hunt was a native of Devon who came to Cornwall through his involvement with the mining industry, and developed a passion for folklore collection. He came to know the miners and their lore well, but Hunt also took an interest in those supernatural tales and traditions not connected so intimately with the mining communities. In 1865 Hunt published *The Drolls and Superstitions of Old Cornwall: Popular Romances of the West of England*, which remains as the classic collection of Cornish folklore. Hunt's work later took on an almost religious status for those involved in the Celtic-Cornish Revival, for it was a main source of older traditions to be learned and built upon. It was Hunt who, in a Biblical allusion, first suggested that antiquarians 'gather a fragment here, and gather a fragment there',[15] a maxim which was later to become the creed and mission of the Old Cornwall Societies: 'gather ye the fragments that remain lest nothing be lost.'

That the Cornish were Celtic was not a point to be argued by Hunt. In fact, it was their very Celticity that accounted for their 'backward' and 'superstitious' nature:

> I have possessed the best possible opportunities for gathering up the folk-lore of a people, who, but a few generations since, had a language peculiarly their own, a people who, like all the Celts, cling with sincere affection to the memories of the past, and who even now regard with jealousy the introduction of any novelty and accept improvements slowly.[16]

In describing what prompted his collecting mission, his characterization of a 'Celtic' people is typical:

> From early youth accidental circumstances have led to my acquiring a taste for collecting the waifs floating upon the sea of time, which tell us of those ancient peoples who have not a written history. The rude traditions of a race who appear to have possessed much native intelligence, minds wildly poetical, and great fertility of imagination, united with a deep feeling for the mysteries by which life is girdled, especially interested me.[17]

When our Celtic ancestors—in the very darkness of their ignorance—were taught, through their fears, a Pantheistic religion, and saw a god in every grand phenomenon . . . then was moulded the Celtic mind, and the early impressions have not entirely been obliterated . . . Notwithstanding the influences which can be—not very obscurely—traced of Roman and Saxon, Danish and Norman civilisations, the Celtic superstitions lingered on:—varied perhaps in their clothing, but in all essentials the same. Those wild dreams which swayed with irresistible force the skin-clad Briton of the Cornish hills, have not entirely lost their power where even the National and the British schools are busy with the people, and the Mechanic's [*sic*] Institutions are diffusing the truths of science.[18]

The subject matter of Hunt's collection was not Pan-Celtic, as such. He did not concentrate on the formal similarities between Cornish narratives, beliefs and festivals, and other 'Celtic' phenomena. For Hunt, this matter did not need to be justified by comparative evidence. The Cornish material was Celtic, because the Cornish were Celts. This sentiment was also Robert Morton Nance's philosophy, when he took the lead in the Cornish-Celtic Revival in the 1920s.

On top of all this external classification of the indigenous culture, there remained the sense of difference that the Cornish themselves experienced from the dominant English culture that surrounded them. It was thus a logical step for the Cornish to self-define as 'Celtic', following suit with others in similar circumstances in developing a sense of Celtic identity, together with a growing desire to express it. Although there may not then have been in Cornwall a widespread grass-roots consciousness of Celticity, especially when compared to other Celtic areas, there were (it is thought) Cornish representatives at what was the first-ever modern Pan-Celtic event, held at St Brieuc in Brittany in 1867. Thereafter, the notion of 'Celtic Cornwall' gained increasing currency, precipitating the Cornish-Celtic Revival and moulding a variety of cultural constructions of Cornwall. But given that such constructions rapidly became commonplace, then why—we are entitled to ask—has there been such as fuss about it ever since? The answer, I propose, is twofold. Firstly, and most importantly, the need to continually rehearse Cornwall's Celticity has had a great deal to do with the hierarchy of acceptable 'Celtic' attributes and expressions that have emerged as trends in Pan-Celtic cultural innovation. Additionally, there is the potential conflict between Cornwall's industrial heritage and popular perceptions of Celts as non-industrial peoples.

THE CULTURAL POLITICS OF PAN-CELTICISM

As Pan-Celtic politics developed at the end of the nineteenth century, the main players in the movement, those with the money, the stylish cultural institutions and publishing ability, were the Irish and the Welsh, with the Bretons coming in a little later. As it happened, the languages became the central issues (even though most of the discourse occurred in English), and for activists as well as scholars, having a spoken Celtic language was the prime identifier of a 'genuine' Celtic identity. Naturally, the now widely understood fact that language is not always an accurate marker of ethnicity was not being debated at that time. Thus language was seen as an indicator of 'Celtic purity', especially for the Irish at the turn of the century as their political crisis took centre stage, when the Irish language became a strategic playing card. Of course, because Cornish had been pronounced 'dead', Cornwall was at a distinct disadvantage as the international playing field began to be contested more hotly.

Almost as important as language, however, were the other issues of 'Celtic style' that in Cornwall are often labelled as 'invented' or 'inauthentic', such as kilt-wearing and pipe-playing, even the Gorseth, which was originally Welsh. Are the Cornish copycats? Why do they need to wear tartan? Isn't that a Scottish tradition? Well, not any more. The Cornish would argue that they are no less Celtic for having had to adopt these traditions, because all the contemporary Celts have made similar adaptions.

In the early years of the twentieth century, the main organ of the Pan-Celtic movement was the Celtic Association, which was, for all of its disclaimers, a hotbed of incipient Romantic nationalism. The Celtic Association, of which the Anglo-Irish Lord Castletown was president, was attempting to fortify Celtic cultures by reviving and/or inventing 'Celtic' traditions, and thereby strengthening their visible symbols of 'difference'. Re-establishing the Celtic languages was a prime objective of the Association but, as has often been the pattern in cultural nationalist movements, great emphasis was placed on establishing 'folk' traditions such as festivals, music, costume and sport. While the Celtic Association certainly encouraged each constituent 'nation' to develop distinctively, it did set clear parameters for the development of 'national' traditions. For instance, the July 1901 issue of *Celtia* contained an article on the best way to establish an Irish national festival costume. The article states:

> The essential requisites of an Irish festival costume are the
> following:
> 1. It must be historically correct.

2. It must be convenient and "wearable".
3. It must be artistic and becoming.
4. It must be made of Irish material.
5. It must be distinctively Irish.[19]

The August 1901 *Celtia* gives the programme for the Pan-Celtic Congress' business meeting. Aside from the language, philology and archaeological sections, there was a section devoted to 'Celtic Costume, Custom, Games and Folk-Lore', the matter of which was much more overtly prescriptive than academic. The agenda for the meeting of this section was as follows:

(a) On what occasions should a national costume generally be worn?
(b) What period should be adhered to in the choice of an Irish, Manx or Welsh national costume?
(c) What Celtic games and customs are worthy of preservation?
(d) In what directions should folk-lore researches be chiefly made in the immediate future?

Clearly, for the Celtic Association 'tradition' was a strategy that needed to be well thought-out and effectively presented, and it was in this environment that variations on Pan-Celtic traditions arose, and certain aspects of culture were highlighted for revival. For instance, Celtic music and poetry festivals patterned after the Welsh Eisteddfod and the Gorsedd, became an important part of Celtic tradition formation. At first it was thought that all Celtic nations would adopt the Eisteddfod and Gorsedd format. In the end only the Brythonic nations (i.e. Cornwall and Brittany, following the example of Wales) held to it, although the Eisteddfod directly influenced the Scottish Mod, a Scots Gaelic song and music competition and festival.

Sport, too, was thought to be important by the Celtic Association, and certain games were earmarked as particularly Celtic. We see this in the revised pedigree of Cornish wrestling, which went from 'Classical' to 'Celtic' in the estimation of its adherents. This may have been inspired by the formation of the Gaelic Athletic Association (GAA) by Michael Cusack in 1884. The purpose of the GAA was to revive traditional Irish sports such as Irish football and hurling that had waned in popularity in the face of English sports such as cricket and tennis.[21] Its tremendous influence on the revival in Ireland may have caused the Pan-Celtic movement to put sports on its agenda. Then there was the matter of the kilt. The Celtic Association decided that the kilt was the most appropriate and distinctively different costume to be adopted by all modern Celts, not just the Scots, an insistence that was even reflected in the British Army whose Irish regiments wore the 'saffron kilt'. Indeed, in 1902 L.C. Duncombe-Jewell, founder of the Cornish-Celtic Society, and Stuart Erskine were put in charge of developing a Pan-Celtic tartan, and the first suggestion to formulate a Cornish national costume based on the kilt actually emerged around the same time.[22] Early Cornish kilts were in fact black or saffron, the now familiar Cornish National Tartan (and later family tartans, such as the Curnow and the Roseveare) not emerging until after the Second World War.

The 'emerging' Celtic countries needed each other for support and inspiration, and that was the climate in which the earliest Cornish activists entered the debate. Unfortunately, perhaps, on the international stage Cornish activists did not promote the native symbols of Cornish identity already in use by the Cornish themselves, which were often derived from a strong industrial past. Why was this? Were the early leaders of the Revival such as Duncombe- Jewell and Henry Jenner out of touch with everyday working-class Cornwall? Most likely, yes. However, as noted above, 'industrial' and 'Celtic' do not generally share the same semantic space, and many of those working to forge 'new' Celtic nations relied on a more pastoral vision, which was actually incongruent with the reality of Cornish history. Good Celts were not supposed to be modern industrialists; they were to be rural, simple, spiritual peasants working in harmony with the land. This construction is demonstrated at its most reified, perhaps, in the social policies of the early Irish Republic, based on visions of Celtic Ireland as essentially rural, centred on small homesteads. Commentators have argued that this vision greatly held back Ireland's economic development (as well as further alienating the Protestant industrial culture of Ulster), yet for what it is worth it may be noted that Irish is often that nationality most commonly thought of as 'Celtic'.[23]

AUTHENTICITY, TRADITION AND FOLKLORE

So if this 'grab bag' of Celtic tradition exists, and the Cornish have dipped their hands in during the course of their 'Revival', does it mean that the Cornish versions are less authentic? Is there still a sense that some Celts are more 'Celtic' than others? If ultimately we were to prove that the Celts invented all their traditions, then does that mean that the Celts do not exist? Are we best to attempt to reduce the word 'Celtic' to refer to a bunch of disembodied languages and texts, because this is a concept that is easier to handle and understand? Although some people may indeed be more comfortable with this approach, it denies some important ethnographic facts—primarily, that there are people in Cornwall, speaking English and sometimes, too, forms of revived Cornish, who call themselves Celts. This fact should not be ignored and yet it is still often met with derision, even by those who ought to know better. For example, when I told a medievalist colleague of mine that I was working with the 'contemporary Cornish' she said, 'oh, so you're not studying real Celts then'. But what, one retorts, is a 'real' Celt?

Again, the answer to this difficult question will ultimately involve judgements by both those inside and outside the academic arena, but those judgements need to be informed on a much wider range of phenomena than has often been admitted hitherto. First of all, I believe we must re-evaluate the 'linguistic criterion' for assessing 'genuine' Celtic peoples. Ethnographically, it is inconsistant with the lived experiences of many Celts. Although language is an important marker of difference, we realistically need to ask, just how important? I speak English, yet I am not English (I am American), and if I spoke nothing but French from now on, I would never be French. If the Welsh language should disappear tomorrow (which, of course, I hope it does not), the Welsh still would not be English. The same logic can and has to be used in understanding Celtic-Cornish identities.

When examining contemporary forms of Celtic expression, Cornish or otherwise, critics also need to reconsider what we mean by terms like 'authenticity' and 'tradition', and how these have been used, not only to construct cultures but also by academics to judge other people's lived experience. Hobsbawm and Ranger's 1983 collection of essays *The Invention of Tradition* was, admittedly, a seminal work. It has been a starting point for many scholars trying to unpack exactly how the concept of tradition has been used and manipulated, either by activists attempting to establish national cultures or by states trying to legitimize institutions. Hobsbawm defines an 'invented tradition' as 'a set of practices, normally governed by overtly or tacitly accepted rules and of a ritual or symbolic nature, which seek to inculcate certain values and norms of behaviour by repetition, which automatically implies continuity with the past'.[24] The work was of interest for students of Celtic material as it contained essays 'debunking' Highland dress as an English invention and 'exposing' the Welsh Gorsedd as invented, which in 1983 was not news to many.[25] *The Invention of Tradition* made us think about how important tradition is as a construct, and how it functions for people in the quest for identity and even power. However, the work has one major flaw: Hobsbawm makes a rather arbitrary distinction between 'tradition' and 'custom', the latter being seen as the primary mode of operation for 'traditional' societies. Implicit in his argument is the notion that some traditions are invented and thus 'false'

while others are not invented, and therefore 'genuine'. But all traditions, and even languages, are invented. Sometimes we may forget who
made them up, when, and even why, which creates an illusion of
common ownership, anonymity, and organic creation.

Deliberations concerning 'genuine' and 'spurious' folklore have
been elaborated by folklorists since the 1950s, and perhaps the most
articulate discussions have been those conducted by German folklorists
since the 1960s. In 1962 Hans Moser introduced the term *folklorismus*
(English: folklorism) to describe the phenomenon of folklore 'out of
context', or that which has been invented or altered for specific
purposes.[26] This can cover anything from state-funded 'folk' performances and 'folk' festivals to professional storytelling, or cultural
preservation efforts generally understood as revival. However, Herman
Bausinger later offered a critique of this concept, which has resulted
in nothing less than a challenge to the underlying precepts upon which
the field of folklore had been founded. Several of his points seem
particularly relevant here, and I would like to paraphrase loosely. First
he notes that explaining folklorism as purely the result of economic
factors overestimates the commercial aspect of invented traditions and
can obstruct the essence and function of the phenomenon (and, one
might add, the aesthetic response to it).[27] Thus, to assume that Celtic
revivalist traditions in Cornwall arose only in response to the economic
crisis brought about by the collapse of the mining industry, reduces the
emotional and aesthetic components of their genesis. Bausinger states:

> It seems to me to be important that all these manifestations are an
> aspect of leisure time . . . and that they must be seen in this light.
> This activity can be looked upon, on the one hand, as a contrast to
> the world of work in its monotony and bareness. These things bring
> color to people's lives, and yet there is at the same time the
> impression and the appearance of simplicity, the natural, the old.[28]

Bausinger also notes the effect that invented traditions have in terms
of mobilizing minority cultures and increasing group consciousness.[29]
Through cultural invention people can engage in creating their own
representations and telling their own stories.

Further, those who contrast folklorism (invented traditions) with
'genuine' folk culture draw attention to the latter in such a way that it
too must inevitably tend toward folklorism.[30] Put simply, once a
folklorist identifies a 'real' folk tradition, it becomes marked behaviour
and is suddenly more self- conscious, frozen in time. Suddenly 'genuine'
culture becomes manipulated 'out of context', leaving us to ask what
'genuine' culture was in the first place and what criteria we might have

used to evaluate it. Regina Bendix sums up these arguments by stating that 'those who insist on studying "genuine" folklore imply that they know the boundaries of such a folk culture, and that they implicitly wished to preserve their field of study within these limits'.[31] In other words, the fear of folklorists, anthropologists, and even Celticists, is that the actual processes of culture may slip over the boundaries that they (the academics) have set for them. Bausinger notes the potential for these arguments to be used to critique key concepts such as 'tradition', 'custom' and 'community', all of which are usually taken to be fixed discrete units at the mercy of social scientists and folklorists, but in reality are shifting and governed by ideological precepts. He suggests that inquiry into these concepts should be within the contexts of transmission, meaning, historical context, popular culture, and mass media.[32]

CONCLUSION

So let us come back to Celtic Cornwall for a moment. First, let us agree that the category of 'Celtic', like all other cultural designations, has a history and has been governed by a set of ideologies, agendas and discourses that have changed over time. Second, let us be clear that Cornwall and the Cornish have, historically, participated in these Celtic discourses. Third, we should also note that Celtic traditions in Cornwall have been influenced by a wider Pan-Celtic network and adapted to a specifically Cornish context. And fourthly, let us acknowledge that Celtic expressions in Cornwall are meaningful, multi-vocalic, and constantly undergoing change and negotiation. In order to understand how the concept of 'Celtic' works in late twentieth-century Cornwall, it will be crucial to know how it affects the expressive behaviour and stylistic responses of those individuals who self-identify with a Celtic ethnicity, or perhaps with other forms of perceived Celtic inheritance, such as spirituality. We need to find out what 'Celtic' means to them, how they interpret it, what elements are most effective for them, and which are most contentious. Most importantly, however, on our Celtic quests we must approach the material and the people with cool heads and sensitivity, without being in any way judgemental. Whether we are observing an old man in a Cornish kilt singing 'Trelawny', a language bard in a blue robe and droopy headdress, or even Goddess worshippers chanting at the Merry Maidens under a full moon, we must be aware that these aesthetic responses are the result of deep convictions and personal choices that need to be treated with the utmost respect.

NOTES AND REFERENCES

1. Charles Thomas' address to the Fifth International Congress of Celtic Studies, 1975 Penzance, Cornwall.
2. Richard Handler, *Nationalism and the Politics of Culture in Quebec*, Madison, 1988, p. 8.
3. Malcolm Chapman, *The Celts: The Construction of a Myth*, London, 1992, pp. 24–54.
4. Stuart Piggott, *The Druids*, New York, 1975, p. 123.
5. Chapman, 1993, pp. 120–145. See also Richard M. Dorson, *The British Folklorists: A History*, London, 1968, p. 393.
6. William A.Wilson, 'Herder, Folklore and Romantic Nationalism', *The Journal of Popular Culture*, 1973, Vol. 6, no. 4, pp. 819–835.
7. For discussions of the role of folklore research in Finnish and German nation building see William A. Wilson 'The Kalevala and Finnish Politics' *Journal of the Folklore Institute*, 1975, Vol. 12, nos. 2 & 3, pp. 131–153 and Christa Kamenetsky, 'The German Folklore Revival in the Eighteenth Century: Herder's Theory of Naturpoesie', *Journal of Popular Culture*, 1973, Vol. 6, No. 4 pp. 836–847.
8. William Borlase, *Antiquities and Monuments of the County of Cornwall*, 1973, p. 73.
9. Borlase 1973, pp. 2, 129, 136.
10. William Copeland Borlase, *Naenia Cornubae: The Cromlechs and Tumuli of Cornwall*, London, 1872, p. 176.
11. William Copeland Borlase, *The Age of the Saints: A Monograph of Early Christianity in Cornwall, with the Legends of the Cornish Saints and an Introduction illustrative of the Ethnology of the District*, Truro, 1893, p. xvi.
12. Borlase, 1893, p. xvi.
13. Borlase, 1893, p. xviii
14. Borlase, 1893, p. xviii, xix.
15. Robert Hunt, *The Drolls and Superstitions of Old Cornwall: Popular Romances of the West of England*, First Series, Lampeter, 1993, p. 32.
16. Hunt, 1993, p. 23.
17. Hunt, 1993, p. 22.
18. Hunt, 1993, pp. 24, 25.
19. *Celtia*, July 1901, p. 108.
20. *Celtia*, August 1901, p. 123.
21. John Hutchinson, *The Dynamics of Cultural Nationlism: The Gaelic Revival and the Creation of the Irish Nation State*, London, 1987, p. 158.
22. *Celtia*, September 1902, p. 134.
23. For discussions of the effects of 'ruralism' in shaping the modern Irish economy, see Hutchinson 1987 pp. 320–24 and Roy H.W. Johnston, 'Science and Technology in Celtic Nation Building', in Cathal O'Luain (ed.), *For a Celtic Future*, Dublin, 1983, pp. 201–17.
24. E. Hobsbawm and T. Ranger (eds), *The Invention of Tradition*, London, 1983, p. 1.
25. See Hugh Trevor-Roper, 'The Highland Tradition of Scotland' and Prys

Morgan 'From Death to a View: The Hunt for the Welsh Past in the Romantic Period' in Hobsbawm and Ranger (eds), 1983.

26. Regina Bendix 'Folklorism: The Challenge of a Concept', *International Folklore Review*, vol. 6 1988, p. 5.
27. Hermann Bausinger, 'Toward a Critique of Folklorism Criticism' in James R. Dow and Hannjost Lixfeld, eds, *German Volkskunde*, Bloomington, 1986, p. 116.
28. Bausinger, 1986, pp. 116–117.
29. Bausinger, 1986, p. 117.
30. Bausinger, 1986, p. 120.
31. Bendix, 1988, p. 8.
32. Hermann Bausinger, 'A Critique of Tradition: Observations on the Situation of Volkskunde', *German Volkskunde*, 1986, pp. 26–40.

GENESIS OF THE CELTO-CORNISH REVIVAL? L.C. DUNCOMBE-JEWELL AND THE COWETHAS KELTO-KERNUAK

Amy Hale

INTRODUCTION

The Cowethas Kelto-Kernuak (Celtic-Cornish Society, or CKK) was founded in 1901 by L.C. Duncombe-Jewell, who acted as the Society's Honorary Secretary. Duncombe-Jewell presented the aims and intentions of the Society in the May 1902 edition of *Celtia*, the publication of the Celtic Association (later the Pan-Celtic Association). He stated that the Society was founded 'for the study and preseration of the Celtic remains in the Duchy of Cornwall'. There were four main aims.[1]

1. To preserve from damage and destruction and to study the stone-circles, cromlechs, menhirs, hut circles, beehive dwellings, camps, hill forts, castles, logan and crick stones, crosses, oratories, holy wells, cemeteries, barrows, and inscribed stones.
2. To keep carefully every National Custom and above all the truly Cornish sports of Wrestling and Hurling, by presenting every year a Belt to be contended for by Cornish wrestlers, and inscribed silver Hurling balls to each Parish in the Duchy that will ordain an annual Hurling match on its feast day.
3. To revive the Cornish Language as a spoken tongue, by publishing a grammar and Dictionary of the Language, by printing all Cornish manuscripts not yet printed, by giving prizes for fresh competitions in Cornish, by paying a premium for teaching Cornish to Schoolmasters able to satisfy the Council of their fitness, and also [4.] by reviving the ancient Cornish Miracle Plays and re-establishing the Cornish Gorsedd of the Bards at Boscawen-Un.

For the first time, we see here the solid articulation of the cultural aims of the Celtic Revival in Cornwall, yet the CKK is often dismissed as having little or no impact, and L.C. Duncombe-Jewell is certainly not a household name associated with the Celtic-Cornish Revival. The CKK does not appear to have had a newsletter or journal, and there are no apparent records of Society activities or meetings. In fact, the pages of *Celtia* seem to have been where the Society was most active. Still, the CKK may have been more pivotal to the Celtic Revival in Cornwall than is popularly thought, and its members and mission statement deserve a closer look.

THE PAN-CELTIC MOVEMENT

First, however, it is important to understand some of the cultural aims of the early twentieth-century Pan-Celtic movement and its primary vehicle, the Celtic Association, in order to place the Celtic-Cornish Revival in a wider context. The Celtic Association was firmly involved in the enterprise of cultural nationalism, also known as romantic nationalism. Unlike political nationalism, which organizes the nation-state around principles of collective will, cultural nationalism holds that humanity is divided into discrete 'natural' units, or nations, that are distinguished on the grounds of a shared language, culture, religion, race, and most often territory.[2] As Hutchinson notes, in the attempt to secure independent nation-states, cultural nationalism often takes the form of preserving the unique cultural traits that define the 'nation'.

Folklore and expressive culture (for example, dance, music, costume, food) have often been enlisted for use in cultural nationalist movements in order to underscore the 'uniqueness' of the 'nation'. Johann Herder, credited with disseminating the ideals of cultural nationalism, in the eighteenth century proposed that for each nation to develop along its own individual path it must be in touch with its 'folk soul', which was best expressed in the customs of the 'common people', generally meaning the peasants. Just as this concept helped to stimulate the study of folklore, so the study of folklore gave—and still gives—life and structure to cultural nationalist movements around the globe.

These were (and are) some of the precepts underlying the practice of the Celtic revivals in each of the Celtic nations. The Celtic Association, of which the Anglo-Irish Lord Castletown was president, attempted to revive or invent 'Celtic' traditions as important symbols of 'difference'. Language was a major preoccupation, but there was also emphasis upon 'folk' traditions such as festivals, music, costume and sport. Here the Celtic Association could be highly prescriptive, setting parameters and guidelines for each of the Celtic nations in its publication *Celtia*.[3]

It was thus against the background of the agenda set by the Celtic Association that Duncombe-Jewell and other Cornish revivalists entered the Pan-Celtic arena in the early part of the twentieth century. Each Celtic nation sought inspiration from the others, and the organizers of the Celtic Association clearly hoped that they could determine cultural strategies for visible success by acting as a clearing-house for the marshalling, construction and diffusion of 'tradition'. It was here, in the larger framework of Pan-Celtic acceptance, that Duncombe-Jewell formulated his Celtic-Cornish platform.

Very little is known about L.C. Duncombe-Jewell or his interests in Cornwall. An autobiographical essay in the 5 July 1902 edition of *The Candid Friend and the Traveller* states that he was born in Cornwall in 1866, although he does not specify where, into 'one of those old, but unimportant, families of mixed yeoman and bankers'.[4] He was not educated, by his own admission, and was a banker and later journalist in London for several papers, before becoming a military correspondent for the *Daily Mail* and the *Morning Post*. He claimed to have written several novels, including a 'Cornu-Breton novel that will voice the aspiration of the Celts of the two Cornwalls',[5] and some non-fiction works on Cornish earthworks and Cornish pedigrees. He also produced a 1901 travel guide to Fowey.

Duncombe-Jewell's personal reasons for starting the CKK are unclear. He does not seem to have resided in Cornwall for an extended period in his adulthood, as he was not listed in the property registers in 1898 or after 1902, yet he credits himself with 'stimulating the nationalist movement in Cornwall'.[6] His choice of terminology here is intriguing, and one must ask just what he means by 'nationalist'. He describes himself as a committed Royalist, yet refers to Cornwall as a Duchy, a nation, and a country. Clearly, for Duncombe-Jewell, as for Jenner and other Pan-Celtic leaders like the politically Unionist Lord Castletown, the categories of loyalism and nationalism were not in conflict.

Duncombe-Jewell seems to have been interested in a number of Pan-Celtic matters. He was active in the Celtic Association, travelled to ceilidhs in Dublin and was as a patron of the Union of the Red Dragon, a society formed to promote the Welsh language. He described the CKK as an association which would 'take rank with the Gaelic League, the Highland Society, the Breton Regional Union, the Union of the Red Dragon, and the Manx Language Society'.[7] The influence of other Celtic cultural platforms on the mission statement of the CKK is clear, and Saunders has remarked on its resemblance to the aims of the Irish Conradh na Gaelige.[8]

A comprehensive list of the membership of the CKK has not been uncovered, but the names of the Officers and Council members are quite impressive, including some of the more prominent Cornish family names at the time. The President was Sir W.L. Salisbury-Trelawny, a baronet, and last of the titled Trelawnys to live at the family estate. T.R. Bolitho, Vice-President in charge of Cornish sports, was a well-known son of one of the great banking and mine-owning families of the time and also had an interest in Cornish antiquities. Henry Jenner, of course, acted as the Vice-President in charge of the Cornish language, yet it is important to note that we have no evidence that he had intended to revive Cornish as a spoken language prior to the formation of the CKK. The Council members included well-known Cornish antiquarians and authors such as Thurstan Peter, J.B Cornish, J. Percy Treasure, who was also active in the Celtic Association, and Arthur Quiller-Couch. From gossip columns and newspaper accounts of society events, it is clear that many of these men were involved in the same social circles, but it is not certain that Duncombe-Jewell shared their social status. The question remains, then, what was it about the CKK that appealed to these men, and what were their expectations of the Society's activities and effectiveness?

THE CORNISH LOBBY

The chronicle of the CKK's appearance is an interesting one. From Duncombe-Jewell's writings in the pages of *Celtia*, it seems that the main purpose of the CKK was to provide substance for Duncombe-Jewell's lobby to have Cornwall recognized as a Celtic nation by the Celtic Association. Certainly, Cornwall was thought of as 'Celtic' long before any pleas to *Celtia* were ever made. There is even evidence that Cornwall was represented at the 1867 Pan-Celtic conference at St Brieuc in Brittany, which is considered to be the first Pan-Celtic conference ever held. Yet, in 1901 when the Pan-Celtic movement was just beginning to articulate cultural and political platforms, Cornwall was nowhere to be seen in the pages of its major journal. According to *Celtia*, there were five Celtic nations, and Ireland was the most Celtic of them all (according to some editorial comments), the visual cue being the prominence of the Irish shield among the Celtic shields on the opening pages of every issue.

In the August 1901 issue of *Celtia*, a letter to the editor appeared from Alfons Parczewski, a Polish national activist with interets in Pan-Celtic affairs. In this letter, Parczewski referred to an article in the

Revue Celtique by Rev. W.S. Lach-Szyrma, a popular vicar of Newlyn and son of a Polish immigrant, in which he maintained that fragments of Cornish were still being spoken in West Cornwall. Parczewski suggested that this could be the springboard for reviving Cornish as a spoken tongue, and that a Cornish language society should be founded, perhaps at the forthcoming Dublin Pan-Celtic Congress. The editor notes on the same page that by 'an extraordinary coincidence', a letter had arrived from Mr Duncombe-Jewell stating his intention to form such a society.

At the Pan-Celtic Congress held on 15 August 1901 a motion was brought before the assembly to consider the recognition of Cornwall as a Celtic nation. The account of the debate in *Celtia* indicates that first, Mr Fournier d'Albe, Secretary of the Association, stated that no nation should be recognized unless a Celtic language was still spoken. He had, however, received a letter from Mr Duncombe-Jewell making a case to the Congress for the inclusion of Cornwall, and he read excerpts from the letter to the assembly. In this letter Duncombe-Jewell stated that Cornish was not dead, as there were still many words still in use, that Cornwall had a rich literary heritage in the Cornish language, that the characteristics of the Cornish people were Celtic, and that Cornwall had many antiquities of Celtic origin.[9] The letter also revealed that a Celtic-Cornish Society had been founded to preserve and revive the Cornish language, and that a Cornish grammar and English–Cornish dictionary were in production. The record reports that M. Le Fustec and Stuart Erskine proposed that Cornwall be recognized, but Lord Castletown, President of the Association, was unsure that Cornish was still actually a living language. He then suggested that the issue be put to one side for the moment with a view to it being tabled at the next Celtic Congress meeting. Mr John Arnall then spoke in favour of Cornwall, and Fournier d'Albe supported the resolution for inclusion. However, when the votes were cast, it was voted 32:22 to postpone the decision until the next meeting of the Congress. Berresford-Ellis reports that at that Congress Cornwall's request for recognition was actually denied, but this is not entirely accurate.[10] The fact that the decision was in fact postponed might today seem a fine point to argue, but at the time it was an important distinction.

Although Cornwall's Celtic status was not then a burning issue in Cornwall itself, the events of the 1901 Pan-Celtic Congress did make news on the homefront. In a couple of instances at about this time, the new CKK was mentioned in local newspapers, and Duncombe-Jewell was often quoted as being the figurehead of the Celtic-Cornish movement. However, the aims of the society were never made explicit in the Cornish press, nor were any of the other members named at this early date. Just prior to the 1901 Congress, a letter from John Arnall appeared in the *West Briton* of August 8, enquiring about who was organizing the Pan-Celtic Congress, and asking why there was to be no consideration of the Cornish.[11] There was never any direct reply to his letter. Still, the Congress decision was reported in the *Royal Cornwall Gazette*, the *Pall Mall Gazette* and the *West Briton* among others, and generally these reports gave a rather full account of the proceedings concerning Cornwall. However, at this time the press was at best ambivalent in its estimation of the worth of CKK, and the issue drew virtually no reponse from the public. Indeed, the conservative *Royal Cornwall Gazette* was rather unfavourably disposed toward the Cornish activists. It stated that the Cornish were better off learning English, and hoped that no serious attempt would be made to reintroduce the language.[12] The liberal *West Briton* put forth similar sentiments, stating that the reintroduction of Cornish would 'be a great hardship'[13] but that the language should be studied for philosophical purposes.

Interestingly, both the *Royal Cornwall Gazette* and the *West Briton* reported on a letter sent to Rev. Percy Treasure by Fournier d'Albe after the Celtic Congress.[14] Fournier d'Albe noted that the 'lack of any duly appointed representative' to the Celtic Congress 'interfered with the Cornish case' but that the speech from Mr Arnall from Dublin, together with the excerpts from Duncombe-Jewell's letter, were nevertheless quite convincing and impassioned. Although in the following months the status of the language, and even the 'Celticity' of Cornish wrestling, was occasionally given small mention in gossip sections of papers in Cornwall, the wider agenda for the Celtic Revival was not yet being articulated to the Cornish public.

FIGHTING CORNWALL'S BATTLES?

This does not mean, however, that it was not being articulated at all, particularly in a Pan-Celtic context. The October 1901 issue of *Celtia* printed Duncombe-Jewell's letter to the Celtic Congress in full, entitled 'Cornwall: One of the Six Celtic Nations'. The essay is certainly a precursor to Jenner's 1904 *Cornwall: A Celtic Nation*, although Jenner's is a more sophisticated piece. Duncombe-Jewell invoked the Cornish language, archaeological remains, folklore and saints to prove Cornwall's Celticity. He attempted to override the 'official' objections to Cornwall's recognition on the grounds that Cornish was a dead language by providing evidence of its continued use from studies by Lach-Szyrma and Jenner. He also drew upon Cornwall's literary tradition, noting *The Ordinalia* and *Beunans Meriasek* as well as

Anglo-Cornish authors such as Quiller-Couch, Arthur Symons and others.

Duncombe-Jewell also touched briefly on religion, stating that the Cornish were always defenders of the Catholic faith, drawing comparisons with the Bretons and Irish. But then, in a further comparison, this time with the Welsh: 'Like the Welsh . . . religionless after the introduction of the Reformed Faith, which they refused to receive at any price, but with that deep sense of personal religion only to be satisfied by Catholicism or Methodism, found a very real saviour in John Wesley'.[15] Payton and Saunders have suggested that the early revivalists in Cornwall such as Jenner, and to some degree Lach-Szyrma, were attracted to Catholicism as part of their revivalist agenda.[16] However, here we see Catholicism used not only to establish difference from the English who ultimately chose the 'Reformed Faith', but also to comment on the religious and spiritual nature of the Celtic peoples, who (it was thought) would by their very nature have need for a religion that was more 'deep' and 'personal'.

Throughout the essay Duncombe-Jewell stated that Cornwall was a separate *nation* and that its people constituted a separate Celtic *nationality*. He drew on the common conceptions of Celtic personality and racial traits that Jenner was to recall in his 1904 piece. Duncombe-Jewell called the Cornish 'dreamers', living in the realm of imagination, and implied the 'homing instinct' that Jenner used in his later essay: 'All the world over there are to be found successful men who make money and return always to die in Cornwall'. He finishes with a dramatic flourish, calling on the Celtic nations to adopt: ' "Onan hag ol", "One and all" to be the war-cry and the counter-sign of the Celtic Race, to be badge of final union and the seal which shall fasten together the Six Nations with a twice-threefold cord, never to be burst asunder.'[17]

Again, this essay is not as eloquent or as well organized as Jenner's. Yet it was the first time that the cultural components of Celtic-Cornwall were assembled, placed in a Pan-Celtic context, and presented to an international audience so forcefully.

Cornwall and the CKK appeared again in the May 1902 issue of *Celtia*. The introductory remarks to the issue mentioned the 'awakening of Cornwall' and hoped for greater interest in its Celtic heritage. Also, in this issue the membership and intentions of the CKK were printed, first in Cornish, then in English. It was stated that CKK was formed on 15 August 1901, and one wonders why it took so long for the details of the Society to be printed—Duncombe-Jewell was usually very quick to get things to press. Aside from the aims mentioned above, the statement of intention announced that 'All Cornish people—men and women—people of Cornish blood, and Celts of other countries are eligible for membership'.[18] It may have been this stipulation that kept Lach-Szyrma from the Society's ranks.

The next issue of *Celtia* reported that Duncombe-Jewell had been elected to the Executive Committee of the Celtic Association (receiving two more votes than Lady Gregory), which the *West Briton* interpreted as recognition of Cornwall as a Celtic nation. There was also a Christmas song written by Jenner in what he called 'seventeenth-century Cornish', translated into English by Duncombe-Jewell. The September 1902 issue reported on a design for a Cornish national costume developed by Duncombe-Jewell. He thought that 'the kilt is, in fact, the distingui- shing article of Celtic attire, and must bulk largely in the revival of national costume among the six Celtic nations'.[19] He further stated that the Cornish national dress was 'fixed by literature' and should take inspiration from the miracle plays. He suggested a kilt of 'homespun dyed woad-blue, a short tunic of the same, blue hose for those who are courageous, and "tights" for those who are not'.[20] Accessories would include a conical blue hat, to which might be pinned a sprig of broom plant.

Around this time, Duncombe-Jewell was becoming more visible in Pan-Celtic affairs. He was a patron of the Union of the Red Dragon. He was also listed in *Celtia* as the official Cornish delegate to the Bangor Eisteddfod of that year. In November, he travelled to the Celtic Association ceilidh in Dublin where he gave a lecture on Cornish literature. Furthermore, he and Stuart Erskine were credited with developing a Pan-Celtic tartan! However, with all the public relations work he seemed to be doing for the cause of Celtic Cornwall within the Pan-Celtic community, he did not seem to be focusing much of his attention on building a following back in Cornwall. The local press in Cornwall seemed to take very little notice of Duncombe-Jewell and his Celtic endeavours, although the *Royal Cornwall Gazette* did contain a plea for an 'effective working membership' for the Celtic-Cornish Society. The short article gave the aims of the society as they were to be published in *Celtia*, and included a short phrase in Cornish at the end, translated ('for the benefit of our weaker brethren who know not or who have forgotten their Cornish') as 'for those who are interested, please contact the Honorary Secretary'.[21] The next week's edition contained a distinguished list of those who responded to the call.[22] This was the fullest published list of membership, apart from that of the Council and Officers, to date. It included Lord St Levan, Sir Richard Tangye, Surgeon General G.J.H. Evatt, Professor John Penberthy, Herbert Vivian, and Professor Dyneley Prince, Dean of the University of New York. Nonetheless, a week later, the *West Briton*, which had repeated the call for membership, considered that 'very little has been heard from the new Celtic-Cornish Society . . . but the fruits of investigation are eagerly awaited'.[23]

Many of Duncombe-Jewell's innovations of that year were not reported by the local press, but there were other issues concerning symbols of Cornish identity at the time that were widely debated by both the Cornish at home and exiles in London and elsewhere. Questions of the origin of St Piran's flag were raised and correspondents to the *West Briton* wondered why its use was not being revived. The *West Briton* also contained a number of letters and opinion pieces that summer about the tune of 'Trelawny', and whether or not its non-Cornish origin was suitable for a Cornish anthem. The debate raged far and wide, drawing letters in dialect from London and Cornwall, and challenges were waged to see if the Cornish could write a better and more appropriate indigenous tune. It is important to note that neither Duncombe-Jewell nor Jenner ever contributed to these debates, and on the one occasion when a letter appeared in the *Royal Cornwall Gazette* asking for the Cornish days of the week and the months of the year, there was no reply to the request.[24]

Yet, for a brief time, Duncombe-Jewell continued to fight Cornish battles in the pages of *Celtia*. In the November 1902 issue, he recounted the introductory remarks to the speech he delivered to the Association's Dublin ceilidh on Cornish literature in a response to a work entitled *The Literature of the Celts* by Dr Magnus McLean. McLean apparently wrote in his work that there was very little Cornish literature, and what there was of it had almost no literary value. Duncombe-Jewell took him to task with harsh words, calling him 'ignorant', 'blind', a 'parasitical posturer', and—perhaps worst of all—'Saxon'.[25] However, it seems that the strength of this letter may have had some unfortunate effects within the Pan-Celtic community. In the January 1903 issue of *Celtia*, Lord Castletown produced a resound- ing blow to Duncombe-Jewell's angry letter, calling it 'acrid' and 'violent'. His agenda became clear when he pulled what he perceived as Celtic rank, both as president of the Celtic Association and perhaps as Irish representative:

> If the first use the Cornish Celts are going to make of their introduction into our larger world of Celtia is to describe our fellow workers in Scotland as 'parasitical posturers', etc., and to abuse and not criticize, I think it would be well if some notice were taken of this attitude.[26]

Lord Castletown never fully endorsed Cornwall's acceptance as a Celtic nation, always voicing hesitancy over the language issue. It seems that this exchange was symbolic of a rift between the two members. Duncombe-Jewell defended himself and Cornwall with a letter to the editor in the April edition. Here, he asserted the validity of his previous statements, and noted that no real attempt had been made to include Cornwall as a Celtic nation:

> You deliberately seek to seek to exclude Cornwall in your phrase '*five* fragments of a race, *five* nations who have retained their portions of the Celtic inheritance'; and again, upon page 16, where you have chosen to apply to Cornwall the wantonly insulting expression, 'our deceased sisters' . . . If this be the effect of Lord Castletown's call for harmony upon you . . . if this be done in the green trees of *Celtia*—what shall be done in the dry—and how shall the reins of peace be tightened upon the necks of the spirited steeds of the Celtic race dispersed to the uttermost ends of a hostile and somewhat stupid world?[27]

After this traumatic exchange, Duncombe-Jewell took a back seat in the world of Pan-Celtic affairs. He appears to have disappeared from the pages of *Celtia* altogether. It is unclear whether this dispute caused him to back away from the movement, or if other obligations distracted him. But he seems to have abandoned the CKK, and to have left Cornwall altogether by 1903. He was made a bard of the Welsh Gorsedd in 1904, but his involvement with Cornwall ceased.

By 1903 Henry Jenner was in position to take over Duncombe-Jewell's role as frontsman for the Celtic-Cornish revival. He had published a couple of pieces in Cornish in *Celtia*, and was a delegate to the Sixth Congress of the Union Regionaliste Bretonne. In 1904, however, the deciding moment came when Jenner addressed the Pan-Celtic Congress with his speech 'Cornwall: A Celtic Nation'. After being seconded by 'a militant and truly Celtic oration' by Rev. Percy Treasure and another plea from Lach-Szyrma, Cornwall became formally accepted by the Celtic Association as a sixth member, although the proceedings of the event show that Castletown at least was still trying to postpone the matter.[28] However, perhaps the most important visible contribution of the CKK was the promotion of Jenner's 1904 *Handbook of the Cornish Language*.[29] Duncombe-Jewell had gone, and it was left to Jenner to carry on the great Celtic-Cornish project.

CONCLUSION
Was the Cowethas Kelto-Kernuak a failure with no visible accomplishments? Not exactly. Most likely it served as the personal vehicle

for one man who found satisfaction in the nebulous world of early Pan-Celtic politics. In terms of the Cornish Revival, however, it was the first articulation of the cultural politics to come within a Pan-Celtic context. Under the auspices of the CKK, Cornwall was participating in the negotiation of symbols and values that were to shape Celtic cultural nationalism in all the Celtic nations for the first half of the twentieth century.

However, the largest problem that the first attempts of the Cornish-Celtic revival encountered was that its leader had failed to draw upon the values and traditions that were already potent symbols of Cornish identity for the Cornish people themselves. Duncombe-Jewell seemingly made no attempt to integrate the revived and invented traditions of the Pan-Celtic movement with popular Cornish symbols and sentiments, an integration which did not happen until much later. Duncombe-Jewell's approach to 'nationalist revival' as he called it, was clearly 'top-down', and his Celtic agenda had no immediate relevance for the bulk of Cornish people—a criticism levelled at the Celtic Revival in Cornwall (and elsewhere) since its inception. It is with the CKK that we can see the first division of cultural symbolic systems of Cornish identity into subcategories that were class-linked in practice, although in theory they were for one and all.

NOTES AND REFERENCES

1. *Celtia*, May 1902, p. 79.
2. John Hutchinson, *The Dynamics of Cultural Nationalism: The Gaelic Revival and the Creation of the Irish Nation State*, London, 1987, p. 11.
3. For example, the July 1901 edition of *Celtia* gives clear guidelines for the establishment of an Irish national costume.
4. L.C. Duncombe-Jewell, in *The Candid Friend and the Traveller*, 5 July 1902, p. 399.
5. Duncombe-Jewell, 1902, p. 399.
6. Duncombe-Jewell, 1902, p. 400.
7. Duncombe-Jewell, 1902, p. 400.
8. Tim Saunders, 'Aspects of the Cornish Revival', unpub. PhD, University of Wales Aberystwyth, 1982.
9. *Celtia*, September 1901.
10. Peter Berresford-Ellis, *The Celtic Dawn: A History of Pan-Celticism*, London, 1993, p. 74.
11. *West. Briton*, 8 August 1901.
12. *Royal Cornwall Gazette*, 5 September 1901.
13. *West Briton*, 12 September 1901.
14. *Royal Cornwall Gazette*, 5 September 1901; *West Briton*, 5 September 1901.
15. *Celtia*, October 1901, p. 153

16. Philip Payton, 'Paralysis and Revival: The Reconstruction of Celtic-Catholic Cornwall 1890–1945', in Ella Westland (ed.), *Cornwall: The Cultural Construction of Place*, Penzance, 1997; Tim Saunders, 'Cornish: Symbol or Substance?', in Cathal O'Luain (ed.), *For a Celtic Future*, Dublin, 1983.
17. *Celtia*, October 1901, p. 159.
18. *Celtia*, May 1902, p. 134.
19. *Celtia*, September 1902, p. 134.
20. *Celtia*, September 1902.
21. *Royal Cornwall Gazette*, 17 April 1901.
22. *Royal Cornwall Gazette*, 24 April 1901.
23. *West Briton*, 1 May 1901.
24. *Royal Cornwall Gazette*, 20 February 1902.
25. *Celtia*, November 1902, n.p.
26. *Celtia*, January 1903, p. 6.
27. *Celtia*, April 1903, pp. 57–58.
28. *Celtia*, 1904, p. 102.
29. Henry Jenner, *Handbook of the Cornish Language*, London, 1904.

CELTIC REVIVAL AND ECONOMIC DEVELOPMENT IN EDWARDIAN CORNWALL

Ronald Perry

'Cornwall in the early 1900s', wrote Philip Payton, 'was a far cry from that vibrant, self-confident land that existed only a half century or so before'.[1] Sapped by emigration, sunk in what Dr Payton and Bernard Deacon described as a culture of poverty and dependency,[2] Cornwall's inner dynamism, its rich tradition of entrepreneurship and innovation seemed to be ebbing away. According to Payton, one of the reasons for this was that the 'Cornish intelligentsia—the educated middle classes—found themselves pulled in opposite directions'.[3] It was not a straightforward clash between tradition and modernity of the kind some Celtic regions experienced, but a struggle between three different visions of the future. Two groups were looking backward to the return of past glories: industrial revivalists who, in Payton's words, channelled resources into 'forlorn attempts to revive the mining corpse',[4] and Celtic Revivalists who, in Deacon's phrase, 'positively wallowed in the un-reason of Romanticism' to a greater extent than in other Celtic lands.[5] Meanwhile, a third group was building a new post-industrial Cornwall, constructing that great chain of hotels, villas and boarding-houses that dominate the coast of Cornwall to this day.

While Deacon and Payton encompass political, social and cultural as well as economic trends over a period stretching from the collapse of mining to the mid-twentieth century, this article concentrates more narrowly upon the opening decade of the twentieth century. It addresses two sets of questions. Firstly, did the Celtic Revivalists recognize a connection between cultural renaissance and industrial regeneration? Some Celtic Revivalist groups—for instance, the Young

Ireland movement of Thomas Davis—treated cultural recovery as a necessary prerequisite for restoring the self-belief needed for entrepreneurial success and self-generating development. Payton and Deacon, on the other hand, saw Cornish Revivalists as imbued with an anti-industrial ethos which set them in conflict with the industrial classes of Cornwall and 'precluded any serious analysis of the condition in which Cornwall had found itself'.[6]

The second question concerns the relationship between revivalist vision and tourist gaze. The predominant influence upon tourist promotion of the first decade of the century was that curious hybrid, the Cornish Riviera concept created by the Great Western Railway. Cornwall, according to the Great Western, was simultaneously remote but easily accessible, lost in the mists of time yet equipped with the very latest in bourgeois comforts, cloaked in Celtic mist and bathed in Mediterranean sunshine. In Deacon's view, tourist operators appropriated Celtic themes and peddled them in a debased guide-book image of Cornwall as a holiday playground peopled by a quaint but backward race, incapable of modernizing themselves.[7] Payton, however, intriguingly suggests collusion between Celtic Revivalists and tourist publicists, to produce 'the predominant influence on the new cultural constructions of Cornwall that emerged in the period before 1945'.[8] This paper examines the evidence for these hypotheses in the years before the First World War.

FOUR ROMANTIC REVIVALISTS

Generalizations about romanticism among Cornish Revivalists of the early years of the twentieth century tend to focus upon the work of four men: The Reverend Sabine Baring-Gould, Sir Arthur Quiller-Couch, Louis C. Duncombe-Jewell and Henry Jenner.[9] The first two were household names at the time. Baring-Gould was familiar to the public as a Devon country parson, novelist, writer of guides such as *The Book of the West*, pioneer collector of folklore, author of imaginative reconstructions of the lives of Celtic Saints and also President of the Royal Institution of Cornwall (RIC). Definite in his opinions, stimulating in his ideas, Baring-Gould was inclined to be selective on fact but rich on conjecture, and his *Cornish Characters and Strange Events* is a case in point. Dr J. Hambly Rowe, a dedicated Cornish Celticist, recommended it as an ideal Christmas present for Cornish exiles, even although it made a hash of the Cornish language, but an RIC reviewer was appalled at the 'nonentities who filled so many pages'.[10]

Quiller-Couch was then at the height of his fame as anthologist, novelist and author of the 'Troytown' tales based on Fowey. Knighted partly for services to the Liberal Party, he was appointed Professor of English Literature at Cambridge University, a post he combined with that of Vice Chairman, and later Chairman of Cornwall Education Committee. Although a founder member of the Council of Cowethas Kelto-Kernuak (the Cornish Celtic Society) and one of the first Bards of the Cornish Gorsedd, he was never an ardent Celticist, and became increasingly sceptical of the Celtic connection, eventually dismissing it as 'speculative fervour outrunning evidence'.[11] His portrait of the Cornish people complemented the paintings of the Newlyn School, immensely popular in fashionable exhibitions and galleries throughout Britain and abroad, in projecting a picture of simple fishermen and rustic villagers going about their age-old tasks.

English readers of the romantic and pre-industrial works of Quiller-Couch and the medieval superstitions of Baring-Gould might perhaps be forgiven for arriving, as Deacon suggests, at a sentimental view of Cornwall as a quaint and backward region, peopled by a credulous peasantry, a place which could not be taken seriously from an economic standpoint. Yet, paradoxically, both authors were well-informed about the state of the Cornish economy and its future prospects. Baring-Gould wrote the volume on Cornwall in the respected Cambridge University Press series of County Geographies.[12] Now, while it must be admitted that a Royal Institution of Cornwall reviewer dismissed it as 'ludicrously inaccurate and inadequate', its analysis of the economy is of interest.[13] It argued that Cornwall was 'too far away from the coalfields to be a manufacturing county', but that woollen textiles, mining equipment and shipbuilding were all in expansion, and that china clay extraction had 'risen by leaps and bounds'. To his credit, therefore, Baring-Gould identified the puzzling nature of the Cornish economy of his day. Cornwall was not a region of unmitigated economic gloom. Industrial growth existed cheek by jowl with industrial decline, and his analysis was not anti-industrial, but anti-mining. This industry, Baring-Gould concluded, without any apparent tinge of regret, was 'practically dead', ruined partly through its own fault by 'too much dishonesty'. Nor had its physical or cultural legacy the slightest appeal for him. Derelict engine houses and crumbling mine chimneys he regarded as 'hideous objects, and as useless as they are ugly'. As for John Harris, the self-taught Dolcoath writer: 'he calls himself a miner poet, he is not even a minor poet'.[14]

A decade earlier, in the dying years of the century, Quiller-Couch had produced a review of the mining economy when he opened the pages of his *Cornish Magazine* to a debate on the future of the mining industry in which many of the leading figures of the time took part.

The usual grievances were aired about 'mining lords', those landowners who milked the mines dry with their royalties, and agents and shareholders who stripped the coffers of every penny of dividend, leaving nothing for modernization. But nevertheless, the general tone was up-beat, and Arthur Strauss, mining investor and MP for Cornwall's mining area, together with J. H. Collins, an authority on Cornish mining, took a confident view.[15] Quiller-Couch was not convinced. Looking at the ruin and desolation that stared him in the face, he could not believe that mining would ever regain its old place. Yet fifteen years later he was brimming over with optimism: 'Today tin and copper are booming again . . . the flood of mining emigration checked . . . the china clay industry around St Austell has leapt into such prosperity . . . fishermen are opening up new markets through the railway . . . a prosperous fruit-growing area now smiles and flower farming in the Isles of Scilly is famous the world over.' Even the farmers were hard put to conceal some signs of recovery.[16]

Although encouraged by this resurgence, both authors were aware that mining employment was far below its former level, and that tourism could help fill the gap, but their attitude to this prospect differed: Baring-Gould viewed it with equanimity, Quiller-Couch with foreboding. In earlier days, Baring-Gould said, the Cornish had been forced to labour long hours in dark caverns to prise out metallic ores. 'Now the coined metal is being brought into Cornwall by trainloads of tourists, by coveys of bicyclists', he observed, 'so life has its compensations.' What is more, he believed that underground life intensified an emotional instability that was part and parcel of the Celtic temperament, so that a post-industrial service economy would not only benefit the Cornishman's purse, but his character as well.[17] Quiller-Couch took the opposite view. He had launched, in his *Cornish Magazine*, a far-ranging debate on the development of tourism in which all shades of opinion, from ardent conservationists to enthusiastic promoters had their say. He concluded, reluctantly, that tourism had to be developed, but even at this early stage he was concerned about the effects of a service economy upon miners, farmers and fishermen used to a tougher life. Any people who set out to cater for the tourist, he warned, was in danger of losing its manliness.[18]

Could Baring-Gould and Quiller-Couch be said to collude with tourist promoters? Both benefited from the tourist public who purchased their books. Great Western Railway guides to the Cornish Riviera publicized their writings, paying Baring-Gould the double compliment of quoting copiously from his *Book of the West*, and dubbing him 'the historian *par excellence* of the Cornish Saint'. For Quiller-Couch they reserved an even greater accolade: 'What Hardy is to Wessex, Quiller-Couch is to this section of the Riviera'.[19] Nevertheless, neither author was happy with the Celto-Cornish Riviera concept. Baring-Gould had actually written a guide to the French Riviera which permitted him to remark that the Cornish Coast was 'advertised as the Cornish Riviera but it is a Riviera without the sun of the Mediterranean'. He was also bold enough to assert that the lost land of Camelot was to be found off the coast of Brittany and not Cornwall.[20] Quiller-Couch, even before the Great Western launched its Cornish Riviera campaign, had rejected the use of what he later termed that 'detestable word Riviera',[21] but he got the best of both worlds by airing his concern about the growing impact of tourism in one set of publications while encouraging the inflow of visitors through his tales of the Delectable Duchy. But his choice of this more decorous phrase, rather than the image of a Celto-Cornish Riviera, suggested a rejection of the assumptions of Celticity and Mediterranean luxuriance.

So far we have discussed two major players upon the Edwardian literary stage. In contrast, Duncombe-Jewell and Henry Jenner were relatively obscure. Jenner was an official of the British Museum who lived and worked in London, and had given up Cornish studies some twenty years earlier, only returning to them at Duncombe-Jewell's request. The latter was a journalist who, in 1901, gathered some distinguished Cornish names under the banner of Cowethas Kelto-Kernuak, and applied, on Cornwall's behalf, for admission to the recently formed Celtic Association in Dublin. When acceptance was postponed, he embarked upon a campaign to press Cornwall's case, repulsing fellow-Celts who dared to doubt it with such venom that the president of the Association, Lord Castletown, rebuked him for spreading dissent in the Celtic Ranks, to which Duncombe-Jewell replied that if Celts were to vanquish their enemies, they needed to warm up with some in-fighting. Since the key to acceptance into the Celtic Association was possession of a living Celtic language, Duncombe-Jewell (apart from designing a Cornish costume) con-centrated upon linguistic matters, and made no economic pronouncements. However, we may conclude that he was pro-tourist, since he published a guide to Fowey, and we might further assume that he objected to the exploitation of Celtic themes for tourist promotion, because he specifically set out in the guide to 'destroy', in his word, the fanciful myths found in other writings. The prosaic tone of his guide contrasted starkly with his airily romantic phraseology in the Celtic Association journal, and his references to the Cornish language and Celtic remains in the guide book were brief and matter-of-fact.[22] Curiously, while leaving no stone unturned to bring Cornwall (and himself) to the notice of Celts outside the region, he neither wrote articles for local journals, nor engaged in those discussions of Celto-Cornish matters which were a feature of local newspapers like the *Cornish Telegraph*, and soon he was to disappear from the Celto-Cornish scene as enigmatically as he had arrived.[23]

So it is hardly surprising that, in October 1903, a letter appeared in the *Telegraph* over the *nom de plume* of 'Fifteen Bezants', one of the many employed by J. Hambly Rowe. 'What has become of Cowethas Kelto-Kernuak?' he enquired. 'Is it still in existence?' To which a letter from Henry Jenner, one of its Vice Presidents, replied that it was not dead, but that, 'owing to illness and a variety of other circumstances', Duncombe-Jewell was no longer acting as secretary and Jenner was taking his place while looking for a replacement. Jenner also happened to mention that he had prepared a Cornish grammar which was ready for publication if only enough advance subscriptions could be obtained.[24] Whereupon E. Whitfield Crofts, who conducted a weekly column in the *Telegraph* on Celto-Cornish affairs, took on the task of drumming up the two hundred subscribers needed. After a dozen or so appeals in the press, and with the help of fellow Celts and Cornish exiles, he managed to reach the target just in time for the *Handbook of the Cornish Language* to make its appearance at the Celtic Association Congress of 1904. Meanwhile, Jenner, a Breton Bard, had addressed a gathering in Brittany in the Cornish tongue. When he repeated this performance at the Congress, armed with his *Handbook* and supported by members of Cowethas Kelto-Kernuak including its President, the two other Vice Presidents and some members of its Council, Cornwall was unanimously elected as a Celtic member. Jenner, like Duncombe-Jewell, confined himself to linguistic issues, and, far from linking cultural renaissance with economic recovery, seemed to go out of his way to deny such a connection. 'Why should Cornishmen learn Cornish?' he asked. 'There is no money in it, it serves no practical purpose. . .'.[25] But this did not prevent suspicion of the Cornish movement among the general public. Given the state of the Cornish economy, they argued, there were better things to do than resuscitate a dead language, especially since language revival might be tied up with political separatism, as some believed to be the case in Ireland and Brittany. J. Hambly Rowe and E. Whitfield Crofts had to issue disclaimers that there was no hidden agenda and that the study of Cornish, like that of ancient Latin or Greek, was just a harmless exercise, undertaken by respectable members of the establishment.[26]

ESTABLISHMENT ANTIQUARIANS

The initial spadework had been done. Much more was needed before the finishing touches could be applied to a Celtic Movement in Cornwall, even one that was purely cultural in its aims, with no political or economic agenda. But with Duncombe-Jewell sunk without trace, and Jenner busy in London, no one took on their mantle, which has led historians to write off the early Revivalists as an effective force. This does scant justice, however, to other members of Cowethas Kelto-Kernuak, among them the two other Vice-Presidents besides Jenner—Thomas Robins Bolitho and John Davies Enys. Bolitho was an important landowner, partner in one of Cornwall's leading banks, a large shareholder in mines, railways and other enterprises, participating member of all of Cornwall's learned societies, former High Sheriff of Cornwall, Deputy Lieutenant of the County, Justice of the Peace and County Councillor.[27] Enys was also an important landowner as well as a County Councillor and District Councillor, and, at one time or another, President of the Royal Institution of Cornwall, the Royal Cornwall Polytechnic Society and the Royal Geological Society.[28] Succeeding Enys as Editor and then as President of the RIC was a Founder Member of the Cowethas Council, Thurstan Collins Peter, Redruth solicitor, Superintendent Registrar and Clerk to Redruth Urban District Council.[29] Another founder member of Council was John Batten Cornish, who, apart from participating in the proceedings of all of Cornwall's intellectual societies, was Council Member of the Penzance Natural History and Antiquarian Society, and for many years steered the affairs of such institutions as the Newlyn Society of Artists and the West Cornwall Hospital. Among those closely associated with Cowethas was the Reverend L.C. Lach-Szyrma, of Polish extraction, long-time vicar of Carnmenellis and Newlyn, who, as early as 1875, had searched with Henry Jenner for Cornish language speakers in Penwith. Another friend of Jenner's, who shared the task of editing the *Royal Cornwall Polytechnic Society Journal* with him, was Canon Thomas Beville Taylor, for many years vicar of St Just-in-Penwith.[30] Finally, we may mention Dr Thomas Hodgkin, yet another friend of Jenner's, who spent his professional life as partner in a Durham bank, but who was related by marriage to the Foxes of Falmouth, where he retired and became President of the Royal Cornwall Polytechnic Society.[31]

These were men of no little power and influence. Did they use their positions to drag Cornwall back into a pre-industrial past? As a group they published nothing; as individuals or in pairs they wrote hundreds of articles in learned and popular journals, and dozens of books on every aspect of Cornwall's past: Celtic language and literature, dialect and place-names, the history of steam locomotion, mining and pilchard fishing, archaeology, ancient monuments and geology, Arthurian legend and folklore. If this smacks of mere bourgeois dilettantism, both Peter and Taylor were awarded the coveted Henwood Prize of the RIC for their historical research, as was Baring-Gould, while Enys published studies in collaboration with Baring-Gould,[32] and also with Thurstan Peter.[33] Arthur G. Langdon, another founder member of Cowethas' Council, drew on Enys' store of knowledge for his definitive work on Cornish stone crosses,[34] and so did Henry Jenner for his *Handbook of the Cornish Language*.[35] Dr Hodgkin, too, was an acknowledged authority and author on pre-Norman-Conquest Britain, and his Presidential Address compared Celtic Cornwall and Brittany. Enys and Peter served on the RIC committee on mural paintings, Peter and Cornish were co-opted by Cornwall County Council to survey Cornwall's ancient monuments, and Bolitho, Enys, Peter, Cornish, Langdon and Taylor were all invited to participate in the production of the massive *Victoria County History of Cornwall*, intended as the most comprehensive and scholarly account of the region in the Edwardian era.

What is important in the present context, however, is that they combined their deep interest in, and profound knowledge of, Cornwall's pre-industrial past with an equally well-informed concern for Cornwall's industrial future. We can take, as one example, the pressing need for faster and cheaper railway access to deliver fresh fish and horticultural produce from Cornwall to the big cities of England, and transport tourists in the opposite direction. Here we find Bolitho as one of the leaders in the struggle to persuade the Great Western Railway to reduce its tariffs, Thurstan Peter campaigning for a branch line from Redruth to Newquay, and J. B. Cornish interested in a light railway from Marazion to Sennen.[36] Bolitho was also involved in modernizing dairy production and in processing farm produce as a shareholder in a Redruth bacon factory. Thurstan Peter acted as solicitor for the factory and as Company Secretary for a foundry and a brewery.[37] More surprisingly, perhaps, Canon Taylor was given the task of compiling a comprehensive survey of the current state of the Cornish economy for the *Victoria County History*, to which J.B. Cornish contributed the section on the fishing industry. Taylor produced an account of Cornwall as a patchwork of areas at varying stages of economic growth as well as decline, of smelters and foundries closing, and explosive factories and arsenic works opening, of shipbuilding prospering in Falmouth, but failing in Hayle.[38] Taylor's work, like Baring-Gould's and Quiller-Couch's, graphically illustrated how the mixed fortunes of industrial Cornwall in the Edwardian era made it extraordinarily difficult to predict the way ahead. Finally, we might mention that Jenner, when later he was President of the Royal Cornwall Polytechnic Society, served on a committee to survey Cornwall's mining prospects, a task he described as one of the most valuable that the Polytechnic had ever undertaken.[39]

Although they were not directly involved as holiday promoters, the Revivalists also produced suggestions for developing tourism.[40] Enys called for lists of clean accommodation at modest prices to widen the tourist market. Hodgkin argued that Cornwall should emphasize its twin attractions of exoticism and accessibility, its 'unlikeness to the rest of England', its churches dedicated to the Celtic saints, its tin mines, its 'courteous but not servile' people, all available with the comfort and speed of home travel. Here, ready packaged, are most of the ingredients of the Great Western Cornish Riviera recipe, some years before they created it, but without the hint of Mediterranean climate, for Hodgkin was careful to stress the benefits of Atlantic breezes rather than Riviera sunshine.[41] An out-and-out enthusiast for the Cornish Riviera and the Great Western, however, could be found in Lach-Szyrma, whose prodigious literary output included guides and articles in tourist magazines. He praised the railway's publicity, urged them to reduce third-class fares and encourage working-class excursionists, called upon Cornwall to set up an official publicity board and to maintain up-to-date comparisons of winter climate between Cornwall and the French Riviera. He even advocated the growth of Cornish grapes to produce a 'Cornish Riviera Champagne'.

Does all this support the Payton thesis of collusion between Revivalists and tourist publicists to produce a renewed Celtic identity for Cornwall? Certainly at the very period that the Revivalists were successfully pleading Cornwall's case at the Pan-Celtic Assembly in Caernarvon, the Great Western were launching it's Cornish Riviera Express. Coincidence or conspiracy? Quiller-Couch, Baring-Gould, Duncombe-Jewell and Lach-Szyrma derived income from tourist writings, but the Cornish Riviera epithet stuck in Revivalist throats, and only Lach-Szyrma could swallow it hook, line and sinker. To be fair to both the Great Western and the Revivalists, neither indulged in the sentimental and romantic whimsy of some lesser guide-writers of the day, who, Deacon argued, trivialized the Cornish as a childlike people incapable of modernization. On the contrary, Great Western guidebooks devoted an increasing amount of space to Cornish mining and engineering in the years leading up to the First World War. They were also quick to latch on to the bracing 'Atlantic' appeal, and combined it with their 'Riviera' concept.

CULTURAL TRADITION AND ECONOMIC MODERNISM

Past discussion of the role of Celto-Cornish Revivalists in the opening decade or so of the twentieth century has tended to focus on a few well-known cases. This article, by casting the net wider and including a number of other figures of local importance, has led to the conclusion that the movement as a whole could not be regarded as a romantic, anti-industrial group intent upon dragging Cornwall back towards a pre-industrial society. Solid pillars of the local establishment, the Revivalists combined a deep attachment to Cornwall's past with a profound understanding of its economic structure. In addition to an impressive output of linguistic and antiquarian works, some of them analysed Cornwall's industrial problems and prospects, while others engaged in modernizing and diversifying the economy. Yet they kept their revivalist and their modernizing tendencies in separate mental compartments, and never recognized a link between cultural renaissance and economic regeneration, even although such a possibility was common currency among Celtic movements elsewhere. Was this because they approached the issue of economic regeneration from the comfortable cocoon of an affluent, self-confident, anglicized elite, and failed to recognize the depths of self-doubt and pessimism into which some sections of Cornish society had fallen? Did their rejection of any link between socio-cultural and economic recovery reflect an inner conflict between love for ancient Cornish values and the imperatives of an anglicized, imperial upbringing? Or did old- fashioned, Cornish Free Trade Liberalism make them shy away from the protectionist solutions preferred by other Celtic groups? It would be instructive to examine the views of Scottish or Welsh Revivalists who combined antiquarian and industrial interests to see how they compared with their Cornish contemporaries.

Whatever the reason, their revivalism focused upon academic issues rather than the wider cultural context of Celtic sports, pastimes or festivities which might have brought them nearer to the industrial culture of everyday Cornish life. This was not due to lack of awareness, since Bolitho's special responsibility as Vice President of Cowethas Kelto-Kernuak was to foster Celtic sports, but, as Hambly Rowe pointed out in his letter to the *Cornish Telegraph*, this remained a moribund area of the Society's activities.

As for the interface between Revivalists' vision and the tourist gaze, while lesser writers concocted a sentimental and trivializing image of Cornwall and the Cornish on the lines suggested by Deacon, most Revivalists were careful to avoid this kind of whimsy, as were Great Western Railway guide-writers. Although Revivalists published guide-books, and the GWR quoted flatteringly from them, there seemed little direct evidence of the collusion that Payton proposed. The Great Western Railway's creation of the Cornish Riviera Express concept, which, in three words, opened a Pandora's box of cultural, climatic and geographical contradictions, stuck in Revivalist throats, at least in the period up until the First World War.

CONCLUSION

To sum up, these Revivalists were respectable businessmen, land-owners and Church of England dignitaries. They were also respectable antiquarians, not romantic revolutionaries. As cultural revivalists, they had a common agenda, albeit a limited one. As economic revivalists, they had none. But this did not mean they had no underlying common aims, even if their activities were fragmented and unco-ordinated. Like most of their contemporaries, they saw no need for radical change. On their mental map of the economic world, Cornwall seemed part of a prosperous Victorian, imperialist England, rather than the forerunner of a de-industrializing Britain.

It is easy to understand why later Celticists, eager for political and economic independence, have dismissed the work of these Revivialists of the early twentieth century. But in defence of their pragmatic, down-to-earth approach it must be said that the Cornish economy, in the years leading up to the 1914 War, offered grounds for hope without the need for Revivalist fervour. Cornish mining engineers were exporting equipment around the globe with growing success, ship-building was expanding, the mining industry itself was recovering, explosives factories and arsenic works were flourishing, china-clay extraction was booming, horticulture was prospering, tourism was on the increase. In these circumstances, the Revivalists were, each in his or her own way, striving to modernize the Cornish economy. Far from engaging in a kind of ideological tug-of-war to drag it back into the past, they were striving to push it forward. They could not agree upon a common solution. But then, as their own analysis so clearly indicated, the way ahead seemed unusually obscure.[42]

NOTES AND REFERENCES

1. Philip Payton, *The Making of Modern Cornwall: Historical Experience and the Persistence of 'Difference'*, Redruth, 1993, p. 114.
2. Bernard Deacon and Philip Payton, 'Re-inventing Cornwall: Culture Change on the European Periphery', in Philip Payton (ed.) *Cornish Studies One*, Exeter, 1993, p. 68.
3. Payton, 1993, p. 130.
4. Payton, 1992, p. 121.

5. Quoted in Payton, 1992, p. 134.

6. Payton, 1993, p. 130.

7. See, for example, Bernard Deacon, Andrew George and Ronald Perry, *Cornwall at the Crossroads*, Redruth, 1988, p. 105.

8. Philip Payton and Paul Thornton, 'The Great Western Railway and the Cornish-Celtic Revival', in Philip Payton (ed.), *Cornish Studies Three*, Exeter, 1995, p. 96.

9. See, for instance, the treatment of Revivalism by Payton, 1993; Deacon and Payton, 1993; John Lowerson, 'Celtic Tourism', in Philip Payton (ed.), *Cornish Studies Two*, Exeter, 1994, pp. 129–30; Peter Berresford Ellis, *The Celtic Revolution*, Ceredigion, 1985, p. 140.

10. For Hambly's letter to *Cornish Telegraph*, see n. 24; *Journal of the Royal Institution of Cornwall*, JRIC, 1909, p. 406.

11. Sir Arthur Quiller-Couch, introduction to *Cornish Tales* by Charles Lee, London, 1941, p. 6; see also his earlier views in his introduction to *Cornwall: A Survey*, Council for the Preservation of Rural England, 1930.

12. Sabine Baring-Gould, *Cornwall*, Cambridge, 1910.

13. JRIC, 1910, p. 258.

14. Baring-Gould, 1910, pp. 79, 84, 87; *Book of the West: Cornwall*, London, 1899, p. 66; *Cornish Characters and Strange Events*, London, 1908, p. 87.

15. Quiller-Couch, *Cornish Magazine*, Vol. I, 1898, pp. 76–9 and 153–56.

16. Quiller-Couch, Introduction to *Burrow's Guide to Cornwall*, 1913, p. 14.

17. Baring-Gould, 1899, p. 66; 1910, p. 69.

18. Quiller-Couch, *Cornish Magazine* Vol. II, 1899, pp. 237–38.

19. Great Western Railway, *The Cornish Riviera*, 1904, London, p. 20 on Baring-Gould; 1905, p. 35 on Quiller-Couch.

20. Baring-Gould, 1899, p. 337.

21. Quiller-Couch, 1913, p. 12.

22. L.C. Duncombe-Jewell, *A Guide to Fowey*, pp. 14, 48.

23. Louis C. Duncombe-Jewell: contributions to *Celtia*, Dublin; August 1901, p. 117; October 1901, pp. 151–59 and 161; September 1902, pp. 141, 144; November 1902, p. 165; April 1903, p. 6.

24. *Cornish Telegraph*, 14 October 1903. See scrapbook by J. Hambly Rowe in Cornish Studies Library, Redruth, for subsequent correspondence.

25. Henry Jenner, *Handbook of the Cornish Language*, London, 1904, preface, p. xii.

26. See n. 24; also *Royal Cornwall Gazette*, 8 September 1904, and 22 September 1904.

27. Thomas Robins Bolitho should not be confused with his cousin, Thomas Bedford Bolitho, MP for Penzance and St Ives, who played an even more prominent part in banking, mining, agriculture, railways and in public affairs in general.

28. For Enys' achievements in Cornwall, see Ernest Gaskill, *Leaders of Cornwall*, 1909; for his earlier life in New Zealand, see JRIC, 1996, pp. 30–40.

29. For Peter's life, see Jenner's description in JRIC Vol. XX, pp. 204–17; also *Cornubian*, 13 September 1917.

30. See 'The Life of Canon Thomas Taylor', *JRIC* 1994, pp. 74–84.

31. Dr Thomas Hodgkin, DCL, LittD (1831–1913) was a partner in the Newcastle Quaker bank of Hodgkin, Barnett, Pease and Spence. Another partner, Sir Joseph Whitwell Pease (1828–1903), Liberal MP for Durham constituencies and Chairman of the North Eastern Railway, also married into the Fox family, and came to live in Falmouth and contributed to Quiller-Couch's debate on tourist development (1899, p. 71). Jenner wrote an appreciation of Hodgkin's contribution in *Royal Cornwall Polytechnic Society Journal*, Vol. 81, p. 30 and pp. 82–100.

32. JRIC, Vol. XVI, p. 73.

33. JRIC, Vol. XV, p. 36.

34. Arthur G. Langdon, introduction to *Old Cornish Crosses*, 1896; also JRIC, Vol. X, p. 33; Vol. XI, p. 214, and contribution to *Victoria County History*, 1906, on 'Early Christian Monuments'.

35. Jenner, 1904, introduction.

36. For Bolitho's contribution (and also that of his cousin), see *Royal Cornwall Gazette*, 16 February 1893, 23 February 1893, 16 March 1893; for Peter's, see *Royal Cornwall Gazette*, 27 August 1896; J.D. Enys also backed the Redruth scheme; for J.B. Cornish, see *Royal Cornwall Gazette*, 18 August 1898.

37. For the involvement of both T.R. Bolitho and T.B. Bolitho and T. Peter in the troubled fortunes of the bacon factory, see *Royal Cornwall Gazette*, 23 December 1897; *Redruth Independent*, 25 September 1891.

38. William Page (ed.), *The Victoria History of County of Cornwall*, Vol. I, Constable, 1906. Sir W. Salisbury Trelawney, President of Cowethas Kelto-Kernuak, was also a member of the Committee. Page singled out Taylor for thanks for his 'constant help' as well as thanking J.D. Enys and Thurstan Peter.

39. Presidential Address to the Royal Cornwall Polytechnic Society, 1916.

40. Quiller-Couch, 1899, p. 159.

41. Quiller-Couch, 1899, p. 158.

42. *Royal Cornwall Gazette*, 22 September 1904; *Cornish Telegraph*, 7 October 1909, 5 May 1910.

THE POLITICS OF THE CELTO-CORNISH REVIVAL, 1886–1939

Garry Tregidga

Whenever we think of the word 'nationalism', our automatic response is probably based on *political* nationalism. Yet this does not appear to have been the case in Cornwall from 1886 to 1939. Although a Celtic Revival movement emerged during these years, it was not until the formation of Mebyon Kernow (Sons of Cornwall) in 1951 that there was an organization which advocated domestic self-government for Cornwall. This article poses two basic questions: why did it take so long before the Revivalists accepted the full implications of Cornish nationalism; and what was the potential for political nationalism within Cornwall itself? The first section considers the wider Celtic framework from a political perspective. This is then developed into a study of developments in Cornwall during this period, focusing on the negative impact of the Irish Home Rule issue on regional politics and the antiquarian nature of the Celto-Cornish movement. The final section, however, suggests that there was some attempt to incorporate the Celtic imagery of the Revivalist movement into the anti-metropolitan stance of regional Liberalism. When this factor was combined with the emergence during the 1930s of a younger generation of Revivalists, who tended to be more interested in political ideas, it created a positive environment for developments after the Second World War.

THE CELTIC FRAMEWORK: 'HOME RULE ALL ROUND'

Before discussing the situation in Cornwall at this time, it is necessary to take a brief look at political developments in the other Celtic nations. The debate over Home Rule for Ireland, arguably the dominant issue in British politics from 1886 to 1914, can be regarded as the catalyst for the rise of nationalism in both Scotland and Wales. The Liberals, weakened by the defection of the Liberal Unionists, were anxious to make the Home Rule issue appear more relevant to mainland Britain, and they encouraged the people of Scotland and Wales to demand a federal system of government: 'Home Rule All Round'. This ensured that nationalism was to develop within a Liberal framework. It was only in the 1920s that disillusionment with the London-based parties led to the formation of Plaid Cymru (1925) and the National Party of Scotland (1928). These events provide the essential background for studying the Cornish experience.

During the early 1880s the issue of nationalism was placed firmly on the political agenda by the success of Charles Stewart Parnell in turning the Irish Home Rule party into a disciplined and effective force at Westminster. The strength of the Irish nationalists, with a permanent force of about eighty MPs in the House of Commons, ensured that there was a greater risk of parliamentary deadlock whenever the Liberals formed a minority government (1886, 1892–5 and 1910–4). This situation was further complicated by a serious split within the Liberal party following Gladstone's conversion to the cause of Irish self-government in December 1885. A Liberal Unionist group was formed under the leadership of Lord Hartington and Joseph Chamberlain, and these dissident MPs voted with the Conservatives in June 1886 to defeat Gladstone's proposals for Irish Home Rule. This Unionist alliance obtained a landslide victory in the general election of that year, and remained in power for much of the period up to 1906. By 1910, however, the Irish issue had reappeared. The massive Liberal majority of 1906 was lost in the elections of January and December 1910, and the government was dependent upon the Irish MPs for a majority in the Commons. In April 1912 the Government of Ireland Bill was introduced, and this led to a new crisis in British politics. Attention focused on the Protestant community in Ulster which had a great fear of being ruled by the Roman Catholic majority in Ireland. In 1912 the Unionist leadership seemed to be encouraging open rebellion in the province, and by the summer of 1914 Ulster was apparently on the verge of civil war. Internal conflict was probably only avoided because of the postponement of Irish Home Rule on the outbreak of the First World War.[1]

The 'Irish Question' had implications for the wider development of Celtic nationalism. As Gladstone remarked, since the 1886 election had been 'fought upon the question of nationality', it was an ideal opportunity to reconsider the entire political structure of the United Kingdom. According to Hanham, the positive attitude of the Liberal leader proved to be a key factor in the rise of political nationalism in

Scotland since support for the idea of domestic self-government was 'confined to a tiny minority before 1886'.[2] A Scottish Home Rule Association was formed at Edinburgh during that year, and support for devolution 'steadily mounted' in the Scottish Liberal associations and the early Labour movement. But it was only in April 1912, when Herbert Asquith committed his Liberal government to a programme of devolution bills, that self-government for Scotland became a practical issue. A Scottish National Committee of Liberal MPs had been formed in 1910 to campaign for Home Rule, and in February 1914 a Government of Scotland Bill was granted a first reading.[3] Similar developments took place in Wales. Morgan has remarked that Wales was just regarded as a 'geographical expression' in the mid-nineteenth century, but the radicalisation of Welsh politics after 1868 led to a nationalist agenda in the 1880s based on Home Rule and the disestablishment of the Anglican church. Between 1886 and 1896 a nationalist movement, Cymru Fydd, flourished within the Liberal party under the leadership of Welsh MPs like Tom Ellis and the young David Lloyd George. Although the collapse of Cymru Fydd led to a period of stagnation for Welsh nationalism, historians like Morgan and Jones have commented upon a renewed interest in the devolution issue during the years from 1910 to 1914.[4]

The widening of the debate over Home Rule gave an advantage to the Liberals, at least in their Celtic strongholds. The party could argue that a federal system of government would remove the burden of local administration and make Westminster more effective in regard to foreign and imperial policy. 'Home Rule All Round' was also a solution to the serious constitutional problems raised by just creating a separate parliament for Ireland, yet at the same time allowing Irish MPs to continue to sit at Westminster. Once the Government of Ireland Bill had been accepted by the House of Commons in 1913, it was possible to proceed with such a strategy. Indeed, it is no coincidence that the main periods of nationalist activity in Scotland and Wales occurred at times when the political controversy over Ireland was at its highest. The political interests of the Celtic nations were directly connected, and 'Liberal' and 'Nationalist' became virtually interchangeable words in both Scotland and Wales. As Lloyd George had declared in 1890, the 'current of the time [was] sweeping to nationalism. Wales, in throwing in her lot with Ireland in the self-government struggle, [had] struck a blow not only for the national rights of another Celtic country, but also for her own'.[5]

This bond between Celtic nationalism and Liberalism was weakened after the First World War. The formation of the first Labour administration in 1924 signalled the demise of the Liberals as a party of government. In the changing political climate of the inter-war period the party was simply in no position to lead the campaign for Home Rule. In addition, the Welsh and Scottish nationalists felt that the Liberals were losing interest in the devolution issue. This concern also applied to Labour, which in theory was committed to the objective of a federal Britain in the 1920s but made no real attempt to implement a programme of constitutional reform.[6] The apathy of the London-based parties apparently reflected a wider loss of interest in nationalist ideas. This was certainly the case in areas such as South Wales where the electorate was more concerned with social issues like poverty and high unemployment. Above all, the creation of the Irish Free State in 1922, as Philip noted, 'ended the previous home rule deadlock which had allowed talk of Scottish and Welsh home rule to flourish'.[7]

Nevertheless, a nationalist tradition had been established. Many activists decided that they had to operate outside the Liberal and Labour parties, and in 1925 this sentiment led to the creation of Plaid Genedlaethol Cymru (Welsh Nationalist Party). While the party put forward its first candidate in the 1929 election, it is perhaps surprising that it was not until 1932 that Plaid Cymru adopted the offical aim of self-government. The party's initial objective was to defend the Welsh language, and 'material considerations [including the need for a coherent economic programme] were notably absent from the thinking' of many of its original members.[8] The Scottish nationalists were from the very beginning committed to full independence. This aim was modified to domestic self-government when the National Party of Scotland merged with the Scottish Party in 1934, but the new Scottish National Party remained more concerned with political rather than cultural objectives. Plaid Cymru and the SNP enjoyed little electoral success during the inter-war period, but the ground had been prepared for the rise of the nationalist parties after 1945.[9]

'YOU WON'T VOTE FOR HOME RULE, WILL YOU?'
Although the years after 1886 represented the formative period for political nationalism in Wales and Scotland, this was apparently not the case in Cornwall. The 'Irish Question', far from stimulating a debate over devolution, had a negative impact on local Liberalism in the late 1880s and 1890s. Cornish voters, due to a combination of religious and economic concerns, had a reputation throughout Britain for their opposition to Home Rule for Ireland, and Liberal Unionism was a powerful force in the region. It could be said that this hostility towards Irish self-government also influenced the unique development of the Celto-Cornish Revival. There was a reluctance to link the Cornish

movement with the political nationalism of Ireland, and activists tended to restrict their activities to a cultural and antiquarian agenda. This created the background for events during the 1920s and 1930s. The older Revivalists were still sensitive over the situation in Ireland, and on an official level, at least, there was a failure to combine politics with cultural nationalism.

The Irish issue certainly undermined the electoral position of Cornish Liberalism. In 1885 the Liberals had monopolised the parliamentary representation of Cornwall with victories in all seven divisions, but the split over Home Rule led to a local Unionist majority from 1886 to 1900. Virtually all of these Unionist MPs, as Pelling noted, were Liberal Unionists, and their political beliefs, 'radical on domestic questions [but] conservative on Imperial matters', ensured that they were in a strong position to attract the support of Cornish voters.[10] The Gladstonian Liberals, reduced to three seats, remained a powerful force, but the essential point was that, unlike their counterparts in Scotland and Wales, they were now the minority party. Although the Liberals were the dominant force in Cornish politics after their landslide victory in 1906, they were still on the defensive over the Irish issue. In 1910, for example, Liberal voters in the fishing communities of the St Ives seat said to their candidate: 'you won't vote for Home Rule, will you?'[11] It is significant that even some Liberal MPs, such as the Hon. Thomas C.R. Agar Robartes (Bodmin, 1906 and St Austell, 1908–15) and Clifford Cory (St Ives, 1906–22), were also opposed to self-government for Ireland.[12]

There was a number of reasons for this inherent hostility towards Home Rule. To begin with, the Cornish Methodists felt a special affinity towards the Protestant community in Ulster. When Robartes warned in January 1914 of the 'power of the Pope', he was appealing to the basic fundamentalist instincts of regional nonconformity. The cry 'Home Rule means Rome Rule' was heard in Cornwall as well as Ulster, and a good example of this occurred in July 1910 when the only opposition in the Commons to the government's Declaration Bill, a measure which removed anti-Catholic references in the Royal Declaration of Accession, came from 'Ulster and Liverpool and a few Cornish members on the Radical side'.[13] There were also economic concerns. The Unionists claimed that Home Rule would ultimately lead to total independence for Ireland, and that a situation could emerge in which the Cornish fishing industry was excluded from Irish waters.[14] Finally, Payton has shown that the Cornish took a particular interest in Imperial policy since the region's prosperity depended on the stability of the British Empire. Many families, impoverished by the collapse of the mining industry in Cornwall, relied on financial support from relatives working in the colonies, particularly South Africa. The Unionists argued that the political fragmentation of the United Kingdom would ultimately threaten the Empire itself, and that party's election slogan, 'The Empire in Danger', was clearly designed to exploit the fears of Cornish voters.[15]

An indirect consequence of the Irish issue was that the Liberals lost their local leadership. In 1886 a large proportion of the party's activists in Cornwall, including three MPs, defected to the Liberal Unionists. The Liberals found it difficult to obtain high-calibre candidates from the local community, and they had to select virtually all of their candidates from other regions of Britain. Indeed, Robartes was the only Liberal MP from 1887 to 1915 to be born and bred in Cornwall.[16] This was important considering that the other Celtic nations could all depend on a strong bloc of native MPs who could instinctively appeal to patriotic sentiment. Although it was quite possible for 'outsiders' to play a prominent role in nationalist politics, such as Stuart Rendel in Wales during the 1880s, they were obviously at a disadvantage. This suggests that the lack of an indigenous leadership for Cornish Liberalism made it far more difficult to translate the popular concept of 'Cornishness' into clear nationalist objectives. The Unionists, in contrast, were in a far stronger position to appeal to local patriotism. The vast majority of the Liberal Unionist MPs, such as Leonard Courtney (MP for Bodmin, 1885–1900 and later Lord Courtney of Penwith), Thomas B. Bolitho (MP for St Ives, 1887–1900) and Sir Edwin Durning-Lawrence (MP for Truro, 1895–1906), had strong Cornish connections. Even Neville Chamberlain, the nephew of Joseph Chamberlain and the Unionist candidate for Camborne in December 1910, took pride in having 'Cornish blood in his veins'.[17] These candidates emphasised a sentimental loyalty to their county. They accused their Liberal opponents of being 'foreigners', and claimed that Cornwall was becoming the 'Scrap Heap' of British politics as 'outsiders' moved to the area in search of a safe seat. A typical example of this patriotic appeal was the way in which a Unionist candidate was described in 1910:

> They had the certain fact that he was a Cornishman (hear, hear) and he could not too strongly urge the importance which he thought they all ought to attach to having representatives in Parliament. Men who belonged to the county, men who were Cornishmen born and bred, who knew what Cornishmen wanted, who went about them and who understood their feelings and who could be trusted to represent their needs and wishes truly and faithfully in Parliament (Applause).[18]

But in practical terms this meant very little since the Unionists were opposed to a federal system of government for the British Isles. Some activists accepted the need for a limited devolution of power on a county basis, but this was different from the federal proposals of the Liberal party which would lead to the 'disintegration of the United Kingdom into separate cantons'.[19] Moreover, the Cornish Unionists did not recognise any need to show their solidarity with the political aspirations of the other Celtic nations. The Home Rule debate, as Boyce observed, had created a 'crude simplification' of politics, based on Victorian ideas of racial differences, with the ' "Celtic" lands ranged against the "Saxon" '.[20] The local Unionists, who regarded themselves as both 'Cornish' and 'English' patriots, even used anti-Celtic imagery in their speeches. In their view the Celts were incapable of self-government, and they accused the Liberals of handing England over to a 'band of Irish rebels'. G.F. Thomas-Peter, the prospective Unionist candidate for Camborne in 1912, believed that the Asquith government was more concerned with the Celtic fringe than with the needs of England, and he concluded that it was 'Ireland for the Irish, Scotland for the Scottish, Wales for the Welsh and England for the foreigner'.[21] Even Courtney, who was sympathetic towards the aims of the Celto-Cornish movement, believed that regional diversity threatened the political unity of the United Kingdom. In 1886 he declared that 'we were fusing the people of the British Isles into one great nationality, which was rapidly filling the waste places of the earth with the English-speaking races. Was it not a greater aim to develop one nationality than to maintain the divisions between the two Islands?'.[22]

The Cornish experience was quite different from the situation in Wales where local candidates, patriotism and nationalist ideas could be combined. As Morgan has shown, the vast majority of Welsh MPs by 1892 were able to identify with their constituencies. 'Over two-thirds were Welsh-born, many of humble origins', while young patriots like Lloyd George were able to construct a Liberal–Nationalist agenda at the local level by linking the 'power of the chapels [and] the local press'.[23] By comparison, the Cornish Liberals were unable to replace those local landowners, such as Sir John St. Aubyn (MP for St Ives, 1885–7) and J.C. Williams (MP for Truro, 1892–5), who defected to the Unionists. This was quite possibly due to the enervating climate that existed in Cornwall following the collapse of the region's industrial base in the nineteenth century. It has been estimated that 'Cornwall lost at least one third of its population' during the 1800s, and this 'Great Emigration' ensured that, as Payton put it, the 'driving force of Cornwall's mining-Methodist culture lost its momentum. As the mines closed, so Cornwall's ablest and most articulate sons and daughters

(. . . whose leadership qualities had made them local preachers, class leaders, Sunday school teachers) had emigrated'.[24] This was the very environment from which an indigenous parliamentary leadership for Cornish Liberalism might have emerged. Yet even in the St Austell division, where some prosperous employers in the clay industry still supported the Liberal cause, it is interesting that party activists in 1908 selected Robartes, a member of another landed family, to replace William McArthur, an Ulster Protestant and MP since 1887.

The Irish issue, both directly and indirectly, was therefore a major obstacle to the rise of nationalism in Cornish politics. The Liberal Unionists, with their concern over the possible 'disintegration' of the United Kingdom, were hardly likely to champion the cause of Home Rule for Cornwall, while the Liberals were deprived of an indigenous leadership after 1886. It could also be said that the reluctance of Liberal candidates to discuss the 'Irish Question' prevented any real debate in Cornwall, certainly compared to Scotland and Wales in the late 1880s and 1890s, over the wider issue of devolution. There is evidence to suggest that many Liberal activists were quite prepared to accept Home Rule for Ireland. Courtney in 1886 was accused by his erstwhile supporters of betraying Gladstone, while in 1912 the St Ives Liberals voted to deselect Cory because of his opposition to Home Rule.[25] The problem, however, was that many candidates believed that a strong defence of Home Rule would alienate the local electorate. Even supporters of Irish self-government, such as George Hay Morgan, Liberal MP for Truro (1906–18) and a former member of Cymru Fydd, tended to adopt an 'open mind on the subject'.[26] The Welsh and Scottish Liberals tended to be strong supporters of Home Rule since they recognised the wider significance of the rise of Irish nationalism in the 1880s. Cornish politics, to put it simply, lacked a 'Parnell' or a 'Lloyd George' who could provide the leadership to make a similar transition from patriotism to nationalism.

Another vital factor was the failure of the Celto-Cornish movement to move to a political agenda. The nineteenth century had witnessed a 'Celtic Revival' based on studies of the Cornish language by individuals like Robert Williams, *Lexicon Cornu-Britannicum* (1865), and the Rev. W.S. Lach-Szyrma, *The Last Lost Language of Europe* (1890). In 1901 the Revivalists were able to establish a focus for their activities with the formation of Cowethas Kelto- Kernuak (the Celtic Cornish Society), while Cornwall was accepted in 1904 as a member of the Celtic Congress. According to Robert Morton Nance, Cowethas Kelto-Kernuak had 'fizzled out [by the First World War] because it was too flamboyant in its aims for the prevalent Cornish taste', but the Old Cornwall movement was formed in the 1920s in order, as Payton put it, to give the Revival a 'grass-roots dimension'.[27] An opportunity for political nationalism had been created.

However, it is generally accepted that the Revivalist movement operated on a non-political basis until after the Second World War.[28] Cowethas Kelto-Kernuak was created to promote the idea of Cornish nationality, while even before the First World War some activists were claiming that Cornwall had become 'merged into the English mass'. Yet the group preferred to concentrate on the 'study and discussion of Celtic relics', and to put forward such schemes as an anthropological survey of all schoolchildren in Cornwall.[29] This concern with antiquarian and cultural issues did occasionally lead to an interest in the condition of modern Cornwall. Lach-Szyrma, for example, suggested in 1903 that Cornwall should 'follow the example of "gallant little Wales" and . . . have a Cornish University like the University of Wales'.[30] Nonetheless, the full implications of Cornish nationalism were ignored. The leading activists believed that their main concern had to be with the almost impossible task of reviving the Cornish language, and it is understandable that the real heroes of Cornish nationalism during this period should be language enthusiasts, like Henry Jenner and Morton Nance, rather than politicians.

Developments after the First World War merely confirmed the antiquarian nature of the Revival. The creation of the Federation of Old Cornwall Societies in 1924 represented a serious attempt to disseminate the ideas of the movement to a wider audience, with the emphasis being placed on linking the popular interest in dialect sketches and local history to the preservation of the Celtic identity of Cornwall. By 1935 Morton Nance was expressing his concern that some local societies were even neglecting their cultural role. He added that the movement was attracting 'people who will never learn, or do, or collect, anything, but at the same time join a society because it is a Cornish one and they have a vague Cornish sentiment'.[31] The annual Cornish Gorsedd, which first met in 1928, was also intended as a 'medium between academic scholarship and popular culture'. Admittedly, William Tregonning Hooper, one of the first bards and a founder member of the Old Cornwall movement, wanted the 1933 Gorsedd to campaign for a government commission to rebuild the Cornish tin industry. But Jack Clemo's comments on that year's Gorsedd sum up the escapist nature of the event: 'I know of no ceremony or function which makes one forget so completely the present world muddle—which enables one to glimpse so clearly the past from which we have come'.[32]

The Revivalists were therefore able to attract a considerable amount of support from individuals with Unionist sympathies. This was certainly the case with those organisations associated with the Revival. As Deacon notes, the London Cornish Association (LCA) arose out of a dinner held in 1886 by supporters of a defeated Conservative candidate in Cornwall.[33] While the association of Cornish exiles later attracted Liberals like the Rev. Silas Hocking, the well-known author and parliamentary candidate for Mid Buckinghamshire (1906) and Coventry (January 1910), the Unionist influence remained. A revealing example of this bias occurred at the annual meeting of the LCA in 1910. When it was announced that the Liberal MPs for Cornwall were unable to attend, a member of the association cried out 'Good job too'.[34] Even the Royal Institution of Cornwall, a learned and non-political body, appointed several Unionist MPs to the office of president after 1886 (John Tremayne, 1887–9; Leonard Courtney, 1895–7; J.C. Williams, 1899–1901; and Sir Edwin Durning-Lawrence, 1903–5), but not a single Liberal.[35] While this was probably not intentional, given the virtual absence of Cornish-born Liberal MPs, it does suggest that the Unionists were in a strong position to ensure that the Cornish movement restricted its activities to cultural objectives.

It appears that the Unionist argument was accepted by many of the leading Revivalists. Thurstan Collins Peter, a founder member of Cowethas Kelto-Kernuak and president of the Royal Institution of Cornwall (1912–7), declared in 1906 that 'we have no desire to see Cornwall aping the larger countries of Ireland, Wales and Brittany in their efforts after what they mistakenly suppose will lead to home rule'.[36] The views of Lach-Szyrma, a prominent figure in the early years of the Revival, are revealing. Morrish has concluded that Lach-Szyrma played a major role in the successful campaign for a separate Anglican diocese for Cornwall in the 1860s and 1870s. In a pamphlet written in 1869 he argued that the Cornish had 'far more connection' with the people of Wales and Brittany than with their Anglo-Saxon 'neighbours in Devon'. He added that a 'distinct race requires a distinct mode of treatment'.[37] While Lach-Szyrma was in favour of ecclesiastical independence for the local Anglican church, his loyalty to the Unionist cause meant that he could not become a political nationalist. In 1910 he sent a letter to the *Royal Cornwall Gazette* in which he expressed his clear support for a united Empire, opposition to free trade, the need for a strong House of Lords, and an extreme dislike of Lloyd George and progressive politics.[38] Jenner was also opposed to a political agenda. As a Vice-President of Cowethas Kelto-Kernuak and president of the Federation of Old Cornwall Societies, he was in a key position to influence the development of the Revival. In an article in the *Old Cornwall* journal in 1926 he declared that there was 'no wish on anyone's part to translate the Irish political expression "Sinn Fein" into Cornish, to agitate for Home Rule for Cornwall, . . . forment disloyalty to England's King or to the British Empire'. Jenner clearly believed that it was essential for the Cornish Revival to be regarded as completely separate from the situation in Ireland, especially after that country's civil war (1922–3). He argued that there could be a difference between cultural and political nationalism, and his remarks sum up the official attitude of the Revivalist movement throughout this period: 'of Ireland and its attitude it is better to say nothing here, one way or the other, for in that direction politics lie'.[39]

'IF IRELAND, WHY NOT CORNWALL?'

Yet there is a neglected side to the history of the Revival. Far from being an essentially uneventful time for political nationalism, this period witnessed the gradual fusion of Celtic and anti-metropolitan ideas within a Liberal–Nonconformist framework. It is perhaps surprising that many of the themes of the Celtic Revival, apparently a marginal force in Cornish society, were filtering through to a wider audience before the First World War. The Liberals, unlike the Unionists, were willing to use Celtic imagery on the election platform, while issues like devolution and the local disestablishment of the Anglican church were starting to make an impact. Although it appears that this early debate came to an abrupt end on the outbreak of war, the developments of the inter-war period created a more secure environment to discuss a political agenda.

The Welsh experience suggests that if a popular nationalist movement had emerged in Cornwall during this period, it would have been associated with religious nonconformity. Stein Rokkan, the Norwegian academic, concluded that religious issues in Western Europe were often integrated into the culture of a 'subject' province, and became a key factor in, what he termed, the 'politics of cultural defense'.[40] Welsh nationalism was a good example since it was directly linked at this stage to the political demands of the Free Churches. This ensured that education, temperance, land reform and the disestablishment of the Anglican church were all regarded as nationalist causes. These issues were debated in England, but the Welsh nonconformists resented the idea of waiting for a 'change of policy in Anglican Britain'. They claimed that the numerical superiority of the Free Churches in Wales meant that they should be treated differently. This led to a demand for separate legislation, such as the Welsh Sunday Closing Act of 1881, or even self-government in order for Wales to implement its own programme of domestic reform.[41] This bond between nationalism and religious nonconformity ensured that the Irish issue was a positive factor in the rise of Cymru Fydd. The Welsh nonconformists, just like their counterparts in Cornwall, were concerned with the power of the Catholic Church in Ireland. The difference was that during the 1880s many Welsh nationalists began to recognize, as Morgan remarks, that on a 'wide range of issues [such as disestablishment, land reform and self-government], the requirements of Wales seemed to find a direct parallel in Ireland'. The Liberals could claim that once Irish Home Rule had been accepted it would be possible to proceed to the Welsh nonconformist–nationalist agenda. This helps to explain why the Liberal Unionists in Wales, in contrast to Cornwall, enjoyed little success in 1886.[42]

It could be argued that a nonconformist–nationalist nexus was not really possible in Cornwall. Deacon concluded that the rise of Methodism had 'shattered the older traditions [and] established a crucial historical break between modern Cornish and "Celtic" pre-industrial Cornwall'.[43] In addition, Payton has contrasted the success of the Welsh Revivalists, 'who managed to address their aspirations to the Methodist majority', with the failure of the Cornish movement to appeal to the 'mass of Cornish people'. This reflected the fact that many of the leading figures associated with the Celto-Cornish Revival were either Roman Catholics, such as Jenner and L.C. Duncombe Jewell, or else High Anglicans (Anglo-Catholics), like Lach-Szyrma and the Rev. G.H. Doble. The romantic objective of many Revivalists, according to Payton, was to 'rebuild a pre-industrial Celtic-Catholic culture in Cornwall'.[44] Doble, in particular, upset many nonconformists in the 1920s when he declared that 'in Methodist Cornwall the standard of morality was very low'. The only hope, he believed, was to copy the 'discipline' of the Celto-Catholic nations of Ireland and Brittany.[45] Anti- Catholic sentiment was particularly acute in Cornwall at this time because many nonconformists were concerned about the 'Romanist' rituals introduced into Cornish churches by Walter Frere, the Bishop of Truro. Even the question of whether the Rev. Robert Stephen Hawker had died in 1875 as a Roman Catholic or an Anglican was still a controversial subject in the local press in 1933.[46] This suggests that the Revivalists had made a serious mistake in linking their movement to Anglo-Catholicism. By looking back to a pre-industrial and Catholic past they were distancing themselves from the Liberal Nonconformists: the only group which could possibly lead Cornwall into a Celtic future.

Nevertheless, there were individuals who wanted to link the Celtic Revival to the nonconformist cause. Even in 1865 it was claimed that Wesleyan Methodism was successful in Cornwall because its population had the same racial temperament as the people of Wales, while in 1883 the antiquarian correspondent of the *Royal Cornwall Gazette* could remark that the Breton Catholics and the Cornish Methodists shared a strong religious sentiment that was derived from their common Celtic past.[47] With the passage of time Methodism came to be regarded as a traditional and distinctive feature of Cornish society. Harris Stone in 1912 dismissed the view that 'all Celts are Catholics and all Saxons are Protestants . . . since the Cornish Celts are strongly Protestant'. The real point, he believed, was that the Celts, Catholic or Protestant, were more enthusiastic than the English in expressing their religious beliefs.[48] The experience of Tyr ha Tavas (Land and Language), a language pressure group formed in 1932 by young Cornish exiles in the London area, suggests that nonconformists could relate to the Revival. Although the group attracted some Anglo-Catholic support, the main organisers were all nonconformists: Edmund Hambly, the group's leader, was a Quaker; Cecil Beer, general secretary and treasurer, was a Baptist; while the other key activists were Methodists. Hambly made a conscious attempt to attract the Methodist community. In 1933 he declared that it was a tragedy that John Wesley had not lived a century earlier, since the 'religious zeal that he aroused might have arrested the decay of the language' if it had been used in religious services. He added that 'one can easily picture the eloquence the local preachers might have reached in the use of the native tongue'.[49]

It appears that such ideas were accepted by prominent Cornish-born nonconformists. For example, the Rev. Mark Guy Pearce, the well-known author and Wesleyan minister. took a keen interest in the Celtic Revival. He combined his Methodist beliefs with a pride in being able to say the Lord's Prayer in Cornish. Even in the 1890s he spoke of the 'Celtic fervour, the imagination [and] the passion' of the Cornish people, and in 1929, a year before his death, he was made a Bard of the Cornish Gorsedd.[50] Alfred Browning Lyne was another interesting, but less well-known, supporter of the Cornish movement. As the editor and proprieter of the pro-Liberal *Cornish Guardian* newspaper, he was an influential figure in Mid and East Cornwall. Lyne was also a Methodist preacher, President of the Bodmin Free Church Council, Chairman of Bodmin Liberal Association during the inter-war period and a prominent County and Borough Councillor. Even before the First World War, Lyne was keen to link the Celtic Revival to Liberal Nonconformity. In February 1914 he declared that Cornish Methodism and the 'dynamic political force' of Lloyd George were motivated by the same 'Celtic temperament'. He added that while it was possible for a 'pure Saxon' to become a Methodist, only a Celt could really be inspired by Methodism.[51] During the inter-war period Lyne supported the Federation of Old Cornwall Societies, while the *Cornish Guardian* published sympathetic articles on the Gorsedd and Tyr ha Tavas.[52]

The distinctive identity of Cornwall was also exploited by the Liberal party for electoral purposes. Robartes, for example, consistently appealed to local patriotism, and he campaigned in the St Austell division on the slogan 'A Cornishman for Cornishmen'. In January 1910 he declared that the Cornish, 'from Land's End to the Tamar', would vote against the power and influence of the House of Lords. He added that the 'chief characteristic of Cornishmen is their love of independence. As a nation we dislike being trampled on'.[53] Sir Arthur Quiller-Couch, the president of Bodmin Liberal Association at this time, was a founder member of Cowethas Kelto-Kernuak. Although he lacked the enthusiasm of the leading Revivalists, his political instincts meant that he could defend Home Rule for Ireland on Pan-Celtic grounds. Sir Reginald Pole-Carew, the Unionist candidate for Bodmin, had remarked in December 1910 that the Irish were Celts, and thus incapable of self-government. Quiller-Couch ridiculed this statement at an election meeting. He declared that the Cornish themselves were Celts, and he added that Pole-Carew was the 'greatest Celt in Cornwall (Laughter)'. Quiller-Couch also regarded it as an insult to think that the Cornish people, by implication, were incapable of self-government.[54] Even Lloyd George was prepared to use Celtic rhetoric on the election platform. In January 1910 on an election visit to Falmouth he declared that the Cornish and the Welsh shared the 'same Celtic passion for liberty', and he regarded the meeting, to the cheers of the crowd, as a 'gathering of his fellow [Celtic] countrymen'.[55] This image of a Cornwall that was both Celtic *and* Liberal Nonconformist formed the basis of a report by the political correspondent of the *Observer* at the time of Isaac Foot's victory for the Liberal party in the 1922 Bodmin by- election:

> The scenes on Saturday afternoon at the declaration of the poll beggared description . . . the enthusiasm of nonconformist farmers, of earnest young preachers, of dark-eyed women and fiery Celtic youth had something religious about it. No such fervour could be seen elsewhere outside Wales.[56]

What did this mean in practical terms? In the first place it was perhaps inevitable that the Cornish, like the Welsh, should link regional diversity with religious issues. The campaign for a Cornish Sunday Closing Bill in 1883, just prior to our period, was a classic example of the use of local patriotism for temperance purposes. In itself the campaign reflected the basic arguments of the Welsh nonconformists: England was not yet ready for such a radical measure, but there was a consensus in Cornwall in favour of reform. It was stated that the

Cornish people had 'taken the lead' in Sunday closing, and that the county had 'made up its mind to have the bill'. A speaker at a public meeting in February 1883 declared that the promoters of the bill were 'animated by the same spirit as those hardy miners of two hundred years ago, who joined in the song: "And shall Trelawny die"'.[57] Similarly, the Welsh Disestablishment Bill of 1912 caused particular concern for Cornish Anglicans since they feared that the next step of the Liberal Party would be to disestablish the Church of England in Cornwall. The Methodists had claimed for many years that they were the real 'Church of Cornwall', and by 1912 the Anglicans were warning that there were 'few arguments—if any—which were applied to Welsh disestablishment . . . which could not be applied with equal reason to Cornwall'. Arthur Carkeek, the chairman of Redruth Liberal Association, was actually demanding Cornish disestablishment at this time.[58]

During the period immediately prior to the First World War there was even some discussion of the question of Home Rule for Cornwall. This was linked to a major speech on devolution by Winston Churchill in September 1912. He argued that while there was no real difficulty in applying a federal system to Ireland, Scotland and Wales, it was simply not practical to administer the rest of Britain with a single provincial government, and he suggested the creation of regional legislatures.[59] Churchill's so-called Heptarchy speech, a reference to the old Anglo-Saxon Kingdoms of England, provided an opportunity to demand greater self-government for Cornwall. Although the Irish issue had prevented the Cornish Liberals from imitating their counterparts in Scotland and Wales, there was always a vague belief that 'Home Rule All Round' could be applied on a county basis. For example, George Marks, Liberal MP for North Cornwall (1906–24), declared in 1906 that the creation of an Irish Parliament should be accompanied by a devolution of power to the county councils in England.[60] More significance should be attached to an interview with Lloyd George in the *Pall Mall Magazine* in June 1905:

> 'As for Home Rule, I want local self-government not only for Ireland, but for Scotland, Wales.' At this point the interviewer interjected . . . 'Cornwall?' To Mr. Lloyd George's objection that Cornwall was small, the interviewer rejoined that it was a separate race.[61]

This quotation neatly demonstrates the problem that Cornwall has always posed in any debate over devolution. Lloyd George's belief that the county was too small to be granted the right to domestic self-government reflects the conventional view that regional status depends on size and population. But the interviewer states the alternative argument: the ethnic identity of Cornwall meant that it should automatically follow the other Celtic nations in obtaining Home Rule. Yet the most fascinating aspect of this debate is that the question of self-government for Cornwall should even be discussed at this time! It was mentioned earlier that the Cornish movement restricted its activities to antiquarian and cultural affairs, while leading Revivalists like Jenner and Peter were totally opposed to the idea of political nationalism. The Lloyd George interview, however, suggests that some Cornish Revivalists were starting to make a connection between political and cultural nationalism. Evidence for this view can be seen in an article by Lyne in the *Cornish Guardian* in September 1912:

> There is another Home Rule movement on the horizon. Self-government for Cornwall will be the next move . . . It is true that the programme sketched out for the [Celto-Cornish] Association at present is simply 'the study and discussion of Celtic relics, literary, artistic, and legendary'. But who can doubt that it means 'separation'?

> We [have] considerable sympathy with the protest of these fiery Celts against the excessive centralisation, not only of Government but of culture in these days. The Metropolis is coming to mean everything, and all the provinces approximate towards the fashion of the centre . . . We think this is much to be deplored, and we do not see why Cornwall should not join in the 'Regionalist' movement which is striving in various parts of Western Europe to revive local patriotism.[62]

The timing of this article is significant since the immediate pre-war period represented a unique opportunity for the advocates of regional autonomy. By 1912 it was generally accepted that the Cornish Nonconformists were losing interest in the Irish issue. The pro-Liberal *West Briton* claimed that there had been a 'deep change in the Nonconformist outlook upon the problem, a matter which makes all the difference in connection with a Cornish electorate', while even in 1910 the Unionists had lamented that the 'Irish Roman Catholics [were] helped by Nonconformist Cornwall'.[63] The extent of this change should not be exaggerated. Issac Foot believed that he had failed to win Bodmin in December 1910 because some nonconformists had voted Unionist because of the Irish issue, while Cory and Robartes refused to support the Government of Ireland Bill in 1912.[64] Nonetheless, it is significant that even former opponents of Irish self-government, such as Joseph Hocking and Lord Courtney, were prepared to support the

Bill on the grounds that there were now sufficient safeguards for the Protestant minority. Local democracy, it was claimed, would actually reduce the 'power of the Priest'.[65] Even Robartes was prepared to accept a federal solution to the Irish question, especially as it would remove the legislative 'congestion' in the Imperial Parliament.[66] The changing nature of the Home Rule issue meant that it was now possible to discuss some form of self-government for Cornwall.

Furthermore, there was a growing concern on the part of many leading Liberals that Cornwall was being neglected by central government. Robartes claimed that the fishermen and small farmers of Cornwall were receiving very little assistance from the government in comparison to the financial support given to similar industries in Ireland and Scotland, while Francis Acland, MP for Camborne (1910–22), believed that the local issue of leasehold enfranchisement was being ignored because it was less important in other parts of Britain.[67] In January 1912 Quiller-Couch declared that government legislation was usually biased towards the interests of the 'great industrial centres', and this ensured that rural areas like Cornwall were neglected.[68] These views are interesting since he provided an official link with the Revivalist movement. It is quite possible that Quiller-Couch was also a major influence on the ideas of Lyne since both men were well acquainted with each other through their active involvement in Bodmin Liberal Association. Indeed, in July 1912 Lyne supported Quiller-Couch's claim that central government was ignoring the 'needs of such places as Cornwall'. Two months later, Lyne was linking anti-metropolitan sentiment to Churchill's call for 'Home Rule All Round':

> Cornwall seems to be regarded 'up the country' as a rather insignificant place, more or less 'off the map'. There may be an idea that we have some sort of local problems—perhaps it is thought the natives eat a missionary now and then—but it would be far beneath the dignity of the Imperial Parliament to concern itself with these things. Here, surely, is a case where that delegation of power suggested by Mr. Churchill might be justified.[69]

Lyne was not alone in recognising the opportunity presented by the idea of a new Heptarchy. On the previous day the journalist for Cornish affairs in the *West Briton* had declared that if the government extended its programme of 'Home Rule for Ireland, Scotland and Wales then, from the historical point of view, Cornwall can hardly be neglected. It is now recognised as one of the six Celtic nations, and it has the claims of a once separate existence.'[70] Even at this early stage, then, some individuals were linking Celtic themes to constitutional objectives, and it is quite possible, given the sympathetic support of the local Liberal press, that this would have led to the emergence of a devolution movement within Cornish Liberalism. However, the outbreak of the First World War removed those conditions which had allowed these Home Rule ideas to flourish. The focus in British politics gradually shifted away after 1914 towards social and economic subjects, and it was not until the 1960s and 1970s that devolution again became a major issue at Westminster. The loss of this external stimulus was crucial. Cornwall, in contrast to the other Celtic nations, lacked a recent tradition of political nationalism, and the debate over Cornish self-government had not developed sufficiently to make a lasting impact on party politics.

One consolation was that the political experience of Cornwall during the inter-war period was to ensure that the centre-periphery process continued. The 1920s witnessed a dramatic realignment in British politics. Labour's electoral breakthrough in the immediate post-war period led to the creation of a class-based electoral system. The Conservatives were able to find a new role as the principal anti-socialist force, but the Liberals, divided between the supporters of Asquith and Lloyd George, were forced into third place. Yet Labour failed to establish itself as a leading force in Cornish politics. In 1945, when that party swept to a landslide victory at the national level, it was still in third place in Cornwall with only a quarter of the vote. Radical politics was still based on the the the traditional agenda of the Liberal–Methodist nexus, while the absence of a strong trade-union movement meant that Labour was unable to establish a secure electoral base. Economic decline and depopulation had created, as Payton put it, 'The Politics of Paralysis'.[71]

Although the social base of Cornish Liberalism was still quite strong, with the Liberals winning all five seats in 1923 and 1929, the party had to define a role for the future. Critics, such as A.L. Rowse, Labour candidate for Penryn and Falmouth in the 1930s, claimed that Cornwall was losing power and influence at Westminster by supporting the Liberal Party. Paradoxically, Rowse's claim that Cornwall had become the 'home of lost causes' could also be turned into an argument to justify the survival of Liberalism. The Liberals claimed that their party, unlike the new Labour–Conservative alignment at Westminster, could 'understand Cornish folk and be in sympathy with their traditions and outlook on life'.[72] Lyne, now the Chairman of Bodmin Liberal Association, developed this anti-metropolitan theme when he wrote in 1923 that Isaac Foot, with his ability to relate to the radical and nonconformist interests of the community, was the natural champion of Cornwall. He added that the region was 'a long way from London and unless the powers that be are made to realise that Cornwall does really exist and is entitled to some of the money that goes up from Cornwall . . . we shall not get what is our fair proportion of public expenditure'.[73]

This attempt to devise an anti-metropolitan image for Cornish Liberalism was perhaps most evident during the brief period from 1929 to 1931. In the first place the Liberal campaign in 1929 had placed regional issues well to the fore. The attempted revision of the Prayer Book in 1928, of little importance in Britain as a whole, was a controversial issue for Cornish voters since it was associated with the Anglo-Catholic movement. Public meetings were disrupted by the cry 'we want to keep away from Rome'. The Liberals also campaigned for a Cornish Local Option Bill, with echoes of the Sunday Closing campaign of 1883, which would have placed the licensing of public houses under the democratic control of the community. In addition, the party criticised the Conservative government's policy of moving unemployed workers to the area. Despite the fact that Cornwall itself was suffering from high unemployment, local councils were forced to accept workers from other regions in order to qualify for financial support from the government for public work schemes. This policy obviously caused resentment amongst Cornish voters, and enabled the Liberals to pose as the natural defenders of Cornwall against central government.[74]

The actual results of the 1929 election ensured that the political isolation of Cornwall was more starkly portrayed than before. While the Liberals were able to monopolise the area's parliamentary representation, they remained firmly in third place at Westminster. The idea that 'Good Old Cornwall' was now the 'last refuge of Liberalism' created an inward-looking attitude on the part of many Liberal activists.[75] This was complemented by the decision of the Cornish MPs to co-ordinate their activities by creating a so-called Duchy Committee, also known as the Duchy Parliamentary Group. It was announced that the immediate priority of the Committee was to devise public work schemes to reduce unemployment, but the MPs also resolved to 'promote the [wider] interests of Cornwall', and key groups like the Cornish Farmers' Union took a keen interest in its work. By 1931 the Duchy Committee could claim some successes. For example, in March 1930 the Cornish MPs forced the new Labour government to abandon the policy of including 'outsiders' on public work schemes.[76] By working together the five MPs could consolidate their position by claiming that they formed a united group that was defending Cornish interests at Westminster. The emphasis on the word 'Duchy', which played on the idea that Cornwall was more than just a mere 'county', also suggested a way in which the Cornish identity could be given political recognition. Indeed, Peter Bessell, Liberal MP for Bodmin (1964–70) and a member of Mebyon Kernow, was to revive the idea of a Duchy Committee in 1958 when he called for the Cornish MPs to be given special powers to legislate on local issues.[77]

But the Duchy Commitee was to fail in its attempts to pursue a united approach to national and regional issues because of internal differences within the Liberal Party. The events surrounding the formation of the National Government in 1931 divided the Liberals into three factions at Westminster: a group of independent Liberals under the leadership of Herbert Samuel; the Liberal National allies of the Conservative party led by Sir John Simon; and the supporters of Lloyd George. After the general election of that year the parliamentary representation of Cornwall consisted of two independent Liberals, two Conservatives, and one Liberal National. The Liberal decline continued in 1935. While the party was still the main alternative to the Conservatives in Cornwall, only one independent Liberal candidate, Sir Francis Acland in North Cornwall, was elected. The essential point, however, is that Liberalism was firmly associated by the late 1930s with the Cornish identity and anti-metropolitanism. This fact was to be demonstrated in 1952 when senior Liberals like John Foot, the son of Isaac Foot, and Stuart Roseveare, the party's candidate for Bodmin, supported Mebyon Kernow's demand for Home Rule on the grounds that Cornwall was a 'separate nation'.[78]

The impact of Celtic imagery and the centre–periphery cleavage on the Liberal party is even more remarkable considering that the Cornish movement had no political objectives at this time. If the Revivalists had operated as an active pressure group, like Mebyon Kernow in the 1950s and 1960s, a nationalist agenda might well have become an integral feature of Cornish Liberalism. Instead, it was left to individuals like Lyne, on the fringes of the Revivalist movement, to advocate the cause of Home Rule for Cornwall nearly forty years before the formation of Mebyon Kernow, while the opportunity presented by the patriotic stance of Cornish Liberalism during the inter-war period was ignored. This suggests that the real obstacle to political nationalism lay with the Revivalist movement itself. Not only was the movement unable to relate to the 'mass' of the Cornish population, it actually failed to recognize, or quite possibly did not even want to exploit, the clear potential for political nationalism.

However, there were indications by the 1930s that even the Celto-Cornish movement was finally, albeit slowly, moving in a political direction. The creation of the Irish Free State in 1922 ensured that the Irish issue was increasingly less relevant for those younger activists who gradually began to take the place of the early Revivalists. Similarly, Cornwall's membership of the Celtic Congress meant that the Revivalists were operating within a wider framework, and were now more likely to be influenced by political ideas from the other Celtic nations. For example, when Robert Morton Nance reported on the 1924 Celtic Congress he expressed his concern that the Breton culture was being undermined by the over-centralised nature of the French system of government.[79] The formation of Tyr ha Tavas in 1932, which was inspired by a similar group in the Isle of Man, represented an important stage in this evolution of Cornish nationalism. Although ostensibly a language pressure group, its members certainly placed a greater emphasis on ideas like nationality. Edwin Chirgwin, for example, noted in his diary in February 1933 that Tyr ha Tavas was 'nationalist in essence'.[80] These individuals may have thought primarily in terms of cultural nationalism, but wider developments and the evolution of ideas meant that there was now a natural progression to political nationalism. Some younger members of Tyr ha Tavas, notably E.G. Retallack Hooper and Francis Cargeeg, wanted the organization to have political objectives from the very beginning. By the late 1930s a number of activists were starting to link their defence of the culture of 'our ancient kingdom' to the national struggles of other ethnic minorities:

> Does the Jew wish to keep his Passover? Make his existence a burden to him! Does the Basque wish to maintain his national characteristics? Decimate him! Does the Breton wish to preserve his language? Ban it from public instruction! Is there a Cornishman who is interested in the ancient tongue of Cornwall? Tell him that he is wasting his time. . .! There is a tendency everywhere . . . to crush personal and national individuality.[81]

But the fact remains that Tyr ha Tavas did not become a fully-fledged political movement. The group was formed with the intention of making the Cornish language and culture more accessible to the general public, and it was believed that an active involvement in politics would prevent members from concentrating on its primary task. Timing was also important. The 1930s, of course, witnessed the rise of Hitler, and this meant that nationalism became, as Beer put it, a 'dirty word'. The Cornish MPs, now predominately Conservative, adopted a cautious attitude towards the group, while even some sympathisers, such as Lyne, were concerned that the Cornish movement might move in a fascist direction. Beer, in particular, wanted Tyr ha Tavas to avoid a 'wildcat' image. In his view the organization had to remain non-political, and in order to develop a respectable image he persuaded

J.W. Hunkin, the Bishop of Truro, and Sir John Langdon Bonython, a wealthy Cornish exile in South Australia, to become patrons of the organization.[82] In addition, politics threatened the unity of Tyr ha Tavas. It appears that some leading activists were already divided over personal issues, while there were also differences between Tyr ha Tavas and the wider Cornish movement. For example, Morton Nance in 1935 was opposed to Tyr ha Tavas' decision to call itself the 'World Cornish Movement'. He declared that it was totally unacceptable that the 'centre of any Cornish movement on a world scale should be shifted into [London] which from a national point of view is a foreign capital'.[83] Political nationalism would have further complicated this situation.

Even on an official level, however, Tyr ha Tavas was not just concerned with language and cultural issues. Hambly used his social contacts to put pressure on the Cornish MPs to deal with social-economic problems in the county. By 1935 the members of the group were being actively encouraged to take an interest in the 'socio-conditions and industry of the motherland. It was their desire to see that the education, the daily and industrial life . . . was the best that Cornwall could provide'.[84] This suggests that the development of Tyr ha Tavas, which came to a premature end on the outbreak of the Second World War, was fairly similar to the early experience of Plaid Cymru: an initial concern with the language issue which was then extended to economic and political objectives. It is significant that most of the active members of the group, including Beer, eventually joined Mebyon Kernow.[85] Tyr ha Tavas can be regarded as a bridge from the purely cultural and academic concerns of individuals like Jenner to the political objectives of Mebyon Kernow in the 1950s.

CONCLUSION

While there is clearly a need for a more detailed analysis of the politics of the Celto-Cornish Revival, we can establish that the impact of the 'Irish Question' is central to any discussion of this subject. To start with, the split within the Liberal Party in 1886 led to a Unionist majority in Cornwall which lasted until the early years of the twentieth century, while the Revivalist movement, with its antiquarian and even Unionist leanings, was simply in no position to develop a political agenda. This issue was still relevant after the First World War since the older Revivalists, influenced by the divisive nature of the issue, refused to discuss publicly the question of a constitutional objective for Cornish nationalism. Paradoxically, the debate over the Irish issue also stimulated an early interest in the idea of Home Rule for Cornwall. It is intriguing that the Celtic imagery of the Revival was not restricted to the Cornish movement, but was actually being used by the Liberal Party for electoral purposes before the First World War. In the changing environment of the immediate pre-war period it was perfectly natural for individuals with anti-Unionist beliefs to demand that Cornwall should be included in any devolution programme based on the concept of 'Home Rule All Round'. This process continued during the inter-war period since the Liberals, no longer a party of central government, were able to consolidate their electoral position by adopting an anti-metropolitan role in Cornish politics. The basic problem was that the Revivalists failed to exploit these opportunities. Nonetheless, the changing nature of the Revival during the 1930s meant that a more positive environment was finally being created. A framework now existed for the Cornish movement to take advantage of the unique development of regional politics in the 1950s and 1960s.

NOTES AND REFERENCES

1. For further information on the Irish issue see D.G. Boyce, *The Irish Question and British Politics, 1868–1986*, London, 1988, and K.T. Hoppen, *Ireland since 1800: Conflict and Conformity*, London, 1989. I would like to thank Dr Philip Payton and the other members of the New Cornish Studies Forum who commented on an earlier version of this paper at a seminar in December 1996. I would also like to thank Major Cecil Beer, Dr Andrew Thorpe at the University of Exeter, and the staff of Cornwall Record Office, Courtney Library (Royal Institution of Cornwall), Liskeard Liberal Democrat office, Redruth Cornish Studies Library and local libraries at Bodmin, St Austell and Truro.
2. H.J. Hanham, *Scottish Nationalism*, London, 1969, pp. 91 and 92.
3. Hanham, 1969, pp. 91–107.
4. Based on K.O. Morgan, *Wales in British Politics, 1868–1922*, Cardiff, 1970; J. Graham Jones, 'E.T. John and Welsh Home Rule, 1910–14', *The Welsh History Review/Cylchgrawn Hanes Cymru*, Vol. 13, No. 4, 1987, pp. 453–67; see also A.B. Philip, *The Welsh Question: Nationalism in Welsh Politics, 1945–1970*, Cardiff, pp. 3–10.
5. Hanham, 1969, pp. 96–8; P.B. Ellis, *The Celtic Revolution: A Study in Anti-Imperialism*, Ceredigon, 1985, p. 83; *West Briton*, 23 May 1912.
6. R.J. Finlay, *Independent and Free: Scottish Politics and the Origins of the Scottish National Party, 1918–1945*, Edinburgh, 1994, pp. 1–24; Philip, 1975, pp. 10–13.
7. Philip, 1975, pp. 11–13.
8. Philip, 1975, pp. 13–22.
9. Hanham, 1969, pp. 150–66; see also Finlay, 1994.
10. H. Pelling, *Social Geography of British Elections, 1885–1910*, London, 1967, pp. 163–74.
11. *Royal Cornwall Gazette*, 29 February 1912.

12. *Royal Cornwall Gazette*, 14 July 1892 and 29 February 1912; Robartes also had personal reasons for his opposition to Irish Home Rule. In 1910 he had declared: 'Irish! I don't like them a bit: I have always said I did not like them' (*Royal Cornwall Gazette*, 21 February 1910). The Robartes family owned land in Ireland, and he was possibly concerned about the potential threat of land reform. See J. Gillespie (ed.), *Our Cornwall: The Stories of Cornish Men and Women*, Padstow, 1988, p. 108.

13. *Royal Cornwall Gazette*, 22 February and 19 April 1912; *Cornish Guardian*, 31 May 1912 and 23 January 1914; J. Loughlin, *Ulster Unionism and British National Identity Since 1885*, London, 1995, p. 59.

14. Pelling, 1967, p. 174; *Royal Cornwall Gazette*, 22 February 1912.

15. P. Payton, *The Making of Modern Cornwall: Historical Experience and the Persistence of 'Difference'*, Redruth, 1992, pp. 107–14 and 152–55; *Royal Cornwall Gazette*, 4 July 1895 and 15 February 1912; *West Briton*, 11 January 1906.

16. *The Times*, 2 February 1892; *Royal Cornwall Gazette*, 30 June 1892; based on newspaper reports and J. Vincent & M. Stenton (eds.), *McCalmont's Parliamentary Poll Book: British Election Results, 1832–1918*, Brighton, 1971, pp. 49–51 and 196.

17. Pelling, 1967, pp. 165 and 166; *West Briton*, 10 January 1910.

18. *Royal Cornwall Gazette*, 13 January 1910 and 8 February 1912.

19. *Cornish Guardian*, 3 May 1912.

20. Boyce, 1988, p. 33.

21. *Royal Cornwall Gazette*, 27 January and 3 February 1910; 29 February 1912.

22. W.H. Hudson, *The Land's End: A Naturalist's Impression in West Cornwall*, London, 1908, p. 182; *The Times*, 14 June 1886.

23. Morgan, 1970, pp. 112–19; K.O. Morgan, *The Age of Lloyd George: The Liberal Party and British Politics, 1890–1929*, London, 1971, pp. 18-21.

24. Payton, 1992, pp. 107 and 128.

25. *The Times*, 14 and 15 June 1886; *Cornish Guardian*, 16 February 1912.

26. *Royal Cornwall Gazette*, 11 January 1912.

27. Ellis, 1985, pp. 139–42; Payton, 1992, pp. 128–35; P. Payton, *Cornwall*, Fowey, 1996, pp. 266–73; Robert Morton Nance to Cecil Beer, 14 June 1935 (private collection of letters in the possession of Cecil Beer, Newquay).

28. Payton, 1996, pp. 273 and 284 and Payton, 1992, pp. 159, 193 and 194; B. Deacon, 'The Cornish Revival: An Analysis', unpublished paper in Cornish Studies Library, Redruth, 1985, p. 1.

29. *Cornish Guardian*, 6 September 1912; presidential address by T.C. Peter, *Journal of the Royal Institution of Cornwall*, 1913–14, p. 346; Payton, 1996, p. 267.

30. *Royal Cornwall Gazette*, 26 March 1903. T.C. Peter was another early advocate of a Cornish University: see the presidential address by Peter in *Journal of the Royal Institution of Cornwall*, 1916–17, p. 161.

31. *Old Cornwall*, No. 3 (April 1926), pp. 11 and 31–33; No. 4 (October 1926), pp. 40–42; Nance to Beer, 24 June 1935 (Beer collection).
32. *Cornish Guardian*, 31 August 1933.
33. *Cornish Guardian*, 28 January 1910; Deacon, 1985, p. 16.
34. *Royal Cornwall Gazette*, 24 February 1910.
35. Information derived from annual editions of the *Journal of the Royal Institution of Cornwall* before the First World War.
36. T.C. Peter, *A Compendium of the History and Geography of Cornwall*, London, 1906, p. 202.
37. P.S. Morrish, 'History, Celticism and Propaganda in the Formation of the Diocese of Truro', *Southern History*, Vol. 5, 1983, pp. 238–66.
38. *Royal Cornwall Gazette*, 6 January 1910.
39. H. Jenner, 'Who are the Celts and what has Cornwall to do with them?', *Old Cornwall*, No. 1, 1926, pp. 3–42.
40. S. Rokkan, *Citizens, Elections, Parties: Approaches to the Comparative Study of the Processes of Development*, Oslo, 1970, pp. 100–6.
41. Philip, 1970, pp. 3–10; *Cornish Guardian*, 22 July 1904.
42. Morgan, 1970, pp. 68-75; W. Ormsby Gore, 'Welsh Disestablishment and Disendowment', *The National Review*, Vol. LIX, 1912, pp. 50–51.
43. Deacon, 1985, p. 44.
44. Payton, 1996, pp. 267–69; Payton, 1992, p. 132; Deacon, 1985, p. 8.
45. *Royal Cornwall Gazette*, 20 and 27 August 1924.
46. *Cornish Guardian*, 16 and 23 March 1933.
47. Morrish, 1983, p. 247; *Royal Cornwall Gazette*, 9 February 1883.
48. J. Harris Stone, *England's Riviera*, London, 1912, p. 430.
49. Interview with Cecil Beer, 25 November 1996; *Cornish Guardian*, 17 August 1933.
50. Arthur Lawrence, 'Rev. Mark Guy Pearse', *Cornish Magazine*, Vol. II, 1899, pp. 243–52; Rev. T. Shaw, *A History of Cornish Methodism*, Truro, 1967, pp. 128–29.
51. *Cornish Guardian*, 19 August 1904; 13 and 20 February 1914.
52. *Cornish Guardian*, 2 February, 15 March, 1 June and 17 August 1933; 21 July 1938.
53. *West Briton*, 7 and 21 January 1910.
54. Payton, 1996, p. 271; *Cornish Guardian*, 16 December 1910.
55. *West Briton*, 7 and 13 January 1910.
56. *Cornish Guardian*, 3 March 1922.
57. *Royal Cornwall Gazette*, 26 and 30 January; 9 and 16 February 1883.
58. *Royal Cornwall Gazette*, 16 January 1885; 24 February 1910; 29 February 1912.
59. *The Times*, 13 September 1912; Hanham, 1969, pp. 97 and 98.
60. *Cornish Guardian*, 5 January 1906.
61. Quoted in *The Times*, 28 October 1912.
62. *Cornish Guardian*, 6 September 1912.
63. *West Briton*, 29 February 1912; *Royal Cornwall Gazette*, 3 February 1910 and 18 April 1912.

64. *Cornish Guardian*, 16 December 1910; *Royal Cornwall Gazette*, 18 April 1912.
65. *Cornish Guardian*, 15 March, 12 July and 1 November 1912.
66. *Cornish Guardian*, 19 January 1912.
67. *Cornish Guardian*, 26 January and 19 July 1912.
68. *Cornish Guardian*, 12 January and 19 July 1912.
69. *Cornish Guardian*, 20 September 1912.
70. *West Briton*, 19 September 1912.
71. Payton, 1992, p. 139; G. Tregidga, 'The Survival of Cornish Liberalism, 1918–45', *Journal of the Royal Institution of Cornwall*, new series II, Vol. 1, Pt. 2, 1992, pp. 211–32; P. Payton, 'Labour Failure and Liberal Tenacity: Radical Politics and Cornish Political Culture, 1880–1939', *Cornish Studies: Two*, Exeter, 1994, pp. 83–95.
72. *Cornish Guardian*, 9 January 1930; Penryn & Falmouth Conservative Association papers (Cornwall Record Office) DDX/551/11, electoral address of the Liberal candidate for Penryn & Falmouth in 1935.
73. *Cornish Guardian*, 16 February 1923.
74. *West Briton*, 7 February, 14 and 21 March, 25 April, 2 and 23 May 1929; Camborne Conservative Association papers (CRO), DDX/387/3, executive committee minutes, 21 October 1929.
75. *Cornish Guardian*, 6 and 13 June 1929.
76. *Cornish Guardian*, 4 July 1929 and 16 January 1930; *Western Morning News*, 6 March 1930.
77. Bodmin Liberal Association papers (Liskeard Liberal Democrat Office), newspaper article in *Cornish Times*, 22 August 1958.
78. *Cornish Guardian*, 8 May 1952; 27 May, 22 July and 19 August 1954.
79. R. Morton Nance, 'The Celtic Congress, Quimper 1924', *Journal of the Royal Institution of Cornwall*, Vol. XXI, 1925, p. 454.
80. *Western Morning News*, 18 February 1933: diary of Edwin Chirgwin (February 1933) in the possession of John Jenkin.
81. Interview with Beer, 25 November 1996; E.G. Retallack Hooper (Talek) to Beer, 3 July 1935; *Cornish Guardian*, 25 August 1938.
82. Interview with Beer, 25 November 1996; *Cornish Guardian*, 17 August 1933.
83. Nance to Beer, 10 June 1935 (Beer collection).
84. *Cornish Guardian*, 30 May 1935.
85. Interview with Beer, 25 November 1996.

A PASSION TO EXIST: CULTURAL HEGEMONY AND THE ROOTS OF CORNISH IDENTITY

Rob Burton

Whatever its origins or level, that particular 'combination' of cultural elements is the intellectual heritage of a particular social group. The group lives it and makes use of it from the inside, without realizing its contradictoriness, or at any rate not realizing it in the same way as somebody looking in from the outside. Thus, any combination of cultural elements which is embodied by an identifiable social group comes to constitute a kind of '*de facto* unity'. It can be looked at from the point of view of the group which recognises itself in and so can legitimately be called a 'conception of the world' because, even if it is not so *for us* it is *for others*.[1]

INTRODUCTION

There is a seemingly never-ending debate concerning the nature of the Cornish identity, not least in the local press in papers such as the *Western Morning News, West Briton* and *Cornish Times* where there is a continual assertion of 'Cornish difference'. But what is the nature of this 'Cornishness' which attracts such eloquent articulation? And why is it, we may ask, that 'Cornishness' is an issue at all? After all, in the condition of what many academics call 'late-modernity', we live in a world of compressed global communications and transactions with an apparently relentless drive towards cultural homogeneity in which the assertion of separate identity appears both eccentric and perverse.

And yet, one cannot walk the streets of Cornwall today and deny that there is a 'group of people who define themselves as "Cornish" '.[2] According to Deacon, this Cornish identity is dynamic and has been for some years re-asserting itself. Deacon argues that 'the

sense of belonging . . . now rests on a wider set of symbols than before;
a changing repertoire' of elements from other cultures and newly
re-invented traditions.[3] However, notwithstanding the works of
Deacon, Payton et al. in elaborating this 'difference', and despite the
deployment of such symbols as the Cornish tartan, the bards and the
Gorsedd, Cornwall is still ostensibly an English county and is clearly
an integral part of the United Kingdom. The people who live in
Cornwall receive the same media and cultural exposure as the rest of
Britain and are subject to the same political debates and influences. So
how can we understand such insistence that a Cornish identity does
exist, and if *not for us* but *for others*?

     This article draws upon the perspective presented by the Italian
Marxist Antonio Gramsci, in which the Italian proletariat is depicted
as a subordinate group that can simultaneously hold two distinct
conceptions of the world. It is argued here that this analysis can be
utilized to show how the Cornish, as another subordinate group, can
also hold two conceptions of the world. One is the 'official' conception,
or dominant English viewpoint. The other is the 'popular' conception
of the world, i.e. a Cornish conception which, despite the dominance
of the English viewpoint, has its own vigour and its own spontaneous
life.

GRAMSCI, CULTURAL HEGEMONY AND CORNWALL

The work of Gramsci on cultural hegemony[4] allows us, according to
Jackson-Lears, to 'analyze the systemic features of a society character-
ised by inequalities of power without reducing that society to a system'.[5]
Thus:

> By clarifying the political functions of cultural symbols, the concept
> of cultural hegemony can aid [in] . . . trying to understand how ideas
> reinforce or undermine existing social structures . . . and seek . . .
> to reconcile the apparent contradiction between the power wielded
> by dominant groups and the relative cultural autonomy of sub-
> ordinate groups whom they victimize.[6]

     In this way, it is possible for us to recognize and acknowledge the
existence of a Cornish version of the Gramscian 'popular consciousness'
in which the consciousness of exploited populations is seen as turbulent,
fluctuating, incoherent and (most notably) contradictory.

     However, in order to achieve a fuller analysis of Cornish culture
and Cornish identity, we need to probe more deeply into what Gramsci
called the 'popular consciousness' and to follow his suggestion that the
'spontaneous philosophies' of 'forklores' expressed in the thought of

the common people need to be understood. In undertaking such an analysis, we should note that the 'philosophies' of the subordinated Cornish population draw upon fragments of many ideologies: Celticism, Catholicism, Capitalism, Methodism, old customs, folklore and so on. Each vie for domination. And it is these conceptions that find themselves at odds with the dominant or hegemonic culture—that of the English state. Myriad fragments of ideologies may be absorbed by a Cornish individual to create a 'mosaic of meaning' which in many ways if unsystematic, lacks coherence and is subject to external influence, particularly from the hegemonic culture.[7] Often everyday experience will contradict or challenge this mosaic of meaning, producing a frustrating and contradictory consciousness which may facilitate the domination of more powerful ideologies and cultures (e.g. 'Englishness') and yet may also construct an internal (albeit inconsistent) ideology of resistance or rebellion.[8]

Gramsci was above all concerned with the concept of cultural hegemony:

> the 'spontaneous' consent given by the great masses of the population to the general direction imposed on social life by the dominant fundamental group; this consent is 'historically' caused by the prestige (and consequent confidence) which the dominant group enjoys because of its position and function in the world of production.[9]

Although Gramsci acknowledged that the power of the state was vested ultimately in its monopoly on the means of violence,[10] he argued that in practice the ruling elites in modern parliamentary democracies win their authority (hegemony) not through the explicit domination of their peoples through violence (or even through legitimizing symbols) but through the consent of the subordinate groups. Thus:

> In the bourgeois state, which is the first to use an extensive hegemonic apparatus, the autonomous castes of the pre-modern state become transformed into the voluntary associations—parties, unions, cultural institutions, etc,—which serve as hegemonic instruments.[11]

THE CONSTRUCTION OF ENGLISHNESS
The contemporary hegemonic social construct of 'Englishness' can be located within nineteenth-century society. During this period, with its rapidly industrializing economy and its mass of industrial workers, the bourgeoisie of southern England imagined a romantic past, a 'golden

age' of 'merrie England', a reaction against those 'cosmopolitan forces within industry and empire building'.[12] It was a time when there was an 'assertion of a sense of English cultural and national identity . . . the roots of the English national idea'.[13]

The new industrial society also saw the burgeoning of the so-called 'voluntary organizations' in England, the emergence of a distinct industrial working class, the development of political parties around class interests, and of course the trade unions. But the English state was still 'weak' (in Gramscian terminology) in its approach to the assimilation of the Cornish people, despite its attempts over many centuries at domination through violence (as in its response to the Cornish rebellions of 1497 and 1549, and in the Civil War). In the eighteenth century, the Cornish were still feared as rebels by the English ruling classes, as the records of Bodmin Assizes suggest (in April 1796 one alarmed observed of Cornish behaviour wrote that 'I hope the military will settle your rebellion and rejoice they [the rebels] have been kept from Truro').

Thompson sees this period, with its widespread tinners' riots, as a final 'desperate effort by the [Cornish] people to reimpose the older moral economy as against the economy of the free market'.[14] Such disturbances were not confined to Cornwall, however, and elsewhere there were also riots of a consumerist nature, concerned more with the cost of bread than with wages.[15] But while the riotous nature of the late eighteenth century was (Thompson argues) crucial in securing the dominance of the *laissez-faire* economics that dominated industrial society, it was also a period that saw the assimilation of the English working classes into their class identity—an identity inherently linked to England and all things English in both a political and social sense.

CULTURAL HEGEMONY AND 'NEW TRADITIONS'

The apparent paradox of a 'weak' assimilation of the Cornish at a time of powerful English working-class identity formation is resolved in Gramsci's recognition that cultural hegemony is never closed. It is never a complete and static ideology (such as Marx or Lenin might have conceived). Rather, it is 'a process of continuous creation which, given its massive scale, is bound to be uneven in the degree of legitimacy it commands and to leave some room for antagonistic cultural expressions to develop.'[16] This is precisely the position in which the Cornish found themselves, and one does not have to look far for examples of attempts by the English state to achieve cultural hegemony in Cornwall. In the sixteenth century, for instance, the decline of the Cornish language was exacerbated by the refusal of the state to introduce a Cornish Prayer

Book and Bible. Halliday's assessment of the outcome of this process is surprisingly Gramscian in tone. He writes:

> Now, with an obsolescent language, symbol at once of their distinction and of their conservative Catholicism, they [the Cornish] began to identify themselves with the gentry and middle classes, English speaking and protestant. Cornish nationalism was merged, though never submerged, in a greater English nationalism.[17]

Later examples of attempts at cultural hegemony can be found in the English state's use of the education system to try to absorb the Cornish into mass civil society by centralizing culture and by eradicating distinctiveness and diversity. Indeed, Green has argued that the 1870 Education Act represented: 'a culturally elitist perspective which is recorded all over Celtic Britain as a "murder machine" for native language and culture, and its operation in Cornwall made everything Cornish seem "rough ready and rude".'[18]

At the same time, the new industrial English hegemonic culture produced a repertoire of 'new traditions'. These were disseminated in Cornwall as they were elsewhere, but they were based on English values and English norms, perceptions, beliefs, sentiments and prejudices. Brass bands, male voice choirs and rugby football were particular phenomena associated with industrialized areas throughout nineteenth-century Britain, notably Wales and the North-east of England, and in Cornwall they were superimposed upon the existing raft of Cornish cultural artefacts and expressions. It is this imposition of 'new traditions', suggests Gramsci in his *Prison Notebooks*, that causes the typifying ambiguities and conflicts within a group's historical consciousness and serves to inform the complexity of popular consciousness under capitalism.

A DUAL CONSIOUSNESS

As noted above, Gramsci considers that a subordinate group holds dual consciousness, one that is not its own and is 'borrowed' from another group—in this case the English. The other is 'its own conception of the world, even if only embryonic;' a conception which manifests itself in action, 'but occasionally and in flashes'.[19] If this duality is applied to Cornwall, then a Cornish person has thus:

> two theoretical consciousness (or one contradictory consciousness): one which is implicit in his activity and which in reality unites him [sic] with all his fellow workers in the practical transformation of the real world; and one, superficially explicit or verbal, which he has

inherited from the past and uncritically absorbed. But this verbal conception is not without consequences. It holds together a specific social group, it influences moral conduct and the direction of will, with varying efficacy but often powerfully enough to produce a situation in which the contradictory state of consciousness does not permit any action, any decision or any choice, and produces a condition of moral and political passivity.[20]

Consequently, the cultural hegemonic imperatives which exist within the modernizing process have 'incorporated' many of the older ways of the Cornish, their language, customs and religion, but paradoxically it is (according to Gramsci's analysis) these very forces of incorporation which have been central to the preservation of the notion of 'difference' amongst the Cornish. The process of hegemony, and the reactions to it which are located in the historically fragmented ideologies of the language, customs and religion, create a 'spontaneous philosophy' which—according to Gramsci—can embody all sorts of prejudices that have particular meaning apart from and outside of the normal realms of power relations.

This Cornish identity or particular world view is to be found within what Gramsci calls a 'historical bloc', and is a shared belief that possesses a cultural and an economic solidarity which:

> departs significantly from notions of class embedded in the Marxist tradition: it promotes analysis of social formations that cut across categories of ownership and nonownership and that are bound by religious or other ideological ties as well as those of economic interest.[21]

Thus in Cornwall the new cultures of industrialization worked together with the impact of the older traditions of the Celt and the shared experiences of tinning, mining, fishing, clayworking, folklore and so on, to ensure that the distinct Cornish identity of the Cornish people was perpetuated. Elsewhere, in England, the hegemonic modernizing forces of industrialization encouraged people to think of themselves in the general terms of class and of Englishness (or Britishness) rather than as a specifically identifiable status group or moral order.

A POPULAR CONSCIOUSNESS AND A SYMBOLIC UNIVERSE
Writing in the inter-war period in this century, Hamilton-Jenkin suggested that, despite 'the many modernizing influences',[22] the Cornish still retained a belief in the ancient custom, curious practices and beliefs of times past. He went on to assert that: 'Conservative by

nature and deeply attached to the way of his own country, the chain of custom and tradition which linked the Cornish miner to his forefathers of untold generations was, until recent years, an unbroken one.'[23] This Cornish 'popular consciousness' was one that had reformulated the earlier hegemonic ideological constructions of the Cornish as 'inferior rebels'. This was not as a passive acceptance by the Cornish of such negative constructions but neither was it a revolutionary consciousness intent on challenging such constructions. Rather, it was a force which allowed people to give meaning to their own reality, to make life understandable and tolerable—in short, to create their own symbolic universe.

Nonetheless, English state hegemony and encroaching industrialization and modernization did precipitate the decline of an older way of life. The Methodists, as an integral part of this process, were vigorously opposed to Cornish folk ceremonies, folklore and superstitions, and discouraged traditional activities like hurling and wrestling. They disliked Maypole dances and the Helston furry dance, considering that these and other activities such as the Padstow Hobby Horse and Celtic saints' days were 'rooted in pagan antiquity'.[24] The forces of modernization and their associated cultural attacks were by and large successful. Wesley himself came to be seen as a 'courageous insurgent against inert traditional institutions'.[25]

It is little wonder that Cornish 'popular consciousness' railed against this encroachment and occasionally rose in protest—Gramsci's 'flashes'.[26] For example, in their dealings with 'up-country' capitalists, it seems that many a Cornish mining 'adventurer' had no qualms in swindling the English. Upon being 'gulled' into buying mines by Cornish agents, one director complained: 'It really appears to me that they looked upon us as foreigners, and considered us fair game to be plucked at their pleasure'.[27] Meanwhile, in the 1830s and 1840s hungry miners were still paying 'visits' to Wadebridge and Padstow to prevent corn being 'exported' to England. Indeed, Hobsbawn and Rudé argue that throughout the eighteenth century and well into the midnineteenth, Cornish miners were 'regarded as almost beyond the pale of civilisation'.[28]

THE ROLE OF FOLKLORE

Gramsci suggests that the study of folklore is a legitimate and indispensable method of understanding the structure of a society, its tensions and its conflicts. He argues that 'There exists a "popular morality" which is understood as a certain whole (in space and time) of maxims of practical conduct and customs which have derived from it or have produced it'.[29] Furthermore, he argues that 'There exist imperatives which are much stronger, more tenacious and more effectual than those of official "mortality" '.[30] Consequently, the confrontation between an official state morality and the morality of a subordinate groups at odds with the attack on their culture would, Gramsci argues, inevitably produce conflict, a conflict which we can discern in the resistance of a popular Cornish morality to the intrusions of the official morality of the English state.

Thus confrontation occurred when the 'new order' of the industrial nation-state had to bring the 'threatening gestures' of Cornish popular culture or popular consciousness under control. This was done as it had been done in earlier centuries, by the imposition of hegemonic cultural forces through such state institutions as religion, the law, education and so on. Occasionally, it was attempted through the use of legitimized violence—for example, in the deployment of the police, gunboats or the army to quell popular Cornish uprisings in the form of riot or strike.

In 1817, Gilbert wrote approvingly that 'Desperate wrestling matches, inhuman cock-fights, pitched battles, and riotous revellings, are now happily of much rarer occurrence than heretofore', adding significantly that 'The spirit of sport has evaporated and that of industry [i.e. the English 'moral order] has supplied its place'.[31] Folk activities such as Cornish wrestling, the Padstow Hobby Horse and so on, had to be opposed by the hegemonic accommodating forces of English imperialism simply because they represented and defended a traditional morality that was exclusively Cornish. They showed Cornish people acting under their own initiative, a situation which was potentially a threat to the new, dominant ideas.

Bushaway[32] has suggested that some folk customs and ceremonies in themselves embodied a strong element of confrontation, and that certain rituals in which conflict between groups is a central feature and in which disruptive or anti-social behaviour is tolerated can be interpreted as a demonstration of strength and importance. For example, the Padstow Hobby Horse has a 'confrontational' aspect and encourages behaviour which—though 'anti-social'—also suggests that such rituals occur when particular groups feel threatened or are under some sort of external pressure. It was common, he argues, for these ritual demonstrations of strength to be carried out at certain times of the year; for example, when deprivation threatened, was at its worst, or was soon to disappear.[33]

Indeed, despite the attacks upon their cultural life, the Cornish did retain many of their ancient customs and superstitions, these very folk rituals and folklores acting as vehicles of protest or (in the Gramscian

sense) as 'contadictory ideologies' resisting the destruction of traditional society and asserting a strong identity. We see in Cornwall's
eighteenth- and nineteenth-century history of riots, fights, conflict, the
strong smuggling and wrecking traditions, and folk rituals, a pattern of
folk activity which was robust, aggressive, demanding and far from
deferential, and which cemented the modern Cornish identity into the
earlier soil of Celtic identity.

This burgeoning 'folk' identity or 'popular consciousness' was,
Payton argues, boosted by 'Cornwall's supremary in the realms of
mining and engineering'.[34] Payton indicates that in the late 1800s
the sayings 'Cornwall near England' and 'into Cornwall, our of England' were in common use,[35] while in Cornwall people not of Cornish
descent were described as 'foreigners' as a matter of course.[36] Here,
paradoxically, the apparently threatening 'new order' ideology of
industrialization had been successfully co-opted (at least in part) by
the Cornish, producing a meld which kept the unifying ideologies of
the nation-state at bay throughout the early twentieth century. For the
English too, Cornwall remained 'foreign' and 'different'. As the Rev.
J. J. Daniel wrote:

> In May 1904 . . . [I] . . . met a vegetable dealer in Bath who classed
> his broccoli into two lots, English and foreign. Those from Cornwall
> were placed with the foreign and the man was surprised at its being
> suggested that it was wrong, his father and grandfather had done so
> before him.[37]

In the late twentieth century we can find evidence of a similar culture
of 'difference', a contemporary Cornish identity in which Gramscian
'flashes' of resistance can be discerned, and where folkloric icons are
displayed as cultural symbols. Such activity was very clearly displayed
in the image of 'Trelawny's Army' advancing upon Twickenham for a
rugby final against an English team, while those who in 1997 com-
memorated the 1497 rebellions by marching (either in whole or part
way) to London exhibited an array of 'flashes': the euphoria as the
marchers moved off from St Keverne, the triumph as the 'rebels' took
Polson bridge and marched across the Tamar 'into England', the sense
of achievement and defiance as they planted their colours upon the
battlefield at Blackheath. Redruth Brewery even introduced a line of
Cornish Rebellion beer, with supporting T-shirts to match.

A PASSION TO EXIST

Gramsci argues that, for the people of any given society, culture provides the mechanism for a meaningful conception of their world and their place within it. Culture delineates for them the rules, norms and values that correspond to that conception. He also argues that in a subordinated society (such as the Cornish) there are certain 'popular' imperatives which are much stronger, more tenacious and more effective than those of the official 'morality'. Deacon and Payton recognize this, when they write:

> Cornish culture has a persistent meaning for a large proportion of the population of Cornwall . . . The sense of belonging to an imagined Cornish community now rests upon a wider set of symbols than before; a changing repertoire which includes co-opted elements from other cultures and newly re-invented 'traditions' . . . This may only be a case of any symbol in a storm, or it could be testament to a reinvigorated and still dynamic sense of Cornish cultural identity.[38]

This statement is in effect a Gramscian recognition of Cornish 'popular consciousness', a consciousness that is not exclusively Cornish in its origins, but is neither an exact reflection of the English view of the world. It is, as Deacon and Payton intimate, a mosaic of meaning, a tangled web of contradictory components. It is such contradictory components, Gramsci suggests, which reinforce and shape the popular consciousness, not in the absolutist Marxist sense of a 'false consciousness', but in a way that still leaves subordinated people (such as the Cornish) open to a greater or lesser degree to the myriad influences of the dominant, hegemonic culture.

Some observers, for example, might claim that the apparent 'persistence of difference' in late twentieth-century Cornwall is merely the romantic construction of travel writers, novelists and tourist directors: a 'magical peninsula . . . A Land of legend and romance, dark and mystery and vibrant colours'.[39] From such a perspective, Cornwall has already been effectively assimilated within an English state and within a unified Britain, where the 'Great Arch' between rural society and the modern industrialized state has been completed, and where 'older theories and symbologies have come to terms with this central contradiction'[40] (the creation of the English state). Other readings of this 'difference', however, insist that the perceived distinctiveness is very real and has real significance for many Cornish people: 'a particular history has helped to produce an ethnic consciousness among the Cornish [and has] produce[d] a distinct regional identity.'[41] Such a claim for ethnicity is an echo of the many such claims that characterize the contemporary world but it too must be seen as a 'fragment' of the Gramscian mosaic, these very attempts to explain the 'persistence of difference' and thus assert Cornish ethnic identity, becoming themselves integral parts of the 'contradictory consciousness'. As Caroline Vink has wisely observed:

> 'Invented tradition' is employed to enhance claims of ethnic distinctiveness, and in time elements of that tradition (for example, language revival) are defended by activists as central and legitimate aspects of identity. Certainly, 'being Cornish' has become a plausible alternative to other sources of identity.[42]

CONCLUSION

For Gramasci, the key activity was to examine the ways in which cultural meaning emerges in various 'texts': sermons, advertisements, folklore, popular ritual, novels, even this article. Each of these 'fragments' of the mosaic create the 'spontaneous philosophies' through which individuals develop their 'popular consciousness', which in turn gives meaning to their social situations.

Thus we must recognize very clearly that the Cornish identity and its 'passion to exist' are rooted not only in the historical past but in the contradictions of the present. The pasty, brass bands, bards, piskeys, Trelawny's Army, the tartan, Cornish Rebellion beer and so on, including academic deliberations such as those that grace the pages of *Cornish Studies*, form, all in their own ways, a cultural 'text'—a complex and often paradoxical text wherein lies the roots of Cornish identity.

NOTES AND REFERENCES

1. A. M. Cirese, 'Gramsci's Observations on Folklore', in A. Showstack Sassoon, *Approaches to Gramsci*, London, 1982, p. 244.
2. B. Deacon and P. Payton, 'Re-inventing Cornwall: Culture Change on the European Periphery', in P. Payton (ed.), *Cornish Studies: Two*, Exeter, 1993, p. 63.
3. Deacon and Payton, 1993, p. 77.
4. Hegemony is probably Gramsci's key concept. It is used in the sense of influence, leadership, consent rather than the alternative and opposite meaning of domination. It has to do with the way one social group influences other groups, making certain compromises with them in order to gain their consent for its leadership in society as a whole, Hegemony has cultural, political and economic aspects.
5. T.J. Jackson-Lears, 'Concept of Cultural Hegemony: Problems and Possibilities', *American Historical Review*, 90: 3, p. 572.
6. Jackson-Lears, p. 568.
7. Cirese, 1982, p. 213.

162   *Cornish Studies: Five*

8. A. Gramsci, *Selections from the Prison Notebooks and the Study of Philosophy*, London, 1971, p. 321 et seq.
9. Gramsci, 1971, p. 12.
10. Gramsci, 1971, pp. 56n, and 57.
11. W. Adamson, *Hegemony and Revolution*, Berkeley, California, 1980, pp. 173–4.
12. P. Rich, 'The Quest for Englishness', *History Today*, 37: 25, 1987.
13. Rich, 1987.
14. E.P. Thompson, *The Making of the English Working Class*, London, 1963, p. 73.
15. Thompson, 1963, p. 68.
16. Adamson, 1980, p. 174.
17. F.E. Halliday, *A History of Cornwall*, London, 1959, p. 184.
18. R. Green, 'The National Question in Cornwall', pamphlet, the History Group of the Communist Party, p. 20.
19. Jackson-Lears, p. 569.
20. Hoare and Smith, pp. 326–27, 333.
21. Jackson-Lears, p. 571.
22. A.K. Hamilton Jenkin, *The Cornish Miner*, 1927, repub. Newton Abbot, 1972, p. 292.
23. Hamilton Jenkin, 1972, p. 298.
24. Hamilton Jenkin, 1972, p. 33.
25. John Rowe, *Cornwall in the Age of the Industrial Revolution*, Liverpool, 1953, p. 32.
26. Jackson-Lears, p. 569.
27. *West Briton*, 23 May 1828.
28. E.J. Hobsbawm and G. Rudé, *Captain Swing*, London, 1973, p. 106.
29. A. Davidson, 'Antonio Gramsci; The Man, His Ideas', *Australian New Left Review*, 1968, p. 87.
30. Davidson, 1968.
31. C.S. Gilbert, *History of Cornwall*, cited in Hamilton Jenkin, 1972, p. 218.
32. R.W. Bushaway, 'Ceremony, Custom and Ritual: Some Observations on Social Conflict in the Rural Community 1750–1850', in W. Minchinton (ed.), *Reactions to Social and Economic Change 1750–1939*, Exeter, 1979.
33. Bushaway, 1979.
34. P. Payton, *The Making of Modern Cornwall: Historical Experience and the Persistence of 'Difference'*, Redruth, 1992, p. 93.
35. Payton, 1992, p. 92.
36. Payton, 1992.
37. J.J. Daniell in Thurstan C. Peter, *A Compendium of the History and Geography of Cornwall*, Truro-London, (4th Ed.) 1906, p. 93n.
38. Deacon and Payton, 1993, pp. 76–77.
39. P. Corrigan and D. Sayer, *The Great Arch: English State Formation as Cultural Revolution*, London, 1985, pp. 116–17.
40. Guides to Penzance cited in P. Thornton, 'Cornwall and Changes in the "Tourist Gaze" ', in Payton (ed.), 1993, p. 93.

41. B. Deacon, 'And Shall Trelawny Die? The Cornish Identity', in P. Payton (ed.), *Cornwall Since the War: The Contemporary History of a European Region*, Redruth, 1993.

42. C. Vink, ' "Be Forever Cornish!" Some Observations on the Ethno-regional Movement in Contemporary Cornwall', in P. Payton (ed.), *Cornish Studies: Two*, Exeter, 1994.

CORNISH RUGBY AND CULTURAL IDENTITY: A SOCIO-HISTORICAL PERSPECTIVE

Andy Seward

INTRODUCTION

This article is a preliminary investigation into the origins, status and overall development of 'Cornish rugby', and poses a central question —to what extent has Cornish rugby influenced (or, indeed, become a defining construct of) the contemporary Cornish identity? In taking a socio-historical perspective, this article also responds to a further, more uncomfortable question—what is it that historians are supposed to do?—and places a consideration of Cornish rugby within the wider debates that have emerged about the history of sport and how it should be written.

In 1974 the American historian Hayden White asked, 'Why do historians persist in failing to consider historical narratives . . . as what they most manifestly are—verbal fictions, the contents of which are as much invented as found and the forms of which have more in common with their counterparts in literature than they have with those in science?'[1] More recently, Munslow has taken up this theme, arguing that 'historians always write of the past in the form of a literary genre such as romance, tragedy or farce'. Munslow is very sceptical of 'truthful interpretation' in history and yet states that 'history is fiction but that does not mean it cannot tell truths'.[2] This is an interesting observation which impacts upon the debate about how the history of sport ought to be written. Smith and Williams, for example, have argued that the active intervention of the historian's literary skill is essential if sporting history is to be made meaningful and not reduced to a superficial, dry listing of fixtures, results and personalities:

Athletic style and prowess cannot truly be reflected by a catalogue of games, a litany of victories, a string of statistics or a scatter of similes . . . We have tried to argue, through the style of our prose and the structure of our book, that both the tension between sport and society and the fleeting unrepeatability of thrilling rugby play can be, if not recaptured direct, at least suggested by historical writing that is sensitive to the needs of its subject matter.[3]

But despite this plea for active 'interpretation', Smith and Williams remain sceptical of the 'scientific' interpretation offered by sociological perspectives of sport, objecting especially to its 'inevitable reductionism'. Nonetheless, we might observe that the general approach to the history of sport that they advocate could usefully embrace a wide variety of interdisciplinary techniques (including sociology). Their own work, with its perceptive identification of the nuances of Welsh rugby, has important lessons for would-be students of the Cornish game, and yet—in studying Cornish rugby—it is also clear that a wide variety of inter-disciplinary perspectives is required if all the Cornish nuances are to be teased out. Indeed, a comprehensive model for an analysis of rugby football in Cornwall should take account not only of the historical 'facts' of the game itself but of the wider societal influences which moulded the game's development—religious, geographical, philosophical, socio-cultural, political, economic, scientific. This is the approach adopted by this article (and the larger research project of which it is a part), and it thus adds to the growing body of literature which argues that sport has little value except when viewed and understood in its broader societal context. Indeed, it is in this context that we can begin to consider the relationship between sport and identity.

For example, in the relationship between Cornish rugby and Cornish identity, how does Cornwall compare with the other 'Celtic nations' of Scotland, Wales and Ireland where there is a clear relationship between sporting prowess and the assertion of national identity. Are the (alleged) 'distinctive' characteristics of Cornish rugby merely a reflection of Cornish distinctiveness, or has rugby football been used actively in Cornwall as a device to strengthen cultural identity and to raise consciousness? How important has rugby been in perpetuating what Philip Payton has called the 'persistence of difference' in Cornwall,[4] and does rugby football have a particular resonance within that 'difference'? In the apparent absence of other Cornish institutions with a genuinely wide-ranging popular appeal, does the Cornwall Rugby Football Union and the 'Cornish team' fulfil an important symbolic role as a focus for Cornish sentiment? The study for which this article is a prelude intends to ask (and further refine) these fundamental questions in depth; this piece is intended to raise issues and offer a preliminary discussion.

HISTORICAL CONTEXT

Cornish rugby football has a historical background of a little over 100 years as an ordered and fully codified activity but at least a 400 year development as a folk game. Filbee is the latest in a long line of popular commentators to make the case for the ancient provenance of the Cornish game of hurling, and to note the suggestion in Cornish folklore that prehistoric stone circles such as 'The Hurlers were thought to be members of a group of men playing the popular game of hurling, on the Sabbath, who were punished by being turned to stone'.[5]

Certainly, hurling as a folk game in Cornwall (along with many others the length and breadth of Britain, such as 'camping' in East Anglia or 'knappan' in Wales) was an important precursor of the modern game of rugby football. There has been considerable contention among sports historians as to the exact date when a running and passing game commenced. Did it, as many books relate, begin with a certain William Webb Ellis of Rugby School picking the ball up and running with it in 1823? Or, as the President of the Rugby Football Union in 1952–3, P.M. Holman (a Cornishman!), surmised in his foreword to *Rugby in the Duchy*, did the Cornish game of hurling anticipate many of the laws of rugby?[6] Certainly, Holman's reference to Richard Carew's *Survey of Cornwall* of 1602 makes an interesting point, for the clear exposition of 'Laws' was an unusual development at the time when folk games generally were played without rules. Carew wrote:

> Two bushes are pitched in the ground eight or twelve feet asunder, directly against which at a distance ten or twelve yards apart two more bushes, in like manner, which are called the goals.
> The hurlers to goals are bound to observe these orders or Laws:
> In contending for the ball, if a man's body touches the ground, and he cries 'Hold' and delivers the ball, he is not to be further pressed.
> That the hurler must deal no foreball, or throw it to any partner standing nearer the goal than himself.
> In dealing the ball, if any of the adverse party can catch it flying . . . the property of it is thereby transferred to the catching party; and so assailants become defendants, and defendant assailants.
> A breach made in any of these Articles is motive sufficient for the

hurlers going together by the ears; nor do any seek to take revenge but in the same manner.

Holman points out the equivalents to the goal posts, the mark, the forward pass, the interception, and finally, the scrum—all elements of modern rugby football—were all inherent in Cornish hurling.

Hurling was clearly common in Cornwall in the early modern period. Carew noted that hurling matches were usually organized by local gentlemen, a suggestion repeated by Dunning and Sheard in their 1979 sociological study of the origins of rugby football.[8] The 'goals' were either those gentlemens' houses or two towns some three or four miles apart. Carew added that there was 'nether comparing of numbers nor matching of men' and that the game was played with a silver ball. The aim was to carry the ball 'by force or sleight' to the goal of one's side. Reid is sceptical of Dunning's and Sheard's assertion that 'folk football' (such as hurling) was subject to the 'regular' participation of the 'landed' classes, considering the evidence sparse and unsubstantiated. He maintains that Carew's and other early accounts make it clear that the gentry rarely actively participated in the games, other than organizing the matches, providing the balls (traditionally a silvered one with tassels in the case of Cornish hurling), and allowing their houses to be used as the goals. Reid adds that, even if the gentry did participate more directly in Cornish 'folk football', this can hardly be taken as typical of seventeenth or eighteenth-century Britain, given the 'relative geographical and social isolation of Cornwall from the advanced centres of aristocratic and genteel refinement or civilisation of London or Bath'.[9]

Carew describes two versions of the hurling game. One is to 'goales' and the other to the 'country', the former demonstrating a degree of sophistication in comparison to the 'wild' country version. Hurling as practised in Cornwall seems to have anticipated the later debate in nineteenth- century English public schools as to the relative merits of throwing (or hand passing—'hacking') and kicking, and amongst its rudimentary rules was an attempt at an offside rule and at describing 'blocking' moves similar to those in present-day American Football. In comparison with the Welsh 'knappan', however, Cornish hurling remained a 'pretty wild affair'. As Carew observed,

> At this playe privatt grudges arre revendged, see that for every small occasion they fall by the eares, weh beinge but once kindled betweane two, all persons on both sides become parties, soe that sometymes you shall see fyve or vi hundred naked meen, beatinge in a clusture together.[10]

Be that as it may, Dunning et al conclude that:

> Modern rugby is descended from these types of medieval folk-games
> in which particular matches were played by variable, formally
> unrestricted numbers of people sometimes considerably in excess of
> 1000. There was no equalisation of numbers between the contending
> sides and the boundaries of the playing area were only loosely
> defined and limited by custom. Games were played both over open
> countryside and through the streets of towns. The rules were oral
> and locally specific rather than written and instituted and enforced
> by a central controlling body.[11]

By the 1870s rugby football had spread through the United Kingdom,
its impact regionally being in direct proportion to the influence of local
public schoolboys. Cornwall was no different to other areas in this
respect. A Redruth club was formed in 1875 on the initiative of Henry
Grylls, an old Cliftonian, and W.H. Willimott who had returned from
Marlborough. Working together with local people, they were successful
in obtaining support (including a ground) from the Redruth Brewery
Company.[12] This involvement of public schoolboys was reflected in the
diffusion of the game nationwide and in its 'embourgoisement' (as
Dunning and Sheard called it), 'the gradual emergence of the
bourgeoisie as the ruling class . . . their growing control of major
institutions, and . . . the consequent spread of their values through
society'.[13]

However, in Cornwall places of employment were also important
catalysts: Camborne club (formed in 1878) owed 'its playing strength
to the tin workers of the Dolcoath mine, the largest in Cornwall, with
some assistance from the ex-public school trainers of the Camborne
School of Mines'.[14] Camborne was also keen to rival neighbouring
Redruth (as it is today), another reason for its club's foundation. In its
centenary programme, the Camborne club noted that its early players
'were tough, hard men, who thought nothing of climbing from the 425
fathoms level to the surface on rough and dangerous ladders, in order
not to be late for a gruelling match'.[15] These tough Cornish miners,
from the Camborne-Redruth area, emigrating to South Africa and
Australia, also did much to foster the game in those countries. By
contrast, 'Penzance & Newlyn owed its existence to a literary and
debating society steered by a local vicar'.[16]

It was a defining moment when the Cornish Rugby Football Union
was formed at a meeting, half way through the 1883–4 season, to further
consolidate the game in Cornwall. The Union soon became well
organized and it brought together a number of Cornish football clubs

which had been playing rugby, either regularly or sporadically, for more than a decade. These clubs in the main were concentrated in a small area some twenty-four miles by eight, bounded by Penzance in the west and Truro in the east, with the sea on either side. For a long period this area consisted of nine Senior Clubs. In the1990s, by comparison, rugby football has become a Cornwall-wide game, Launceston in particular having emerged as an important focus of 'Cornish rugby'.

The Union quickly established a strict disciplinary code for players and clubs. At the Union meeting of 21 November 1898 it was 'resolved the Hon. Sec. write to all referees in the league asking them to keep a firm hand on all rough play and to report offenders to the CRFU'.[18] Again, at the 22 December meeting in1898 regulations regarding bad language and spectator violence were imposed; warning notices were to be posted on the various grounds throughout Cornwall stating the penalty for bad language used. It was also resolved that no matches be played on the Penryn ground until 7 January 1899 on account of the bad treatment given to members of the committee by spectators during a Penzance versus Penryn game. A referees' association was mooted (and later formed by Mr B. Nicholls of Falmouth) at the meeting of 13 February 1899 and an accident fund established: 'In the event of any player or players being injured in any County trial or County match —such players be paid a sum not exceeding 10 shillings per week during their total disablement, until £10 is paid away. A medical certificate in all cases to be forwarded with the claim to the Hon. Sec'.[19] This development was well ahead of its time and illustrates the organizational and administrative acumen of the CRFU at such an early stage.

Similarly, at the 28 November 1899 committee meeting it was resolved that in future members of the press be admitted to the committee meetings. The strength of Cornish allegiance was apparent in the resolution of the Annual General Meeting of 26 August 1902: 'All players who play in three county matches in any season or in two county matches in one season shall be provided at the expense of the Union with a County cap.'[20] The CRFU had successfully established its authority in Cornwall and, in encouraging Cornish allegiance, had done much to engender the myth of 'Cornish rugby' as a distinctive phenomenon.

But the Union could hardly be accused of being parochial, establishing as it did regular fixtures during the 1890s against Devon and then either individual Welsh clubs or the Glamorgan county side. The Union also developed contacts with, and played against, national touring teams: the 1st All Blacks in 1905, the 1st Springboks in 1906, and the 1st Wallabies in 1908 (for the Olympic title in London at the White City). This 'internationalism' has been a continuing feature of

Cornish rugby, and further contacts were made. The Union consistently showed a generous spirit in these games, and complimentary dinners for touring sides were commonplace at either Tabbs Hotel, Redruth or the Commercial Hotel, Camborne. The Union was also keen to promote its Cornish identity and, in building its international contacts, to avoid being obscured in wider regional constructs. Thus at the 20 April 1912 meeting held at the Alma Hotel, it was 'Resolved on proposition of Mr Smith, seconded by Mr Tremayne, that if we can get a match with the South Africans as "Cornwall" to do so but not to join a match elected from the other Western Counties'.[21]

One might add that a pride and eagerness in staging international matches in Cornwall has been a continuing feature of CRFU activity —for example, in 1953 the minutes of the Union recount the correspondence and detailed discussions between Devon and Cornwall over staging a game with the touring All Blacks.[22] Devon wanted the game at Home Park, Plymouth, a soccer stadium, whereas Cornwall demanded Camborne—the matter was taken to the English Rugby Union for a decision in October 1953, and the Cornish were sub-sequently asked to stage the game. The independent and Cornucentric nature of Cornish rugby continued to be apparent in the records of the Union, and in the minutes of 1 February 1956 a further example is recorded. This concerned international match Programmes. The Honorary Secretary reported he had been asked to raise the question as to why the names of certain players' home clubs were not included after their own names on international club programmes. He stated that an instance had been brought to his attention where three Cornish were playing for the England XV but where there was nothing to indicate that any of them played for Cornwall, let alone any other Cornish club. It was resolved to suggest that where players had represented their counties, the names of those should also be included.

Indeed, the whole question of representing Cornwall has an 'international flavour'; faithful records have been kept and caps awarded to players since 1883—the first ever Cornwall team to play Devon was on the 12 January 1884. By 1968 a London Cornish Rugby Football club had been established, and it was received into the membership of the Middlesex County Union on 28 June 1968. In 1968 also there was an application by Penryn RFC to visit Nchanga, Zambia, and it was resolved that the Union recommend to the Rugby Football Union that the visit go ahead. In 1989 there was a memorable match between Cornwall and the Soviet Union at Redruth, a game which resulted in a closely-fought draw. One cannot resist the observation that, while the Soviet Union has now collapsed, Cornwall endures. Put another way, the 'persistence of difference' that has characterized modern Cornwall has rested in part on the continuity of the 'international flavour' in Cornish rugby. By the late 1980s the celebration of Cornwall as a 'national' side had become even more overt, reflected in the 'Trelawny's Army' phenomenon where the supposed independence and rebel spirit of the historical Bishop Trelawny —together with the song 'Trelawny', the Cornish 'national anthem'— had been co-opted by present-day Cornish rugby supporters. In the quaintly titled *Tales From Twickenham*, recalling Cornwall's county championship win in 1991, the 'Trelawny factor' is encapsulated in the words of Benji Thomas, the Cornish coach:

> The coach journey to Twickenham was amazing. The police escort had to take us on an alternative route because of traffic jams around Twickenham. I put the Trelawney tape on, and it brought lumps to many throats . . . My dream of fifteen years had been fulfilled . . . the greatest day of my rugby life. A day to savour and one for Cornish history.[23]

By 1997 Trelawny had been joined by An Gof (Michael Joseph, the St Keverne smith and rebel leader), and in the culmination on Blackheath battlefield of the activities associated with the commemoration of the 1497 Cornish rising, the Cornwall rugby team symbolically refought the conflict of 500 years ago in a match with the Kent county side. Cornwall won. The *Western Morning News* headlines decided that 'Cornwall change history on heath', while the *West Briton* reported that 'Cornwall showed the An Gof spirit to seal a thrilling win against Kent at Blackheath Common'.[24]

CULTURAL CONTEXT

'Sport is much more than a pastime or recreation and is an integral part of a society's culture.'[25] Today, Perkin's assertion seems self-evident but, as Grupe has noted, sport has in fact struggled to gain general recognition as a cultural attribute.[26] Against the background of 'culture' defined traditionally as drama, literature, poetry, fine art and classical music, sport was easily marginalized. Yet the development of modern Olympism, built upon the Greek philosophy of a wedding between mind and body and encouraged through the Victorian demand for the 'rationalization' of sport, has (according to Grupe) allowed in our time a more solid cultural acceptance of sport. As Grupe observes, 'despite some reservations, sport has become a world-wide acknowledged, really universal phenomenon'.[27] Along with the recent emergence of a multiplicity of subcultures—youth culture, pop culture, economic culture, and so on—'sport culture' has acquired global meaning which ranges from the pursuit of 'true identity' through Eastern martial arts to what Elias sees as the quest for excitement in individual and adventurous sporting activities in an otherwise unexciting and uneventful society.[28] Grupe goes further, identifying in sport the means of assisting 'mankind in moving together by practising solidarity, and in developing models for more peaceful relationships, active tolerance, diversity, and settling conflicts according to rules while seeking achievement under fair play conditions'.[29]

Mangan considers that culture is 'essentially a set of potent and dynamic normative ideas, beliefs and actions', in which sport forms 'a distinct, persistent and significant cluster of cultural traits isolated in time and space possessing a coherent structure and definite purpose.'[30] He believes that 'Social historians neglect the study of social meanings, purposes and consequences at their peril'.[31] In Victorian and Edwardian Britain, for example, sport was for the British Empire an important 'imperial umbilical cord', a device (amongst others) for perpetuating imperial hegemony. 'Sporting subjugation' defined the subordinate status of many parts of the Empire—especially the emerging Dominions of Canada, Australia, New Zealand and South Africa —and the same was perhaps true within the United Kingdom itself, with Scotland, Ireland and Wales invited to contribute sporting teams as constituent and subordinate parts of the greater whole. This was a double-edged device, however, as Mangan notes, for 'there was a certain zest in beating the mother country . . . a test of manhood, almost a proof of fitness for home rule'.[32] A similar kind of sentiment was apparent in Cornwall's victory in the English Rugby Football Union's county championship in 1908, and, paradoxically, in Cornwall's achievement of an Olympic silver medal in rugby when representing England against Australia in the 1908 Olympics in London.

It is clear that modern sport has exercised a 'nation building' effect, and Guttmann has noted that the 'integrative' consequences of sport are stronger than its 'divisive' effects, an observation illustrated in the 'integrative nature' of Cornish rugby where—despite intense internal rivalries; for example, between Camborne and Redruth—all Cornwall has combined to express what Guttmann calls 'peaks of feeling' in county championships such as 1908 and 1991.[33] The formation of the Cornwall Rugby Football Union was crucial in this respect. The first 100 years of the Union saw a strengthening of the code within Cornwall, so much so that rugby football had soon superseded wrestling as the most popular Cornish sport. Indeed, any serious analysis of rugby union has to acknowledge its particular popularity and strength within Cornwall. For example, in Bale's seminal work on the geography of place and rugby union in Britain, Cornwall emerges clearly as a major focus for the game, almost rivalling South Wales itself.[34] Indeed, Bale outlines what he sees as the 'contiguous' nature of South Wales, the West of England, and Cornwall—a territorial stronghold of rugby football with a proportionately large number of clubs per population, a thread of continuity running through Gloucestershire, Somerset and Devon to link the twin heartlands of Cornwall and South Wales.

CORNISH CULTURAL IDENTITY AND RUGBY FOOTBALL

'Cornish identity' is notoriously difficult to define, yet sport is mentioned consistently as an important component, 'one of the ways in which they see themselves, the quality of feeling Cornish, of belonging to an imagined Cornish community'. Deacon and Payton have sketched the essential bedrock of Cornish culture as it emerged in the nineteenth century. This bedrock consisted principally of a combination of mining and Methodism, 'twin symbols' which were grafted onto an already distinctive Cornish identity, vehicles of modernization which created a society built around the values of thrift, self-help, egalitarianism and democracy. The development of a new Cornish cultural self-confidence went hand in hand with a new self-awareness and a local pride in being the world leader in deep mining. The close-knit nature of a single-industry community, with its strong community support systems (including sporting customs), gave substance to this culture. However, Cornwall's nineteenth-century economy and society did not develop 'unscathed', for the industrial base did not diversify in the face of changing international conditions. Copper crashed in the 1860s and tin was in trouble a decade later, preludes to a period of rapid de-industrialization. Deacon and Payton list four cultural changes observable by the 1880s:[35]

- mass urban cultural forms
- mass emigration of Cornish people
- the changing form of patriarchal structure
- the consequences of material poverty.

In an experience similar to that of working-class communities of the North of England, Midlands and South Wales, the rise of literacy, the completion of the railway network, the appearance of popular newspapers, and the development of mass spectator sport as a male-dominated cultural form, had a significant impact upon late nineteenth-century Cornwall. As we have seen already, rugby football was co-opted early and with great enthusiasm by the working class of West Cornwall. Deacon and Payton refer to a 'making-do' culture in early twentieth-century Cornwall, a culture 'which represented resignation and adaptation to the structures of social domination and an unpredictable, but generally stagnant economy', and yet this 'making-do' co-incided with the 'symbolic' catalyst of rugby football. As Salmon pointed out, periodically in the 1920s, 1940s and 1960s (to which we can now add the 1980s and 1990s), rugby was deployed as a symbol of enduring Cornishness in an otherwise changing world, an outlet (almost the only one) for the collective expression of cultural identity. Trewin recalled the season of 1927–8 when Cornwall almost won the county championship: 'opponents would be alarmed by the arrival of a small regiment of Cornishmen in their rosettes of black and gold; it was their habit to chant Trelawney before the game, and cheer frantically to the end'.[36] Later, in 1997, Steve Bale, rugby editor of the *Daily Express*, acknowledged in his contribution to the programme for the Cornwall versus Hertfordshire match (played at Redruth on 18 January 1997) that Cornwall was 'a nation apart' and 'that rugby is its national game'.[37]

Mason reminds us that 'Sport often contributes to an enhancement of the individual's sense of identity with or belonging to a group or collectivity. It can be district, village, town, city or county. It can be class, colour or country'. Vink notes that there has been a more assertive pride in Cornish cultural activities, particularly rugby football, in the 1980s and 1990s,[38] while Deacon and Payton consider that:

> Socially, the cultural identity again found its expression in the success of the Cornish rugby team after 1988. At first glance, this appeared to be a re-run of the sporadic outbursts of collective popular identity that had marked the years since 1908. However, by the late 1980s, there were significant differences observable in this popular expression of Cornishness. A new synthesis of cultural symbols could be spotted at rugby matches. The spectators had borrowed symbols in a fairly eclectic fashion from a number of different cultures and, in doing so, invested them with Cornish meanings. Traditional symbols of Cornishness such as the song 'Trelawny', the 'obby 'oss and pasties were joined in 1990 at Redruth by the Mexican wave, adopted from televised World Cup soccer, and demonstrated with extraordinary self-confidence by the 40,000 Cornish who witnessed their team's victory at Twickenham in 1991.[39]

Cornish sports culture had become 'dynamic'.

As indicated above, there is an emerging (albeit modest) historiography of Cornish sport, one which is beginning to investigate the extent to which rugby football has moulded or at least contributed to a Cornish regional identity. Williams and Hill have commented that

'In the mid 1990s the problem of identity is becoming a central, even fashionable, one among historians and other social scientists' but they add that, despite a literature that has identified specific political, economic, social and other influences upon sport, 'little attention . . . has been directed to the effects of sport itself upon social consciousness'.[40] There have, however, been accounts of the links between national identities and sport, and Smith and Williams have demonstrated the social significance of the relationship between rugby football and national identity in Wales.[41] Similar studies, such as those of Jarvie and Walker, Sugden and Bairner, and Moorhouse, have identified the link between sport and national identity in both Scotland and Ireland.[42] In a recent article in *The Times*, Barnes described the continuing strength of 'Gaelic' sports in Ireland, and noted that the Gaelic Athletic Association was founded in the nineteenth century as a calculated affront to the British Empire.[43] Gaelic football and hurling were cultivated as distinctly Irish activities, a celebration of the nation but also an increasingly politicized assertion of nationalism.

In the context of regional or local identity, Metcalfe has commented that 'Sports, perhaps better than any other single activity, reflected the reality of community life'.[44] He was evaluating the role that sport had played in the mining communities of East Northumberland during the nineteenth century. An interesting aspect of this study, incidentally, is the discussion of the influx of Cornish miners to the Northumberland mining districts at this time: Metcalfe notes that in 1868 the mine owners locked out local employees and brought nearly 600 miners and their families from Cornwall and Devon. In 1891 the Cramlington district still had a large community of Cornish miners, and amongst their cultural activities was wrestling. Metcalf observed that the exceedingly tough conditions of the miners' lives were ameliorated somewhat by sport, 'one of the few visible symbols that provided the miners with a positive view of themselves and with mechanisms for judging themselves against each other and the outside world'.[45] But relating this to issues of regional identity is not always easy. For example, the sports historian Tony Mason remarks that 'Northern consciousness is a slippery identity',[46] and argues that in the North at least sporting loyalties are inherently local rather than part of a shared, 'integrative' regional identity. Jarvie, however, notes the conditions in which sport can become 'integrative' in the sense of creating wider shared experiences and thus collective identities. He emphasises three aspects[47]:

• a sense of continuity between the experiences of succeeding generations

- shared memories of specific events and personages which have been turning points for a collective regional or national history
- a sense of common destiny on the part of those groups sharing those experiences

As suggested above, the experience of Cornish rugby is highly 'integrative', and there is in this experience much that echoes Jarvie's analysis. Comparisons with Welsh (rather than Northern) rugby would seem to be pertinent here, not least in the relationship between rugby and symbols of masculinity and nationality. Andrews sees gender and nationality as the two most important factors shaping modern notions of identity and emphasizes the significance of sport and 'male hegemony' in the creation of the modern Welsh nation: 'The male gaze of the late nineteenth century—of a Celtic past being lauded—was one of masculine pursuits and characteristics, as once again women were written out of history'.[48] Chandler agrees, stating that 'Rugby, like many other traditional Welsh institutions was explicitly male and patriarchal',[49] an observation which might also strike chords in Cornwall.

CONCLUSION

More work needs to be done before we can say with confidence what is the comparative importance for the study of sport and identity in Cornwall of research already completed in Wales, Scotland, Ireland and elsewhere. However, Bradley makes a universally significant point when he concludes that 'For many people in Scotland, football is a way of displaying separateness and distinctiveness; that is, identity. Football often raises the intensity of certain identities because in such a competitive environment they are not subsumed.'[50] Rugby football, it seems, has a similar significance in Cornwall—it has become an integral part of Cornish culture and offers opportunities for the expression of community loyalties, collective endeavour and common aspirations at a time of dynamic socio-economic change. For Deacon, this has reached acute proportions in the 1990s. He invites us to compare the addresses delivered by the two finalists' Presidents on the eve of the 1991 county championship:

> While the Yorkshireman saw 'county' rugby mainly as a stepping stone to 'English rugby', this emphasis was entirely missing from the Cornish President's address. Instead, he referred to Bishop Trelawny's imprisonment and the legendary events of the seventeenth century and argued that 'the Cornish have the additional motivation of a Celtic people striving to preserve an identity'.[51]

The point, then, is that it is the meaning given to a particular sporting event (rather than the event itself) which is of significance. In Cornwall, rugby football—in its origins, status and development—has been imbued from the beginning with Cornish meaning.

NOTES AND REFERENCES

1. Cited in A. Munslow, 'The Plot Thickens', *Times Higher Education Supplement*, 21 March 1997.
2. Munslow, 1997.
3. D. Smith and G. Williams, *Fields of Praise: The Official History of the Welsh Rugby Union 1881–1981*, Cardiff, 1980, p. vii.
4. P. Payton, *The Making of Modern Cornwall: Historical Experience and the persistence of 'Difference'*, Redruth, 1992.
5. M. Filbee, *Celtic Cornwall*, London, 1996, p. 31.
6. P.M. Holman, 'Foreword', *Rugby in The Duchy*, Camborne, 1952.
7. Sir Richard Carew, *Survey of Cornwall*, 1602, repub. New York, 1969, pp. 147–149.
8. E. Dunning and K. Sheard, *Barbarians, Gentlemen and Players: A Sociological Study of the Development of Rugby*, Oxford, 1979; see chapter 1, esp. pp. 21–45.
9. D.A. Reid, 'Folk Football, the Aristocracy and Cultural Change: A Critique of Dunning and Sheard', *International Journal of the History of Sport*, Vol. 5, No. 2, May 1988, p. 255.
10. Carew, 1602/1969, pp. 147–149.
11. E. Dunning, J.A. Maguire, R.E. Pearton, *The Sports Process: A Comparative and Developmental Approach*, Leeds, 1993, p. 51.
12. T. Salmon, *The First Hundred Years: The Story of Rugby Football in Cornwall 1883–1983*, Camborne, 1983, p. 69.
13. Dunning and Sheard, 1979, p. 306.
14. G. Williams in T. Mason (ed.), *Sport in Britain*, Cambridge, 1988, p. 311.
15. Camborne Rugby Football Club Centenary Programme, 1978.
16. Williams, 1988, p. 311.
17. Salmon, 1983, p. 12.
18. CRFU Minutes, 21 November 1898.
19. CRFU Minutes, 13 February 1899.
20. CRFU Minutes, AGM 26 August 1902.
21. CRFU Minutes, 20 April 1912.
22. CRFU Minutes, October/November 1953.
23. J. Clarke and T. Harry, *Tales From Twickenham*, Reduth, 1991.
24. *Western Morning News*, 23 June 1997; *West Briton*, 26 June 1997.
25. H. Perkin, 'Sport and Society: Empire and Commonwealth', in J.A. Mangan, R.B. Small, E. Spon and F.N. Spon (eds), *Sport, Culture and Society: International Historical and Sociological Perpectives*, London, 1986, p. 3.

26. O. Grupe, 'Sport and Culture: the Culture of Sport', unpub. paper, 3rd Congress, Japan Society of Sport Industry, Tokyo, September 29–30, 1993.
27. Grupe, 1993.
28. N. Elias ad E. Dunning, *Quest for Excitement: Sport and Leisure in the Civilising Process*, Oxford, 1986.
29. Grupe, 1993.
30. J.A. Mangan (ed.), *The Cultural Bond: Sport, Empire, Society*, London, 1992, pp. 5.
31. Mangan, 1992, pp. 5–6
32. Mangan et al., 1986, p. 217.
33. A. Guttman, *Games and Empires: Modern Sports and Cultural Imperialism*, New York, 1994, p. 183.
34. J. Bale, *Sport and Place: A Geography of Sport in England, Scotland and Wales*, London, 1982, pp. 64–65.
35. B. Deacon and P. Payton, 'Re-inventing Cornwall: Culture Change on the European Periphery', in P. Payton (ed.), *Cornish Studies: One*, Exeter, 1993.
36. J.C. Trewin, *Up From The Lizard*, London, 1948, repub. 1982, p. 197.
37. S. Bale, 'Forword', CRFU Cornwall v. Hertfordshire Programme, 18 January 1997.
38. C. Vink, ' "Be Forever Cornish!" Some Observations on the Ethno-regional Movement in Contemporary Cornwall', in Payton (ed.), 1993, p. 119.
39. Deacon and Payton, 1993, p. 76.
40. J. Williams and J. Hill (eds), *Sport and Identity in the North of England*, Keele, 1996, p. 1.
41. Smith and Williams, 1980.
42. J. Sugden and A. Bairner, *Sport, Sectarianism and Society in a Divided Ireland*, Leicester, 1993; G. Jarvie and G. Walker (eds.), *Scottish Sport in the Making of the Nation: Ninety Minute Patriots?*, Leicester, 1994; H.F. Moorhouse, 'Repressed Nationalism and Professional Football: Scotland versus England', in Mangan et al. (eds), 1986.
43. S. Barnes, 'Grand Occasion to Celebrate All Ireland', *The Times*, 30 September 1996.
44. A. Metcalfe, 'Sport and Community: A Case Study of the Mining Villages of East Northumberland, 1800–1914', in Williams and Hill (ed.), 1996.
45. Metcalfe, 1996, p. 15.
46. Mason, 1988, p. 118.
47. G. Jarvie, 'Rugby and the Nostalgia of Masculinity', in J. Nauright and T. Chandler (eds.), *Making Men: Rugby and Masculine Identity*, London, 1996, p. 234.
48. D. Andrews, 'Sport and the Masculine Hegemony of the Modern Nation: Welsh Rugby, Culture and Society 1890–1914', in Nauright and Chandler (eds), 1996, p. 56.
49. Nauright and Chandler, 1996, p. 8.

50. J.M. Bradley, 'Political, Religious and Cultural Identities: The Under-currents of Scottish Football', *Politics*, Vol. 17, No. 1, 1997.
51. B. Deacon, 'And Shall Trelawny Die? The Cornish Identity', in P.Payton (ed.), *Cornwall Since the War: The Contemporary History of a European Region*, Redruth, 1993, p. 207, citing *Falmouth Packet*, 13 April 1991.

RESEARCH NOTE

CORNWALL EDUCATION WEEK: SEVENTY YEARS ON

F. Roff Rayner, F.L. Harris and Philip Payton

INTRODUCTION

In recent years there has been increasing recognition of the importance and value of 'local' studies in the education of schoolchildren. Not only might individual localities provide exemplars of wider themes, allowing children to experience close to home the reality of what might otherwise appear to be hypothetical or even irrelevant concerns, but the elucidation of local historical, cultural, socio-economic and environmental issues can be an important educational device in 'empowering' children —in equipping them to recognize and understand the inherent value of their own social–territorial identity. This, it might be argued, is especially the case in Cornwall, where there is a profusion of local attributes (from prehistoric megaliths to rare wildlife habitats) that invite study, and where the existence of a developed sense of Cornish identity is potentially a significant educational resource.[1]

Recognition of this particular Cornish context has led to important work in a number of areas. Individual schools have made much of their local resources (for example, consider Redruth Community School's emphasis in recent years on Portreath harbour and its place in Cornish—indeed, British—industrial history, as a GCSE case study), while both the Local Education Authority (LEA) advisory service and institutions such as the Royal Cornwall Museum and the Cornwall Wildlife Trust have done much to match local resources to local needs. The collection that comprises *Cornish Studies For Schools* remains a landmark publication,[2] while the Institute of Cornish Studies has itself pioneered several initiatives, such as a resource pack on 'Turkish pirates' and a guide to matching National Curriculum requirements to the key moments of Cornish history. Events such as Keskerdh Kernow (the commemoration in 1997 of the 500th anniversary of the Cornish rebellions of 1497) have also prompted a wide range of activity in Cornish schools.

In 1985 the LEA produced a document, *Developing the Curriculum in Cornish Schools,* designed to develop cross-curriculum links within the teaching of the National Curriculum. This was followed by the LEA's *Completing the Curriculum in Cornish Schools* which (amongst other things) addressed itself to Cornish Studies. Having examined the role of Classical studies, the document turned its attention to things Cornish. Its observations deserve to be quoted in full:

> To turn from the heritage of a civilisation to that of a county may seem strange, even if that county is Cornwall—but the Authority hopes that the children in its schools will also be taught something about the very special character and culture of the place in which they live. The Cornish past offers so many local illustrations of universal human concerns, with the sea and the land, what lies under the land and across the sea, with religion, legend and custom, labour and leisure, that to waste all these opportunities to draw past and present closer together would seem perverse, above all at a time when a premium is rightly placed on the need for social cohesion and a sense of community. Much more can be done to promote Cornish Studies, and to stimulate interest in the study of the Cornish language, by drawing on an increasing range of resources in print. The Authority wishes to encourage every school and every teacher to be alert to the wealth of local material which is available to enrich the experience of Cornish pupils.[3]

THE GLOBAL AND THE LOCAL

However, despite this progress and commitment, there remains significant doubt as to the ability of Cornish institutions to deliver a sustained and effective local dimension in the face of what is seen as a deliberately homogenizing National Curriculum unable, by and large, to admit or consider regional variation. Criticism of the National Curriculum in a Cornish context has ranged from its treatment of 'Roman Britain' to the events of the 'Hungry Forties' (the potato famine),[4] while there is a recognition that the myriad pressures experienced by teachers today allow few opportunities for the experimental adoption of Cornish Studies perspectives. It is also probable that Cornish schools cannot offer sustained attention to Cornish Studies without the active support and encouragement of the community, something that at present is restricted to the periodic intervention of two or three local institutions with much wider briefs. In the realms of adult education, too, despite the success of various Cornish and Local History programmes offered by the Workers' Education Association and the University of Exeter's Department of Continuing and Adult Education, Cornish Studies is only partially visible amongst an array of fee-driven, examination-oriented and often (understandably) vocational courses.

Tragically, these shortcomings exist against the background of what Sir Geoffrey Holland has called the 'curious paradox' of globalization, the reality that 'the more our world becomes one . . . the more people feel the need or seek the opportunity, not least thanks to the powerful tools of the new technologies, to assert their own identity'.[5] As Sir Geoffrey admits,

> Everywhere, people are feeling the need to assert their cultural heritage, their music, their language and their traditions. We see it in Scotland, we see it in Wales, we see it in Cornwall. Looking further afield we see it day to day in the former Yugoslavia and the former Soviet Union.[6]

Holland also considers that 'We live in a world in which you do not have to be big to be powerful', inviting us to 'Consider Singapore, Switzerland, Taiwan and Hong Kong', examples which 'have occupied a position of strength and significance far beyond their size or the size of their populations'.[7] As he observes,

> Today's young people are going . . . to have to manage, somehow or other, to reconcile their felt need and indeed their opportunity to express their individual identity, with being in a world which is a global market-place . . . Are we confident that those emerging from the institutions for which we are responsible are prepared for those major tasks of reconciliation, of living simultaneously with the powerful and big but also the powerful small and powerful individual?[8]

Sir Geoffrey Holland suggests that we still have a long way to go in responding to this educational imperative; not only in Cornwall, of course, but in the wider world. However, there is in this an assumption that the modernity of globalization presents only new questions for which there are no existing answers, an insistence that we do not have in our repertoire of experience existing models which might usefully be applied to the future. We might add that this would seem to be especially so in Cornwall, with attempts in the educational sphere to match Cornish Studies to global themes being restricted firmly to the recent initiatives noted above. Indeed, one might argue that, given the socio-economic and cultural 'paralysis' that apparently characterized Cornwall from the late nineteenth century until after the Second World War, there would in any case have been few opportunities for the application of an innovative Cornish Studies perspective.

THE *HANDBOOK*

It comes as a surprise, then, to discover that seventy years ago Cornwall County Council was in fact very much alive to the significance of a Cornish perspective in the education of its children. Between 30 May and 4 June 1927, a 'Cornwall Education Week' was organized by the County Council, with an exhibition in the City Hall in Truro, an opportunity to review the progress made in Cornish education (especially since Balfour's Act of 1902) and to assess the current state of education in Cornwall. A *Cornwall Education Week Handbook* was published to mark the event, in which Sir Arthur Quiller Couch—then Chairman of Cornwall Education Committee—described the event's rationale:

> Certain Cornishmen and Cornishwomen, believers in Education, who now for twenty-five years—some from the start, others in succession—have worked hard to build a system in our Duchy well and truly laid upon the basis of the Balfour Act of 1902 and using material provided by subsequent Acts of Parliament when these offered more than promises, have agreed that the time has arrived for challenging their countrymen to come and with open eyes judge some results of their labours.[9]

Significantly, the *Handbook* insisted that 'The system of education in Cornwall differs from that of any County in the British Isles'.[10] Although offered as a particular comment on the advanced characteristics of Technical Education in Cornwall (not least with regard to agriculture where 'The Agricultural Education Department of the Cornwall County Council embraces General Agriculture, Dairying, Horticulture, Poultry-Keeping, Farriery and Bee- Keeping'),[11] this assertion reflected a more general mood of Cornish particularism evident throughout the book. For as well as sketching the general development of education within Cornwall, the *Handbook* went out of its way to include and describe the contributions of uniquely Cornish institutions such as the Royal Cornwall Polytechnic Society and the Royal Institution of Cornwall, together with that of the School of Metalliferous Mining (later known as the Camborne School of Mines).

There was also a discussion of what the *Handbook* boldly termed 'Exeter University', the University College of the South West (situated at Exeter in Devon) which could trace its origins to 1893, had begun receipt of State funding in 1922, and which in 1927 was in the midst of an ambitious campaign to raise £100,000 for building and endowment projects. It was noted that some 20 per cent of the University College's 400 students came from Cornwall, a fact reflected in Cornwall County Council's generous annual grant of £500 to the College.[12] Robert Morton Nance added that the recent appointment of Henry Jenner as Honorary St Petrock Lecturer in Celtic Studies at the College, 'may point the way to a future establishment there of a Celtic chair'.[13]

Moreover, the *Handbook* was careful to consider the wider cultural milieu in which Cornish education existed, identifying relevant institutions (such as the Old Cornwall Societies) and devoting space to typifying themes such as the Cornish language, Cornish mining, Cornishmen and the sea, Cornish emigration, Cornish sports and customs, and famous men and women of Cornish history. Thus we learn that,

> Cornish folk, however, had little love for 'foreigners' and no desire to learn the Saxon tongue, preferring their own Celtic tongue, which was in common use until the Reformation, when they rose in rebellion at the introduction of a Prayer Book in the unknown English language.[14]

But at the same time,

> The ancient Cornish rounds or theatres speak of a type of education once common in the Duchy, and the texts of the few Plays which still exist in the ancient language show that the education of the mediaeval Cornish—primitive though it may have been—was extended to the common people.[15]

Elsewhere, the book observed that between 1850 and 1900, while the population of England and Wales doubled, that of Cornwall decreased: 'During that period a quarter of a million of Cornish people left the County for good.'[16] Attempting to grasp and convey the sheer scope of this emigration, the book recounted the story of a

> typical trio [which] set out from the same village and journeyed in a sailing ship to Australia. No. 1 married a colonial girl, lived steadily and soberly, and died in middle age. No. 2 was lost sight of. No. 3

came home and went again, came and went several times—gold digging in Australia, tin mining on Mt. Bischoff, Tasmania—pump man on the Rand—copper mining on Lake Superior—and is now a quiet little elderly man who rarely steps from his small holding in the St Austell parish.[17]

Other themes received similar treatment, and although the language and methodology seem to modern eyes to be singularly lacking in rigour and shot-through with prejudice and romantic musings, the approach is in fact rather sophisticated. To begin with, there is evidence of an attempt to achieve a balance between the then newly emergent 'Revivalist' perspectives of Cornwall (with their emphasis on language and Celticity) and the still prevalent 'industrial' image which continued to stress mining, quarrying, engineering, scientific invention, geology, and the contribution made by the Cornish to international economic development. More than this, however, the *Handbook* demonstrates not only a desire to accommodate Cornish themes within education in Cornwall but a belief—writ large in the sheer volume of space devoted to Cornish material—that such accommodation is an essential component of every Cornish child's liberal education.

It would be wrong, however, to imagine that the appearance of the *Handbook* heralded the dawn of a golden age of Cornish Studies in schools. The *Handbook* itself was rather 'top-down' in its approach, celebrating the contribution of the 'great men' of Cornish education and when, in stooping to consider the schoolchildren themselves, identifying not the ordinary pupils (who are largely invisible) but dwelling upon the success of the extraordinary A.L. Rowse who had gone on to Oxford. Moreover, the 'top-down' approach meant that the *Handbook* identified what it saw as the grand themes of Cornish Studies but did not offer prescription or advice in detail as to how these might actually be pursued in schools. As ever, in the years before and after the Second World War it was left to the imagination of enthusiastic individuals, such as Edwin Chirgwin at St Cleer School and Anne Treneer at Gorran, to attempt as best they could the practical teaching of Cornish subjects. Indeed, despite the very Cornish emphasis of the *Handbook*, by the time the prescriptive *Cornwall Education Committee Handbook 1934–37* appeared, the Cornish Studies perspective had apparently been forgotten altogether, with the exception of a brief note that wrestling might be taught with a Headmaster's consent. Instead, the extra-curricular emphasis was now on Empire Day, which was to be marked by 'Some kind of patriotic teaching in connection with English literature, English history, or geography',[18] together with the singing of 'patriotic songs' and saluting the flag. The Grammar Schools, in particular, were vehicles of the English Imperial tradition; 'Cornishness' was something imparted privately in the home.

Nearly thirty years later, in the series of pamphlets published by Cornwall County Council to mark Cornwall Education Week 1962, the Imperial proccupation had disappeared but Cornish Studies continued to be largely absent. The Penzance pamphlet emphasized the importance of 'EDUCATION for ONE AND ALL'[19] but the evocation of the Cornish motto was about the limit of its Cornish Studies perspective. The companion pamphlets for the other Cornish districts were also silent, although that for Falmouth and Helston noted that at Falmouth Technical College 'One of its most recent efforts to satisfy local demand is a course in the Cornish language, the first such class to be sponsored by the Education Committee'.[20]

CONCLUSION

Nonetheless, even if it had proved a false dawn, the *Cornwall Education Week Handbook* of 1927 was a remarkable document. For all its 'top-down' sensibilities, it had recognized the already distinctive qualities of Cornish education and was a powerful, almost passionate statement of the place of Cornish Studies within that education. Of course, much has changed in the realms of education since 1927. Education has become far more centralized, and Local Education Authorities do not enjoy their former range of competences and freedom of action. However, in our responding to the challenges identified by Sir Geoffrey Holland, the *Cornwall Education Week Handbook* is an important reminder that the emphasis on the 'local' as a significant element of education is not new—especially in Cornwall where it had exercised considerable influence after Balfour's Act of 1902. The *Cornwall Education Week Handbook* is thus a source of inspiration to those of us today seeking the accommodation of Cornish Studies in the National Curriculum as it is taught in Cornwall's schools; it is also an example of what might be achieved in any research project designed to achieve that accommodation. This time, however, the aim should be a permanent accommodation, one which genuinely attempts to balance the 'local' with the 'global'.

NOTES AND REFERENCES

1. See Allen E. Ivey and Philip Payton, 'Towards a Cornish Identity Theory', in Philip Payton (ed.), *Cornish Studies: One*, Exeter, 1993.
2. Anne Trevenen Jenkin (ed.), *Cornish Studies For Schools*, Truro, 2nd ed., 1993.
3. *Completing the Curriculum in Cornish Schools*, Truro, 1989, pp. 16–17.

4. For example, see Charles Thomas, *And Shall These Mute Stones Speak? Post-Roman Inscriptions in Western Britain*, Cardiff, 1994, p. xvii; Philip Payton, *Cornish Studies: Four*, Exeter, 1996, p. 4.
5. Sir Geoffrey Holland, 'Are We Educating our Young People for the 21st Century?', *RSA Journal*, Vol. CXLV, No. 5478, April 1997, p. 44.
6. Holland, 1997, p. 44–45.
7. Holland, 1997, p. 44.
8. Holland, 1997, p. 45.
9. Sir Arthur Quiller-Couch, 'Preface', in *Cornwall Education Week Handbook*, Truro, 1927, p. 15.
10. *Handbook*, 1927, p. 65.
11. *Handbook*, 1927, p. 65.
12. *Handbook*, 1927, pp. 82–84.
13. *Handbook*, 1927, p. 93.
14. *Handbook*, 1927, p. 21.
15. *Handbook*, 1927, p. 21
16. *Handbook*, 1927, p. 139.
17. *Handbook*, 1927, p. 143.
18. *Cornwall Education Committee Handbook 1934–37*, Truro, p. 126.
19. *Cornwall Education Week 1962* (Penzance edition), Truro, 1962, p. 14.
20. *Cornwall Education Week 1962* (Falmouth–Helston edition), Truro, 1962, p. 10.

BOOK REVIEW

Marjorie Filbee, *Celtic Cornwall*, Constable and Company Ltd., 1996, 176 pp. ISBN 0 09 476 090, £16.95.

Once again we seem to be firmly in the clutches of Celto-mania, the likes of which have not been witnessed since the late nineteenth century. Book stores are overflowing with titles ranging from Celtic shamanism and Celtic design to Celtic recipes, Celtic women, and Celtic wisdom. Like sex, the Celts sell. Now Celtophiles have Marjorie Filbee's *Celtic Cornwall* to add to their collection of titles.

Unfortunately, the connection between this book and Celtic Cornwall is tenuous, no matter which definition of the word 'Celtic' one uses. Many of the disparities of content can be symbolized by the selection of the Veryan round houses for the cover photo, a seemingly odd choice for a book on Celtic Cornwall. Yet, Filbee contends that the nineteenth-century round houses are an example of architectural continuity with the round huts built in Cornwall in the Iron Age. As with most of the book, this is a nice thought, but perhaps a stretch of a conclusion.

Filbee begins by providing a brief history of Neolithic, Bronze Age, and Iron Age settlements in Cornwall, then easing into a section about Arthurian legend, and saints' lives. She then proceeds to the topic she clearly feels most comfortable with, manor houses and the lives of the gentry. This book contains many sweeping passages about what the inhabitants of the great homes ate, how the ladies lived, descriptions of the dining halls, and where the privies were. Filbee's biographical notes state that her main interests and former publications have concentrated on manor homes, and that her interest in Cornwall comes from having come here on holiday with her family over the last forty years. With this knowledge, the reader has a better framework in which to place her choice of material and its subsequent presentation.

A primary difficulty with the text is that Filbee attempts to maintain some sort of thematic consistency by attributing aspects of behaviour or aesthetics to the 'Celtic' nature of the people. For instance, she argues that the reason why professional classes in Cornwall would actually mingle with the local tradesmen is due to the Celtic love of feasting (p. 127). It surfaces again when Filbee compares Richard Trevithick to King Arthur, stating that the Cornish seem to generate their heroes and leaders at just the right hour (p. 137). The largest problem with this approach is that Filbee writes of the Cornish Celts in a very essentialist manner, in the same school as the eighteenth- and nineteenth-century antiquarians who wrote of the unruly and superstitious, yet passionate and artistic Celtic 'race'. The result is a simplified, stereotypical treatment of both the Cornish and the major events in Cornish history.

For instance, Filbee attributes Wesley's successes with Methodism in Cornwall to the fact that the Cornish 'Celtic exuberance and spiritual needs' were not met by post-Reformation religion (p. 133), yet she seems unaware of the social and economic factors that influenced Methodism's growth. Likewise, she reduces the history of Cornish Royalism to the 'Celtic reverence for their king' (p. 111). The formation and status of the Duchy somehow does not enter into the account. In fact, it is not mentioned throughout the entire work. Of course this does not imply that Cornwall's Royalist stance during the Civil War and the rise of Methodism have nothing to do with the fact that the Cornish are Celts. Certainly they do, but the impact of Cornish Celtic ethnicity and the 'difference' of Cornish history cannot be explained by romanticized constructions of an imagined essential Celtic nature. Certainly, in a work designed for a popular audience such as this one clearly is, there is not a need for advanced critical analysis of historical events. However, in this case a reader with little or no background about Cornwall would be left needing clarification, and a retreat to 'Celtic' traits does not provide suitable explanations. Although Filbee seems to like the Cornish, she tends to write of them as one would have once written of any well-behaved subjugated people; intensely religious, superstitious, clannish, artistic with a love of great quantities of food and ale, and above all, excellent subjects, always willing to follow a strong leader. This approach ultimately does more harm than good.

Furthermore, Filbee's history is inaccurate in many areas, and in others is simply incorrect. For instance, she states that 'by 931 . . . Athelstan had brought all Cornwall under English rule' (pp. 74–75). Furthermore, her claim that after the restoration of the monarchy 'The Church of England was well established in the minds of the people' (p. 119) could also be argued against. Perhaps Filbee's greatest shortcoming in this book is her complete omission of any works in the Cornish language, the *Ordinalia* tradition, or *Beunans Meriasek*, which in a book called *Celtic Cornwall* is unforgivable. In fact, she implies that the only book in Cornish to survive was the Bodmin Manumissions (p. 75), and that after the Book of Common Prayer was introduced, 'The opportunity to preserve the Cornish language was lost, and it was destined to disappear as the people of Cornwall gradually came to accept the use of English' (p. 99). Furthermore, Filbee gives no mention of contemporary Celtic revivalist activities whatsoever, including the language revival, the Gorseth, Celtic music and dance, literature, or Celtic politics.

Yet for all of Filbee's reductionist tendencies, she recognizes that Cornwall's Celtic identity is strong, resilient and adaptable, which may have been part of the impetus for the book in the first place. She notes the popularity of Cornish surfing, and the growth of indigenous Cornish art. She also emphasizes the struggles of the Cornish to preserve their native industries in the face of an ever encroaching tourism economy. Filbee's interest in and respect for Cornwall is obvious, even if her understanding of its history and people is not all that complete. This book is further proof that even the visitors who come over a lifetime and think they know the place can easily be missing some of the rich complexities that Cornish culture and history have to offer.

Amy Hale
Institute of Cornish Studies

NOTES ON CONTRIBUTORS

Rob Burton is a Tutor and postgraduate student in the Department of Sociology at the University of Exeter, where he is currently completing a PhD on aspects of Cornish identity. He also works for the Open University and the University of Plymouth, and has published widely on sociological themes.

Dick Cole is a professional archaeologist who works for the Cornwall Archaeological Unit at Cornwall County Council. He has produced numerous reports for the Unit and also teaches at two local Further Education colleges. He has undertaken research at the University of Wales Lampeter into the development of the South Pembrokeshire landscape, a subject on which he has written widely.

Bernard Deacon is currently teaching social sciences, local and regional history, and British government at the Open University, the University of Exeter's Department of Continuing and Adult Education (in Truro), and Cornwall College. His recent publications include an essay on the Cornish language debate and postmodernity in *Cornish Studies: Four* (1996) and a chapter in Ella Westland (ed.), *Cornwall: The Cultural Construction of Place* (1997).

Amy Hale is Research Fellow in contemporary Celtic Studies at the Institute of Cornish Studies, University of Exeter, and has recently completed her PhD 'Gathering the Fragments: Performing Contemporary Celtic Identities in Cornwall' at the University of California, Los Angeles. She is currently co-editing a book *New Directions in Celtic Studies*, scheduled for publication in 1998.

F.L. Harris is a graduate of Wadham College, Oxford, where he read History before returning to Cornwall in 1928. He worked initially with the Workers' Educational Association and subsequently with what is now the University of Exeter's Department of Continuing and Adult Education in developing the provision of liberal adult education in Cornwall. He was awarded an OBE in 1953 for his services to education, and in 1986 was admitted to the degree of Doctor of Letters at the University of Exeter. He was the University's Senior Resident Tutor in Cornwall on his retirement in 1969. In the late 1960s he was involved closely in the genesis of the Institute of Cornish Studies, and served as its Honorary Director until the appointment of Professor Charles Thomas in 1971. From 1954–74 he was a Cornwall County Councillor and latterly County Alderman, being Vice-Chairman of the Education Committee from 1964–74. He is co-author (with his late wife, Gladys) of *The Making of a Cornish Town: Torpoint and Neighbourhood Through Two Hundred Years* (1976).

David Harvey is a Tutor in the Department of Geography at the University of Exeter where he has recently completed a doctoral thesis on 'Territoriality and the Territorialisation of West Cornwall'. He has written a number of scholarly articles on this theme, and is currently engaged in research into sources of power, authority and identity.

Lynette Olson is Senior Lecturer in the Department of History at the University of Sydney, and is author of *Early Monasteries in Cornwall: Studies in Celtic History XI* (1989) and a number of related articles on related subjects. Her particular interest in the Cornish medieval play Beunans Meriasek was sparked by several recent student productions of its Cornish episodes at the University of Sydney, Australia.

Philip Payton is Reader in Cornish Studies at the Unversity of Exeter and Director of the Institute of Cornish Studies. His recent publications include *Cornwall* (1996) and chapters in Máiréad Nic Craith (ed.), *Watching One's Tongue: Aspects of Romance and Celtic Languages* (1996) and Ella Westland (ed.), *Cornwall: The Cultural Construction of Place* (1997). He is currently writing *The Cornish Overseas*, to be published in 1998.

Ronald Perry is a founder member of the New Cornish Studies Forum, and was formerly Head of the Faculty of Management at Cornwall College. He has written widely on Cornish subjects, including two core chapters in Philip Payton (ed.), *Cornwall Since the War: The Contemporary History of a European Region* (1993) and (with Ken Dean, Bryan Brown and David Shaw) the influential *Counterurbanisation: International Case Studies of Socio-economic Change in Rural Areas* (1986).

F. Roff Rayner is Honorary University Fellow at the Institute of Cornish Studies, University of Exeter, specialising in Cornish education. After teaching in Suffolk and Hertfordshire, he came to Cornwall in 1957 to work with the Local Education Authority. He retired in 1990 as Deputy Secretary for Education, Cornwall County Council.

Andy Seward is Senior Lecturer in the Department of Physical Education and Sports Sciences at the University College of St Mark and St John, Plymouth. He has worked extensively in sports development in Zambia and Papua New Guinea, and is currently engaged in postgraduate research into Cornish rugby and cultural identity.

Garry Tregidga is Assistant Director of the Institute of Cornish Studies, University of Exeter. His research interests are centred on the political experience of Cornwall since the 1880s. He is currently preparing an edited collection of the correspondence of Sir Francis and Lady Eleanor Acland from 1906 to 1939, and is also joint co-ordinator of a major project on the history of mid-Cornwall.